PALACES
on the Prairie

PALACES
on the Prairie

by Rod Evans

North Dakota Institute for Regional Studies
North Dakota State University

North Dakota Institute for Regional Studies
North Dakota State University

Printed in Canada.

International Standard Book Number (ISBN): 978-0-911042-71-9
Library of Congress Control Number: 2009940379

To Cecily

As you grow and learn,
may your eyes be wide with wonder
as they seek out the hidden mysteries of the past,
the evolving complexities of the present
and the infinite possibilities of the future.

Contents

Contents

Palaces on the Prairie

Acknowledgements

First and foremost I must thank my wife, Vicki, an English instructor at Northern State University, who edits my rough drafts during her morning workout sessions. Others I wish to thank include the following people and organizations listed by states in alphabetical order. My regrets and apologies to those I may have forgotten to mention.

Illinois
Arcola: - Dale Yoder, collector of old photographs
                        - Nancy Rairden of Slack Publications
                        - Arcola Public Library
Bloomington: - Bill Kemp, Librarian/Archivist, McLean County Museum of History
                        - McLean County Historical Society
Peoria: - Peoria Public Library staff
Springfield: - Abraham Lincoln Presidential Library, with special thanks to Mary Michels and Roberta Fairburn

Iowa
Creston: - Union County Historical Society Museum, with special thanks to Don Mosman
Des Moines: - State Archives, with special thanks to Susan Jellinger
Forest City: - Local historians Ruth Liebrand and Carol Whiteis
                        - Forest City *Summit* newspaper
Iowa City: - Special Collections unit of the State Historical Society-Iowa City, with special thanks to
                           Mary Bennett and Charles Scott
Ottumwa: - Wapello County Museum, with special thanks to Rusty Corder, Gloria Sample, Ruth Ferdig, and
                           Milly Morris-Amos
                        - Ottumwa Public Library
Sioux City: - Sioux City Public Library and Sioux City Public Museum

Missouri
Springfield: - Irwin Lyndon, Professor of Agriculture at Missouri State University
St. Joseph: - St. Joseph Museums, Inc., with special thanks to Sarah Elder, Curator,
                           Wyeth-Tootle Mansion

Nebraska
Grand Island: - Stuhr Museum of the Prairie Pioneer
                        - Hall County Historical Society, with special thanks to Fred Roeser
Lincoln: - Nebraska State Historical Society, with special thanks to Mary Jo Miller
Sidney: - Gary Person, the City of Sidney, and the Cheyenne County Historical Association
                        - Sidney Public Library, with special thanks to Eileen Nightingale

North Dakota

Bismarck:
- North Dakota State Archives, with special thanks to Sharon Silengo
- State Historical Society of North Dakota

Fargo:
- North Dakota State University and the North Dakota Institute for Regional Studies, with special thanks to Dr. Tom Riley, Dean, College of Arts, Humanities, and Social Sciences; and Mr. Ross Collins, Associate Professor, Department of Communication
- Special thanks to Deb Tanner, Publication Coordinator/Designer, Agriculture Communication, NDSU

Ray:
- Local historian Doris Langager and Ray Centennial Committee

South Dakota

Aberdeen:
- Dacotah Prairie Museum, with special thanks to Sue Gates and staff
- Alexander Mitchell Library, with special thanks to Shirley Arment and staff, and the late Pam Lingor

Gregory:
- Gregory Public Library, with special thanks to Janis Tilton
- Jeff Johnson, President, Gregory Office of Bank West

Ipswich:
- Dwain and Tena Gibson of the Ipswich *Tribune*
- M.P. Beebe Memorial Library, with special thanks to Ruby Bosanko
- Parmley Museum, with special thanks to Irene Rissmann and the late Candis Kub

Mitchell:
- Carnegie Resource Center and Mitchell Area Historical Society, with special thanks to Lyle Swensen
- Mitchell Public Library

Plankinton:
- South Dakota *Mail* newspaper, with special thanks to Gayle Van Genderen and J.P. Studeny

Pierre:
- South Dakota State Historical Society Archives

Rapid City:
- Rapid City Public Library, with special thanks to Susan Braunstein

Timber Lake:
- Timber Lake Topic, with special thanks to Jim and Kathy Nelson, Timber Lake & Area Historical Society, Timber Lake Area Museum, and the late Frank Cundill, photographer

Texas

Fort Worth:
- Courtesy of the Genealogy, History, and Archives Unit, Fort Worth Public Library, with special thanks to Tom Kellam

Waco:
- Baylor University, with special thanks to Ellen Brown

Wyoming

Douglas:
- Pioneer Memorial Museum, with special thanks to Arlene Ekland-Earnst

Prologue

Palaces on the Prairie seeks to shed light on a little-known chapter in the history of the Great Plains. A sprinkling of Iowans are somewhat familiar with the five corn palaces built in Sioux City from 1887 to 1891, and many people throughout the Midwest know of the present Mitchell Corn Palace. Few, however, know the historical significance of the palaces, and even fewer know of the other palaces spread out among various prairie towns.

From the 1880s to the 1930s, at least 34 "prairie palaces" of one sort or another sprang up in at least 24 towns across the Midwest. Their themes ranged in scope from grasses to grains to minerals, but all sought the same goal — attention! Even before the first train headed west, the railroads pummeled the newspapers with advertisements that brought hyperbole to a new art form. What a wonderful surprise, then, when Midwestern towns came up with the "grain palace" idea, bringing a touch of truth to the railroad's exaggerated claims of prairie life.

The palace phenomenon revealed the essence of frontier life — the hopes, the fears, the successes, the failures, the strength of community, the frailty of individualism. In nearly every instance, it was the town's businessmen who got the ball rolling for the creation of the palaces, and in many cases it was the same businessmen who eventually dropped the ball, leading to the palaces' demise.

This book attempts to tackle many unanswered questions: Why is Mitchell's Corn Palace the only one that has survived, especially when in the beginning it struggled more than either Sioux City's or Aberdeen's? Could Sioux City's Expositions have survived if the city hadn't built a new palace each year? Were any failures due to inadequate management? Could some of the palaces have survived were it not for fires and natural disasters? How many of the towns simply did not have the population to sustain a palace of any magnitude? How much influence did the newspapers have? When is "bigger and better" simply not enough? How often does an event have to totally reinvent itself to keep the interest of its populace and ensure survival? How much did cooperation between towns lead to the success of the Expositions, and how did the rivalries spell their doom? How large a role did the national economy play, and did it affect large and small towns equally?

There are no simple answers, and in some cases there are no answers at all, but the questions raised can be contemplated and are usually relevant to issues confronting communities today. There are always valuable lessons to be learned from the successful ventures of the past, as well as the failures. The entire palace phenomenon makes an interesting study, and for those who don't want to study, just the photographs alone are fascinating.

Section 1
Iowa

Sioux City
Corn Palace
1887

**Early 1887 illustration of
proposed Corn Palace**

(Courtesy of State Historical
Society of Iowa, Special Collections)

Section 1 ❖ Iowa
CHAPTER 1

rior to August of 1887, the biggest stories in the Sioux City *Daily Journal* had dealt with the railroad's expansion in Sioux City,[1] Queen Victoria's Golden Jubilee,[2] Teddy Roosevelt's assessment of women on the plains,[3] Crazy King Ludwig's mysterious and tragic powers over young maidens one year after his death,[4] and a 96-year-old man's feat of fathering 41 children.[5]

On August 11, 1887, the newspaper ran a story detailing the city's beautiful location along the Missouri River; its city rail service (which was unique because Sioux City was the youngest town in the nation to have a street railway); its new $1,500,000 railway bridge; its two new meatpacking houses; and its remarkable growth in general.[6] Then, 10 days later, the paper broke the biggest news of all — that Sioux City was to have a Corn Palace Jubilee beginning October 4.[7]

The first thing the city needed for Jubilee Week was the Corn Palace itself, so a meeting was held in the office of D.T. Hedges to organize the project. Mayor Cleland was elected its chairman, and those present quickly decided to raise a minimum of $5,000 for the exposition. Few specifics were finalized, but the committee determined that not only would a palace be decorated with corn, but also principal streets of the city and the buildings thereon. There were to be parades each day representing the major business interests, with emphasis on the pork packing industry. The *Daily Journal* editor stated, "St. Paul and Montreal can have their ice palaces, which melt at the first approach of spring, but Sioux City is going to build a palace of the product of the soil that is making it the great pork-packing center of the northwest."[8]

The program committee met for a second time on August 23 to report on its solicitation campaign and determine whether funds could be raised to proceed with the Corn Palace project. Members were happy to report that Sioux City residents viewed the venture "with a heartiness that [was] decidedly

Mayor Cleland

The Sioux City *Journal*

(Courtesy of State
Historical Society of Iowa)

encouraging. Men who formerly grumbled at a $5 subscription now [gave] freely $25. Everybody wants to see the Corn Palace a success. And it will be."[9]

The committee had not found the time to draw up a detailed blueprint but did prepare a plan that suggested building a palace with towers and buttresses, covering the palace with corn, wiring the interior for electric lights, and providing entertainment that included horse racing, music and fireworks.[10]

A location had not yet been chosen, though a vacant space on Sixth Street was suggested. Regardless of size or space, the architect, Mr. E.W. Loft, went ahead with drawings to be used for advertising. The original minimum expenditure of $5,000 had already been upped to $15,000, with preparations to go as high as $25,000.[11]

More information was leaked the following day concerning the Corn Palace design. There would be "four corner pavilions, representing Iowa, Dakota, Minnesota and Nebraska, each bearing a state banner. Over the main entrance there will be a platform with a primitive hog killing scene."[12] Hog killing scene? That seems unthinkable in today's world, but we must wonder what common practices today will seem unthinkable in the 22nd century. The article went on to say that the "corner pavilions are to be trimmed with straws of smaller cereals, while the main building will be trimmed with corn."[13]

On August 26, another meeting was held at the Hawkeye Club, and the members present waited with anticipation to view the architect's drawing of the new 60-foot-square Corn Palace. Everyone agreed that the design was very appealing, but they also agreed that it was too small. As enthusiasm grew, so did ideas, and it was quickly suggested that the palace be a minimum of 100 feet square. Several members in attendance thought that Fourth Street would be a good location for the Corn Palace, but they couldn't agree whether it should be at the corner of Jackson, Wall or Court Street. Others thought Fifth Street had a better spot. With five different locations receiving consideration, a committee was appointed to select a site.[14]

While the planned Corn Palace was growing in size, the festival itself was growing in length, stretching from four days to six. Instead of running from October 4-7, the party would commence on October 3 and end on October 8. An historian among the group pointed out that while no one had ever before built a Corn Palace, at least as far as anyone knew, celebrating the corn harvest dated back to Roman times "when the country people dressed in white and crowned with white oak leaves danced and sang harvest songs in honor of the goddess Ceres."[15]

The committee appointed to select a building site acted quickly and within 24 hours picked the corner of Fifth and Jackson Streets. That particular spot seemed to be favored because the Corn Palace could be joined to an existing building, Goldie's Rink, which would provide extra space for agricultural exhibits.[16]

Parade organizers had yet to finalize a route, but they knew there should be a parade every afternoon, and the Winnebago Indians should be in the processions since they were the first producers of corn in the U.S. One organizer thought the parade should be four miles long, though no reason was given.[17]

More details concerning the palace itself were released later in the week as Mr. Loft noted specific dimensions. The top of the flag staff would be 100 feet off the ground, each corner pavilion would be 16 feet square and 55 feet high, and the platform beneath the pig-killing scene would be 40 feet above the ground. Amazingly enough, it was expected to take only a week to build the Corn Palace, and another week to decorate it.[18]

The Corn Palace made the front page of the Sioux City *Daily Journal* for the first time on Friday morning, September 9, 1887, when the architect's sketch was presented to the public.[19] During the following week, businesses began promoting the Corn Palace Jubilee in their newspaper advertisements and playing on the Corn Palace theme. W.H. Livingston Company suddenly had a Dry Goods Palace,[20] White & Howe claimed their Shoe Palace was the Anti-Corn Palace,[21] whatever that meant, and B. Davidson & Co. hinted that President Cleveland and his beautiful wife might visit Sioux City so she could receive one of the handsome souvenirs made available to every lady in attendance during the first two days of the Festival. As it turned out, the president and his wife did tour the Corn Palace, but not until the festivities had come to a close.[22]

True to predictions, by September 19, the structure was up and the north side was mostly decorated, as was much of the central tower. However, there was suddenly a great deal more work ahead when it was decided to add another 100 feet to the west of the main building due to increased demand for exhibit space. The city had offered free freight to all exhibitors in hopes of increased participation, and apparently the plan more than met expectations.[23] The only city not participating was Sioux City's competition to the north, as pointed out in an article titled "Jealous Sioux Falls."[24]

On September 21, a rainstorm struck the city with such severity that it not only stopped the decorative efforts, but caused all meetings to be postponed as well. That left little for the *Daily Journal* to report besides that several 3-foot by 12-foot ears of corn were being built out of an unmentioned material, that Iowa's Governor Larrabee was meeting with President Cleveland to offer a personal invitation to attend the Corn Palace Exposition, that a group of ladies met before the rain hit to organize the interior decorations, and that more corn, other grains and grasses were needed to complete the decorations.[25]

The Sioux City Daily Journal

Wednesday, September 21, 1887

THE CORN PALACE.

Good Meetings Last Night, and Reports of Committees Show Everything all Right.

More Help Needed on Decoration—Some Notices to the Public—Press Observations.

THE PALACE BOOMING.

(Newspaper courtesy of State Historical Society of Iowa)

The Illustration on the left closely resembles the actual structure, as shown on the right.
(Courtesy of State Historical Society of Iowa, Special Collections)

An article appeared in the September 23, 1887, edition of the Sioux City *Daily Journal* that was much more entertaining than anything up to that point concerning the Corn Palace. To edit or paraphrase the article would diminish the humor therein, so it must be quoted in its entirety: "E.P. Johnson, the Pierce street merchant, and a man of unquestioned veracity, tells a JOURNAL reporter of a peculiar accident that happened to one of the mules on the Jennings street car line Wednesday night. The night was not only moist, but very dark, and when the driver quit his labors for the day, about 10 o'clock that night, he started up Pierce street with the mules for the street car stables. When he got in front of Mr. Hoyt's residence he observed that he was one mule short. The circumstance bewildered the fellow. He was willing to make affidavit that he had left the car with two mules only a few moments

before, but count as he would just then he could only find one mule present. To investigate the matter and satisfy himself that he was not insane or intoxicated he took the remaining mule and tied it to the fence, and then went to searching for the missing animal. He soon discovered a large hole in the ground which had occurred in a gas-main trench, and the water was roaring terribly in its submarine passage. He reached the conclusion at once that the mule had disappeared in that hole, but in looking into the recesses of the pit he could see nothing of the lost animal. To say that the driver was in a quandary does not express it. He knew positively that only a few moments before he was driving two mules, but how the one should get away without him observing it bothered the fellow terribly. He went to the fence and counted the mule several times, but only one appeared. Feeling positive that when he struck that hole he had a pair, he finally concluded that the missing beast must have gone into that wash-out, and he went down the hill nearly a block to look for the southern outlet of the tunnel. He found the mouth of this submarine passage, and while trying to find how much of a mouth there was, he was nearly frightened to death to see the missing mule standing in the hole below him. The mule had actually come nearly a block through that underground passage without receiving any injury. He was somewhat muddy, and his ears were pasted back, but he was taken out without very much trouble, and worked on the street car line yesterday."[26]

Also missing, but never found, were good song lyrics to arouse public fervor. The following lyrics were submitted instead:

"The farmer used to heave a sigh
Whenever the price of corn was not high,
But now take your glasses from your eye
And see it 110 feet in the sky.
It will pring — Well, corn is king."[27]

At 7:30 p.m. on October 3, 1887, the Sioux City Corn Palace was officially opened, and many of the city's 30,000 residents filled the streets in anticipation of wonderful things to come. It was reported that "there was no jostling, no crowding, and all moved about at will, enjoying the decorations and displays, and chatting gaily. Never was multitude in better humor or more perfect sympathy."[28] The palace's interior was described as "one grand panorama of delightful imagery, and over all poured the flood of brilliant, yet soft clear light of the electric apparatus, bringing out the beauty of nature's own painting, and throwing over all an indescribably suggestive glamour."[29]

Comments by the spectators included: "I saw the Philadelphia centennial and the Montreal Ice Palace, but they couldn't hold a candle to this." "I'm a St. Paul man, but I've got nothing to say. I'm going home and tell all our folks to come and see this vision." "I'll excuse the newspapers for all they've said. They can't tell it all as good as it is." "Gracious sakes! And do they feed corn to hogs? How can they?"[30]

Of all the attractions, displays and events, those involving Native Americans were among the most popular. Approximately 200 Omaha, Sioux and Winnebagos returned to the city that was once their fine hunting grounds to participate in exhibitions, parades and foot races for men and women. There was also a race between a horse and a bicycle (both with riders), and although the distance was not mentioned, the horse won by about three feet.[31]

On the third and fourth days of the Jubilee, Sioux City nearly doubled in size, thanks to visitors from surrounding states. The locals sometimes felt they were in the minority and joked that they wanted to run over and shake hands if they saw a person they knew. The skies were clear, the weather was warm, and there was little more organizers could ask for.[32]

On the closing day of the Festival, attention was turned to another memorable event for the city — the laying of the corner stone for the new $200,000 Chamber of Commerce building, within which would be housed a grand opera house.[33] There is little question that visitors were viewing a very proud city, though the weather did dampen spirits a bit. Rain poured on guests viewing the palace from the outside and dripped on those admiring the inside. On the bright side, those in attendance on the final day had more room to stroll among the exhibits at their leisure, thanks to the smaller crowds.[34]

The *Daily Journal* editor summed up public sentiment when he said, "The Corn Palace was the best advertisement Sioux City ever had. It was the best, because the most truthful. Sioux City has beat the world before; it has done it again. Buy a lot and build a home."[35]

But while the official Jubilee may have been over, activities were not entirely at an end. On October 10, the Corn Palace was opened to more than 500 people who had been unable to visit the previous week. On the following day, several VIPs were in attendance, including Cornelius

---

The Sioux City Journal

Sunday, October 2, 1887

READY FOR THE JUBILEE.

The Corn Palace Will be Ready for the Formal Opening Monday Evening.

The Palace a Vast Scene of Attractive Decorations—The City in Gay Attire.

IN HONOR OF CERES.

(Newspaper courtesy of State Historical Society of Iowa)

The Sioux City Daily Journal

Friday, October 7, 1887

PALACE CLIMAX.

By all Odds the Biggest Crowd the Northwest Ever Saw.

Grand Display of Iowa and Dakota Military Strength—Twelve Companies in Line.

Civic Demonstration Surpassing all Ovations Ever Held in the West.

(Newspaper courtesy of State Historical Society of Iowa)

(Newspaper courtesy of State Historical Society of Iowa)

Vanderbilt and the presidents of three major railroads. It was noted that they were very cordial and seemed very ordinary in spite of the fact that their combined wealth was more than $200,000,000.[36]

The biggest event, however, was saved for Wednesday, October 12, when President Grover Cleveland and his wife arrived by rail for a half-hour tour of the Corn Palace. Folks in Sioux City were grateful from the beginning because "Mankind never prayed for fine weather and was given a prettier dawn in which to celebrate an event of so much importance and pride to a city than nature gave Sioux City. The sky was entirely cloudless, the air fresh and pure, and over all came a feeling that even rugged old nature was chiming in as an interested party in the important event."[37]

The President and First Lady appeared to enjoy their visit and asked several questions about the various exhibits. President Cleveland seemed surprised at the productivity of the Dakota exhibit. Perhaps he wanted to think of it as a wasteland considering that, due to the area's Republican affiliation, he'd been fighting to prevent the territory from achieving statehood. The couple was showered with several souvenirs, but Mrs. Cleveland specifically requested two apples from the Montana exhibit, and the President asked for a large ear of corn from that state.[38]

With the presidential departure, the Corn Palace officially closed for the season, demolition began on the structure, and it was back to normalcy for the citizens of Sioux City. President Cleveland and his party visited several other cities on the way back to Washington, D.C., and perhaps his stop in Memphis actually proved more memorable than his visit to Sioux City. The President had received a welcoming address from Judge H.T. Ellett and was just finishing his own brief remarks when the judge suddenly died on the spot. The President was rushed from the viewing stand without being told of the judge's tragic fate.[39]

President and Mrs. Cleveland
(Newspaper and photos courtesy of State Historical Society of Iowa)

(Courtesy of State Historical Society
of Iowa, Special Collections)

Sioux City
Corn Palace
1888

Section 1 ❖ Iowa
CHAPTER 1

Sioux City may have triumphed with its Corn Palace venture, but it became obvious the following year that the city was not resting on its laurels, nor was it limiting its efforts for future success only to expositions. An announcement was made in late July that the city would be building an elegant new YMCA building on the corner of Pierce and Seventh Streets for upwards of $100,000. The idea had been discussed and debated for the previous four years, and 1888 seemed to be the right time for the undertaking.[40]

In August there were numerous advertisements and articles to inform city residents of the Peavey Opera House grand opening, with its premier performance to run concurrently with the opening of the Corn Palace Exposition. The *Journal* editor wrote, "It is fitting that a palace city should have a play-house in keeping with its pretension, and the Peavey Grand will be to the theater-going people of Sioux City what the Corn Palace is to the city generally — the chief point of interest and the center of attraction."[41] The Conried Opera Company of Chicago was to perform Strauss' *The Gypsy Baron* with fifty actors plus a full orchestra under the direction of Heinrich Conried, who, with 1,006 plays and operas under his belt, was considered the best manager of comic opera in the country.[42]

(Newspaper courtesy of State Historical Society of Iowa)

(Newspaper courtesy of State Historical Society of Iowa)

YMCA, corner of 7th and Pierce Streets, the Sioux City *Journal,* July 29, 1888

(Courtesy of State Historical Society of Iowa)

The Peavey Grand.

Peavey Opera House, the Sioux City *Journal,* September 25, 1888

(Courtesy of State Historical Society of Iowa)

115 ft. octagonal
center tower

1888 Sioux City Corn Palace
(Courtesy of Mitchell Area Historical Society)

Horse-drawn
omnibus

50 ft. corner tower

TICKET OFFICE

Not a bare head or pair of overalls in sight

On September 2, 1888, the call went out from the mayor to all Sioux City women to join in helping make the new Corn Palace grander than the previous year's,[43] and three days later there was a call to the men in essence saying, "Don't expect the women to do it all!" To drive the point home, the editor stated, "Only twenty days until the Festival opens. Let us decorate."[44] Also in that issue was a letter to Mayor Cleland from a New York City publisher who wanted a picture of the Corn Palace in his magazine. He also asked several questions: "What is the Corn Palace? Is it made of corn cobs or corn husks? or boiled corn on the ear? or cornstalks? Or is it an ordinary building full of corn? Or are the people corned when they get inside of it?"[45]

The answers to those questions, thorough but confusing in their complexity, soon appeared in the Journal: "The Corn Palace is a frame building 150 by 150 feet. It thus covers exactly one-quarter of a block of space. It is situated on the corner of Pierce and Sixth streets. It fronts west on Pierce and south on Sixth street. The main wall of the side is 30 feet high. Rising from each corner of the building is a double tower, 32 feet square, fronting to each side, and projecting outwardly 16 feet from the line of the main wall, and rising to a height of 50 feet from the ground line. Midway on each side of the building between the corner towers is a tower of equal height, but projecting only 6 feet outwardly from the main wall. Under each of these middle towers on the ground floor is an ample exit. The main entrance to the building is on the southwest corner of Pierce and Sixth streets— through the double tower of this corner. Rising above this corner and above its double tower is an octagonal tower 115 feet in height, the southwest face of which is a continuation of the perpendicular line of the face of the lower corner tower over the grand portal. The diameter of the octagonal tower is twenty-four feet. Springing from the inmost line of the almost flat roof over the gallery, which is thirty feet wide, but starting at a perpendicular elevation of six feet clear above that line, rises the roof from each side of the building to a point in the center, each side thus being a triangle and forming a central roof in the form of a pyramid."[46]

As for the decorations, the paper went on to say, "The predominating decorative material of the exterior surface is corn. Ears of corn are sawed lengthwise into halves or into transverse sections about an inch thick. These sections are nailed firmly on the sides into every conceivable pattern and geometrical figure. Sections of all colors of corn ears are used — yellow, white, red, variegated, the deep blue 'squaw corn' and all intermediate colors; corn of all kinds and of all stages of growth."[47]

The following item of interest was in the September 8 issue of the *Journal*: "The flags were ordered yesterday. They consist of a thirty-foot national flag which will be attached to a staff from the main tower and surmounted by a forty-foot streamer. Four lettered burgees will float from lower points on the tower and be inscribed, respectively, Iowa, Dakota, Nebraska, and Minnesota. Two blue stars and eight national burgees will be placed at other prominent points."[48] Decorating had started on the upper exterior of the dome, several loads of millet and pompas grass had been delivered and were awaiting the decorators, measures were taken to guard against fires, and the superintendent announced that no one would be allowed to spit on his carpet so he could keep his office "in apple-pie order for lady visitors."[49]

A brief paragraph appeared in the September 12 issue of the *Journal* that must have shocked a few people. E.W. Loft, Corn Palace architect, sent to the editor an angry notice asserting that the decorators on the Corn Palace were not carrying forth his plan. He stated that he had made no designs of decoration and had positively refused to furnish any for incompetent contractors to mutilate.[50] Ouch! On a more positive note, corn for decorating was coming in so fast that contractors were requested to delay their hauling, and experimentation showed that sorghum seed worked very well for the fancier decorating required to make cornices, architraves and capitals.[51]

Corn-decorated interior, 1888 (Courtesy of State Historical Society of Iowa, Special Collections)

By September 22, the Corn Palace management had heard a request from the Ministers' Association to close the palace on Sundays[52] and had successfully tested 17 of the 28 arc lights being used in addition to several incandescent lights. Corn Palace souvenirs ready for sale at a local jewelry store included presentation medals that sold from $3.50 to $25.00, solid gold pins from $3.00 to $6.00, Waterbury watches with a Corn Palace design at $2.50, solid silver Corn Palace pencils for $2.00, pocketbooks from 25 cents to $1.25, match boxes for 25 cents, and Corn Palace corn cob pipes for 15 cents and

20 cents.[53]

At noon on September 24, 1888, there was an unceremonious opening of the palace doors. "There was no speechmaking, no noise and fuss, but a simple, quiet opening of the famous Corn Palace, which from now on will be viewed by many thousands daily for the next two weeks."[54] But the noontime peace and quiet was suddenly broken when "at 2 o'clock a squad of police went to the Commercial hotel and escorted the famous Elgin Watch Factory Military band, of Elgin, Ill., to the Palace."[55] No explanation was given as to whether or not the escort was

Interior corn-decorated fireplaces, 1888

(Courtesy of State Historical Society of Iowa, Special Collections)

(Newspaper courtesy of State Historical Society of Iowa)

of an honorary nature.

As a whole, officials and visitors alike seemed well pleased with the '88 Exposition. The weather was mostly favorable, and the ministers were somewhat appeased in that, though the palace remained open on Sundays, sacred music was performed and enough noisy activities were abandoned to make it seem as though it were a day of rest. The men's Corn Palace Chorus improved considerably from its first performance to its second, and the women's Corn Palace Chorus was so "well received and so warmly applauded it had to be repeated."[56] As for attendance, crowds were much larger than the previous year, and it was stated that "Half of Iowa, a quarter of Nebraska, and all of south Dakota seem to have gathered here."[57]

As the 1888 Exposition came to a close on October 7, no decision had yet been made on whether to sell the Corn Palace or simply tear it down, though there was a rumor that someone from Utah had offered to buy it for $1,000. It was too early to worry about that, and the general feeling was very simply stated by a sign posted on the palace entrance: "Closed. Everybody is tired."[58]

(Courtesy of State Historical Society of Iowa, Special Collections)

Sioux City Corn Palace 1889

Section 1 ❖ Iowa
CHAPTER 1

The 1889 Exposition proceeded in a similar manner to the first two — a new, bigger and better building was constructed, a bigger and better band was sought, and the women took charge of the interior. The building was barely completed when the Exposition committee found it necessary to build an addition onto the northwest corner due to an increased demand in exhibit space. Because of the increased size of the Corn Palace, as well as the desire to make it more impressive to returning visitors, it was estimated that decorating costs would be up 40 percent from the previous year.[59] Costs no doubt rose even higher when some of the interior decorations were damaged by a heavy rainstorm that struck before the roof was completed.[60]

A delegation from Boston caused a fair amount of excitement when it announced its interest in visiting the Corn Palace. The locals saw it as further proof that their Exposition must be extraordinary because, after all, "A true Bostonian does not pick up and fly over the country on any ordinary occasion. He has seen everything almost, heard everything almost, read everything almost, and made up his mind that nearly everything is vanity and vexation of spirit, except Boston."[61]

An article appearing the following week in the Des Moines *Leader* put a different slant on the story: "Sioux City parties were in this city yesterday, and while here closed a contract with the Raymond Excursion company, of Boston, for a solid train of eight vestibule cars to make the round trip from Boston to the Sioux City Corn Palace exposition, to give easterners an opportunity to view the growth and advantages of Sioux City and northwestern Iowa. The price to be paid for the train is $7,500. What Sioux City does she does in a broad and openhanded way that commands admiration. She spends her money like a queen."[62]

A separate article explained that individuals taking advantage of the excursion train would pay $75 for a sleeping car, meals, and three days in Sioux City. There was no mention whether they also were expected to pay for admission into the Palace. If so, coupon books of 10 or 20 were being offered for the price of $3.50 and $6.00, respectively.[63]

The Sioux City Journal

Thursday, August 29, 1889

THE CORN PALACE.

———

The Ladies Turn Out in Strong Force and Dispose of a Delicate Question.

———

The Palace to Stand Until the South American Visitors See It.

———

Sacred Sunday Concerts, Etc.

The Sioux City Journal

Sunday, September 15, 1889

THE CORN PALACE.

———

The Rain Did But a Trifling Amount of Damage to the Decorations.

The Sioux City Journal

Thursday, September 12, 1889

COMING TO THE PALACE

———

A Special Train Will Bring Some Bostonians to the Corn Palace Carnival.

(Newspapers courtesy of State Historical Society of Iowa)

The Sioux City Journal

Friday, September 20, 1889

SIOUX CITY CORN PALACE

Opens its Portals to the World, Monday, September 23, at Noon.

———

First Grand Concert at 1:30 P.M. by
71st REGIMENT BAND OF NEW YORK,
Prof. Arthur A. Clappe, Director.

———

Formal Opening Monday Evening at 7:30.

———

OPENING ADDRESS BY
HON. J.M. THURSTON
THE MOST GIFTED OF WESTERN ORATORS.

———

MISS DORA HENNINGS
The Well Known Operatic Soprano, Accompanied by the full
71st REGIMENT BAND
In Rosini's Masterpiece, "INFLAMMATUS," from "STABAT MATTER."

———

ADDRESS BY MR. A.W. ERWIN.

———

Coupon Tickets in Books of Ten—$3.50; in Books of Twenty—$6.00
General Admission, 50c. Children, 25c.
Reserved Chairs—Tickets sold only inside the Palace—10c.
Get your Tickets early and avoid the crush at night.

(Newspaper courtesy of State Historical Society of Iowa)

The third Sioux City Corn Palace very nearly earned the headlines "The Exposition That Wasn't" when the nearby Palace barn caught fire three days before the opening of the 1889 Exposition. The two men who discovered the fire at first thought the Palace itself was on fire, but what they found was in a sense even more horrible as they helplessly stood by and watched 68 horses burn to death. The next day's *Journal* could only have made the owners feel worse when they read the tacky subheadlines, "An Early Breakfast of Baked Horseflesh; for Which Sixty-Eight Equines Are Roasted."[64]

The fire was brought under control before it reached the Corn Palace, but superstitious tongues were wagging when it was reported that two previous livery barns had also burned to the ground on that very spot.[65]

The 1889 Exposition opened on September 23 to bleary skies,[66] and it wasn't until the fifth day that sunny skies and warm temperatures greeted the attendees.[67] Crowds were satisfactory during the remainder of the two-week run, but organizers knew it was going to be difficult for the carnival to turn a profit. The event was still declared a success, of course, and plans were quickly made for the upcoming year.[68]

(Newspaper courtesy of State Historical Society of Iowa)

Sioux City businessmen spent $3,500 to decorate a six-car Corn Palace Train that would travel to Washington, D.C., on February 28 for the inauguration of President Benjamin Harrison, March 4, 1889.

(Courtesy Mitchell Area Historical Society)

Sioux City Corn Palace interior, 1889
(Courtesy of State Historical Society of Iowa, Special Collections)

Sioux City Corn Palace, 1889
(Courtesy of State Historical Society of Iowa, Special Collections)

(Courtesy of
Mitchell Area Historical Society)

Sioux City
Corn Palace
1890

Section 1 ❖ Iowa
CHAPTER 1

By the following September 18, the carpenters were nearly finished with their work on the 1890 Corn Palace, and decoration of the exterior was already under way. Hundreds of women were ahead of schedule on the interior decorations, although local businessmen had failed to decorate the main arteries leading to the Corn Palace, leaving them "dull and uninviting to the thousands of visitors who [would] gather daily on the streets."[69]

Other concerns involved disreputable individuals who had already been seen lurking on street corners, so the mayor appointed 20 special officers to deal with them. In the past, additional law enforcement hadn't been hired until the beginning of the Exposition, but that year he was worried about "having the horse stolen before the stable was locked up."[70]

The 1890 Corn Palace was described by the *Journal* as superior to the previous structures and as having "a sort of Gothic style of architecture with Corn Palace treatment — a Mohammedan mosque with Iowa trimmings. The building is almost square, with entrances at the corners; a tall central dome rises high above the roof, and six smaller towers are placed along the sides. The main building is about 200 feet square, though irregular, and having a large annex at the rear."[71] The dome was considered the most imposing spectacle, followed by the six smaller towers that were 120 feet high and 14 feet square. The Corn Palace's chief decorator was probably not too pleased with the editor's statement about a general plan, or the lack thereof: "There is none, except to get as many pretty and novel designs as possible and not to duplicate them."[72]

Sioux City's mayor profited unexpectedly from the Exposition when the city council presented him with a new silk hat in recognition of the substantial increase in city revenues due to fines imposed for illegal liquor sales and consumption.[73] The city was also no doubt profiting from the nearly perfect weather during the first week of the Exposition. Crowds were larger than ever, and the future looked promising.[74] The second week, however, proved less successful and attendance dropped sharply. The event was still considered a success, and the closing day was to finish with a flurry of dignitaries, including governors from Iowa and South Dakota and congressional representatives from each of the surrounding states.[75] Unfortunately, heavy rains set in, the Corn Palace roof leaked, and the only dignitaries who showed up were Governor Mellette of South Dakota and one congressman. It was indeed a dismal end to the festivities.[76]

(Newspapers courtesy of State Historical Society of Iowa)

The Sioux City Journal

Thursday, September 25, 1890

OPEN THIS EVENING.

THE FIRST GRAND CONCERT.

The First Correct Programme for the
Carnival Weeks.

Almost Ready for Public Inspection.

(Newspapers courtesy of
State Historical Society of Iowa)

The Sioux City Journal

Saturday, September 27, 1890

BUSY DAY WITH THE POLICE

A Great Variety of Offenders
Jailed Yesterday.

MANY FINES WERE INFLICTED.

There was a motley throng packed
into the cells of the city jail last night.
The cages have been filling gradually
for some days past, and with yesterday's dose the old cage was packed up
to the top tier.

**Tall central dome (above) and two of the smaller
towers (right)**
(Courtesy of State Historical Society of Iowa, Special Collections)

The Sioux City Journal

Saturday, October 11, 1890

A BOLD DAYLIGHT ROBBERY

———

A Stage Coach Held Up by Cowboys on the Streets of Sioux City.

———

CORN PALACE TO CLOSE TO-DAY

———

Col. Wm. Swarts was in command of the old western stage coach. It was drawn by four horses, was filled with passengers and on top was an armed guard to protect the United States mail and American express treasure box. A troop of twenty-five or thirty cowboys, mounted and armed, followed and when the parade had finished and Fourth street was cleared the coach was driven rapidly up the street pursued by the cowboy gang. Just opposite the Booge the coach was over-taken by the outlaws and firing commenced by both the pursued and the pursuers. A lively fusillade was kept up for a few minutes, the mail bag was demanded and secured, the driver of the coach and all the guard gave up and the robbery was complete. Just then a body of mounted police appeared on the scene and gave chase to the robber gang and after a lively conflict recaptured the mail bag and routed the desperadoes. It was about the liveliest street demonstration yet seen and reflected great credit on its originator.

(Newspaper courtesy of
State Historical Society of Iowa)

Sioux City Corn Palace interior, 1890
(Courtesy of State Historical Society of Iowa,
Special Collections)

(Courtesy of Mitchell Area Historical Society)

Sioux City Corn Palace 1891

Section 1 ❖ Iowa
CHAPTER 1

On September 8, 1891, an announcement was issued for the fifth annual Corn Palace Festival, stating that it would run from October 1-17, and would feature the Mexican National Band.[77] The following week a wide-ranging dancing program was listed, which included the Grand March, waltz, quadrille, polka, lancers, waltz quadrille and schottische.[78]

So many South Dakota counties booked exhibit space at the 1891 Festival that Corn Palace organizers decided they'd better acknowledge the spirit of good will by reciprocating with a visit to the South Dakota State Fair.[79]

Sioux City businessmen started making plans for another South Dakota visit after receiving an invitation from Plankinton. The small community was putting the finishing touches on a Grain Palace and was dedicating the opening day to Sioux City. The larger city accepted the invitation and quickly formed a committee to sell 50 tickets for $10 each to guarantee an engine, coach and sleeper for the trip to Plankinton. The train would leave at 10 p.m. on Monday, September 28, and would arrive early Tuesday morning.[80]

The excursion went off without a hitch, and the Sioux City contingent was treated like royalty. Plankinton residents were urged to purchase their wholesale products from Sioux City, and the Plankinton representatives declared Sioux City a natural market for their produce. The two communities agreed to a lasting treaty of peace and good will, and then the Sioux City delegation returned home bleary-eyed but in good spirits.[81]

A musical concert on the evening of October 3 provided a few of the more interesting moments in the 1891 Exposition. The audience was well represented by both northerners and southerners, and even though less than three decades had passed since the Civil War, the orchestra leader, Captain Payen, added three new numbers to his program.

HOLD YOUR HEAD UP.

The man who wears a Dow Hat can hold his head up proudly in any community. The man with a Shocking bad hat should carry his head under his arm.

The Sioux City *Journal,* July 9, 1891

(Newspapers courtesy of State Historical Society of Iowa)

The Sioux City Journal

Wednesday, September 16, 1891

THE OFFICIAL PROGRAM (partial)

Thursday, October 1
Opening of the Corn Palace and harvest festival.

Friday, October 2 & Saturday, October 3
Two grand concerts by the Mexican National band.

Sunday, October 4
Sacred concert by the Mexican National band.

Monday, October 5
German Day

Tuesday, October 6
Civic society day.

Wednesday, October 7 & Thursday, October 8
Bicycle day.

Friday, October 9
Dakota Day

Saturday, October 10
Traveling men's day.

Sunday, October 11
Sacred concerts by the Mexican national band.

Monday, October 12
Indian day.

Tuesday, October 13
Equipage day
(Significant parade of handsome horses and tasteful turnouts of every variety.)

The Sioux City Journal

Wednesday, September 16, 1891

THE CARNIVAL PROGRAMME

———

Arrangement of the Details for King Corn's Festival.

———

THE OPENING CEREMONIAL

———

German Day October 5—Grand Dress Ball on the 8th—Dakota Day on the 9th—Traveling Men's Day, Indian Day, Etc.—What Will Be Done with the Crowds.

(Courtesy of State Historical Society of Iowa, Special Collections)

The Sioux City Journal

Sunday, September 20, 1891

STATE FAIR AND PALACE

Dakota Exhibits for Sioux Falls and Sioux City.

THE RECIPROCITY FEELING

Looking for Iowa Visitors at the Exhibition This Week—The Black Hills Will Be at Both Places—Yankton Is Getting Ready to Show Itself.

Sioux Falls, Sept. 19.—Special: The state fair managers are anticipating a good sized attendance from the neighboring state of Iowa and Sioux City in particular. Insomuch as the Corn Palace has received heretofore a hearty support from South Dakotans the board are of the opinion that it is no more than just that Sioux City should respond in a manner to be noticed, by taking hold and having a well-attended excursion from the King Corn city on one day of the fair.

The Sioux City Journal

Friday, September 25, 1891

FROM PALACE TO PALACE

An Excursion to Visit the Plankinton Grain Palace.

IT WILL GO MONDAY EVENING

The First Palace City to Interchange Courtesies with One of the Latest—The Black Hills Exhibit at the Corn Palace—Palace Kernels.

The Sioux City Journal

Wednesday, September 30, 1891

PLANKINTON GRAIN PALACE

Formal Opening of the Temple to Ceres Yesterday

SIOUX CITY PARTICIPATED

A Representative Delegation from the Corn Palace City Present.

(Newspapers courtesy of State Historical Society of Iowa)

He started off with "Yankee Doodle," which garnered moderate applause, and followed it with "Dixie," which caused the southerners to go wild. The third piece was "The Star Spangled Banner," and after the song ended there was a period of dead silence until the northerners gave in to their pent-up emotions. The *Journal* editor's description of the scene is worth noting: "It seemed as if every man were ready to draw the sword and every woman ready to cheer him on to the fray. Then one looked at another as if half ashamed of the feeling shown. That glance was reassuring, and as if in mutual commendation or endorsement another volley of applause followed."[82]

Exposition attendees were thrilled with the decorations, the programs, the Indian Corn Dances and the musical programs, but few things thrilled them more than a sunny day, and there were few sunny days with which to be thrilled. Despite the unfortunate weather conditions, the Exposition management claimed total receipts of more than $35,000, which was reported to be the largest gross ever, but it was still not enough to make the Exposition a financial success. The celebration was extended an extra week, but even that didn't help. Organizers had hoped to raffle off the Corn Palace, but that plan was scuttled at the last minute and money was refunded to those holding tickets. Payment on outstanding bills was to be delayed until the close of the Exposition, and the last evening was declared a benefit night, where passes would not be recognized and additional revenues would be used to help reduce a deficit of $25,000.[83]

When the doors closed for the last time on October 25, the *Journal* editor reflected on the sadness of the day: "It was lonely enough under the cold glare of the incandescent lights, and a

The Sioux City *Journal,* October 18, 1891
(Courtesy of State Historical Society of Iowa)

footfall echoed drearily through the vast building, as if echo itself were oppressed at the thought of the day when no two sticks of the great structure should be left together. Yet it was difficult to look upon the magnificent sweep of those arches, and note the massive colonnades from which they spring, to drink in the beauty of the coloring of the wide vaulted roof and the graceful drooping draperies of the proscenium, and at the same time realize that this creation so beautiful and so grand had been called into existence to be the center of a few weeks' festivities, only to be cast aside again before a moon had waned."[84]

And cast aside it was. The Corn Palace Association decided to accept offers for the 1891 Palace, and it wasn't long before they wished they'd gone ahead with the raffle. Not only did they receive no offers, but eventually they had to pay for the dismantling and removal of the building.[85]

In May of 1892, tragedy struck Sioux City in the form of a devastating flood that put an end to the year's Exposition. Economic losses were so severe that a majority of the city's businessmen felt funds could not be spared for a palace plus the reconstruction of the business community. The Palace concept was certain to be revived the following year, but then the great Panic of 1893 created a financial burden too heavy for the city to bear. The Sioux City Corn Palace era had come to an end.[86]

Sioux City Corn Palace interior, 1891 (Courtesy of State Historical Society of Iowa, Special Collections)

Illustration of proposed 1892 Sioux City Corn Palace
(Courtesy of Mitchell Area Historical Society)

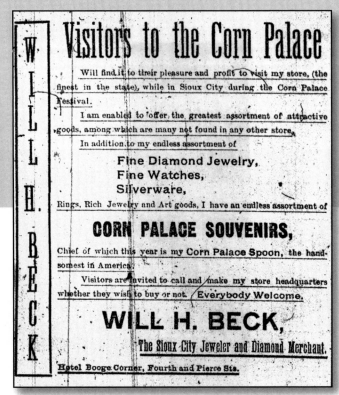

The Sioux City *Journal*, September 23, 1891
(Courtesy of State Historical Society of Iowa)

The Sioux City Journal

Thursday, October 16, 1891

CONTINUED.

THE CORN PALACE.

It will not close until SUNDAY EVENING, OCTOBER 25. The famous Pullman Band, now in Chicago, the greatest musical organization that has ever visited the west, has been engaged for two concerts daily. Special attractions and magnificent parades are being arranged for. The extended week to be made the most attractive of the entire carnival.

(Newspapers courtesy of
State Historical Society of Iowa)

The Sioux City Journal

Monday, October 26, 1891

THE CARNIVAL IS ENDED

———

The Beautiful Corn Palace Soon to Be Demolished.

———

THE BAND'S LAST CONCERT.

———

The Train of Reflection Started by the Contemplation of the Destruction of So Much Beauty that Ran with the Band's Music.

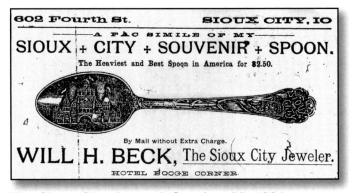

The Sioux City *Journal*, October 26, 1891
(Courtesy of State Historical Society of Iowa)

Footnotes for the Sioux City Corn Palace, 1887-1891

1. Perkins Brothers, "A Start Made," Sioux City *Daily Journal*, June 2, 1887, p. 3.
2. Perkins Brothers, "Victoria's Jubilee," Sioux City *Daily Journal*, June 22, 1887, p. 2.
3. Perkins Brothers, "Queens of the Ranch," Sioux City *Daily Journal*, June 24, 1887, p. 4.
4. Perkins Brothers, "The Vows of Ludwig," Sioux City *Daily Journal*, July 20, 1887, p. 4.
5. Perkins Brothers, "Father of Forty-One," Sioux City *Daily Journal*, July 29, 1887, p. 3.
6. Perkins Brothers, "A Bit of History," Sioux City *Daily Journal*, August 11, 1887, p. 3.
7. Perkins Brothers, "Corn Palace," Sioux City *Daily Journal*, August 21, 1887, p. 3.
8. Ibid.
9. Perkins Brothers, "Everybody Taking Hold," Sioux City *Daily Journal*, August 24, 1887, p. 3.
10. Perkins Brothers, "The Programme," Sioux City *Daily Journal*, August 24, 1887, p. 3.
11. Ibid.
12. Perkins Brothers, "The Corn Palace," Sioux City *Daily Journal*, August 26, 1887, p. 3.
13. Ibid.
14. Perkins Brothers, "A Larger Corn Palace," Sioux City *Daily Journal*, August 27, 1887, p. 3.
15. Ibid.
16. Perkins Brothers, "The Corn Palace Located," Sioux City *Daily Journal*, August 28, 1887, p. 3.
17. Perkins Brothers, "The Parade," Sioux City *Daily Journal*, August 28, 1887, p. 3.
18. Perkins Brothers, "The Plans Adopted," Sioux City *Daily Journal*, August 30, 1887, p. 3.
19. Perkins Brothers, "Sioux City Corn Palace," Sioux City *Daily Journal*, September 9, 1887, p. 1.
20. Perkins Brothers, "Dry-Goods-Palace," Sioux City *Daily Journal*, September 11, 1887, p. 5
21. Perkins Brothers, "The Anti-Corn Palace," Sioux City *Daily Journal*, September 18, 1887, p. 5.
22. Perkins Brothers, "B. Davidson & Co.," Sioux City *Daily Journal*, September 18, 1887, p. 3.
23. Perkins Brothers, "The Corn Palace," Sioux City *Daily Journal*, September 20, 1887, p. 6.
24. Perkins Brothers, "Jealous Sioux Falls," Sioux City *Daily Journal*, September 22, 1887, p. 3.
25. Perkins Brothers, "Palace Items," Sioux City *Daily Journal*, September 22, 1887, p. 6.
26. Perkins Brothers, "A Mule's Excursion," Sioux City *Daily Journal*, September 23, 1887, p. 5.
27. J. G. Smith, "Corn is King," Sioux City *Daily Journal*, September 23, 1887, p. 6.
28. Perkins Brothers, "The Formal Opening," Sioux City *Daily Journal*, October 4, 1887, p. 1.
29. Ibid.
30. Perkins Brothers, "Fragmentary Tributes," Sioux City *Daily Journal*, October 4, 1887, p. 1.
31. Perkins Brothers, "The Second Day," Sioux City *Daily Journal*, October 5, 1887, p. 1.
32. Perkins Brothers, "Growing Greater," Sioux City *Daily Journal*, October 6, 1887, p. 1.
33. Perkins Brothers, "Laying the Corner-Stone," Sioux City *Daily Journal*, October 8, 1887, p. 1.
34. Perkins Brothers, "The Jubilee Ended," Sioux City *Daily Journal*, October 9, 1887, p. 1.
35. Perkins Brothers, "Come Again, Everybody," Sioux City *Daily Journal*, October 9, 1887, p. 4.
36. Perkins Brothers, "A Wealthy Party," Sioux City *Daily Journal*, October 12, 1887, p. 6.
37. Perkins Brothers, "The City's Guests," Sioux City *Daily Journal*, October 13, 1887, p. 1.
38. Ibid.
39. Perkins Brothers, "His Last Speech," Sioux City *Daily Journal*, October 16, 1887, p. 2.
40. Perkins Brothers, "The Y.M.C.A.," Sioux City *Daily Journal*, July 29, 1888, p. 1.
41. Perkins Brothers, "Peavey Grand Opening," Sioux City *Daily Journal*, August 9, 1888, p. 6.
42. Ibid.
43. Perkins Brothers, "The Ladies Invited to Their Work," Sioux City *Daily Journal*, September 2, 1888, p. 6.
44. Perkins Brothers, "Building the Palace," Sioux City *Daily Journal*, September 5, 1888, p. 6.
45. Perkins Brothers, "Wants to Know, You Know," Sioux City *Daily Journal*, September 5, 1888, p. 6.
46. Perkins Brothers, "The Structure: Exterior Decorations," Sioux City *Daily Journal*, September 23, 1888, p. 1.
47. Ibid.
48. Perkins Brothers, "Building the Palace," Sioux City *Daily Journal*, September 8, 1888, p. 8.
49. Ibid.

50. Perkins Brothers, "Corn Palace Gossip," Sioux City *Daily Journal*, September 12, 1888, p. 8.
51. Perkins Brothers, "Some Nubbins," Sioux City *Daily Journal*, September 12, 1888, p. 8.
52. Perkins Brothers, "Opposed to a Sunday Exhibition," Sioux City *Daily Journal*, September 18, 1888, p. 6.
53. Perkins Brothers, "Other Palace Matters," Sioux City *Daily Journal*, September 22, 1888, p. 6.
54. Perkins Brothers, "The Opening," Sioux City *Daily Journal*, September 25, 1888, p. 2.
55. Perkins Brothers, "Band Concert," Sioux City *Daily Journal*, September 25, 1888, p. 2.
56. Perkins Brothers, "Wednesday's Tale," Sioux City *Daily Journal*, October 4, 1888, p. 2.
57. Perkins Brothers, "Sioux City Festival," Sioux City *Daily Journal*, October 7, 1888, p. 3.
58. Perkins Brothers, "Corn Palace Notes," Sioux City *Daily Journal*, October 7, 1888, p. 2.
59. Perkins Brothers, "About the Palace," Sioux City *Daily Journal*, September 14, 1889, p. 6.
60. Perkins Brothers, "The Corn Palace," Sioux City *Daily Journal*, September 15, 1889, p. 7.
61. Perkins Brothers, "Coming to the Palace," Sioux City *Daily Journal*, September 12, 1889, p. 3.
62. Perkins Brothers, "From the Outside Press," Sioux City *Daily Journal*, September 18, 1889, p. 6.
63. Perkins Brothers, "The Boston Excursion," Sioux City *Daily Journal*, September 18, 1889, p. 6.
64. Perkins Brothers, "The Flames' Feast," Sioux City *Daily Journal*, September 21, 1889, p. 6.
65. Ibid.
66. Perkins Brothers, "The Carnival Open," Sioux City *Daily Journal*, September 24, 1889, p. 1.
67. Perkins Brothers, "The Crowd Got Here," Sioux City *Daily Journal*, September 28, 1889, p. 3.
68. Perkins Brothers, "The Corn Palace," Sioux City *Daily Journal*, October 8, 1889, p. 6.
69. Perkins Brothers, "Hundreds of Decorators," Sioux City *Daily Journal*, September 18, 1890, p. 8.
70. Perkins Brothers, "The Corn Palace Fakir," Sioux City *Daily Journal*, September 18, 1890, p. 8.
71. Perkins Brothers, "Open This Evening," Sioux City *Daily Journal*, September 25, 1890, p. 1.
72. Ibid.
73. Perkins Brothers, "The City is Making Money," Sioux City *Daily Journal*, September 27, 1890, p. 5.
74. Perkins Brothers, "A Great Day for Visitors," Sioux City *Daily Journal*, October 3, 1890, p. 6.
75. Perkins Brothers, "Corn Palace to Close Today," Sioux City *Daily Journal*, October 11, 1890, p. 5.
76. William J. Peterson, *The Palimpsest* Vol XLIV (The State Historical Society of Iowa, 1963) 560.
77. Perkins Brothers, "Sioux City Corn Palace," Sioux City *Daily Journal*, September 8, 1891, p. 7.
78. Perkins Brothers, "The Carnival Programme," Sioux City *Daily Journal*, September 16, 1891, p. 5.
79. Perkins Brothers, "State Fair and Palace," Sioux City *Daily Journal*, September 20, 1891, p. 6.
80. Perkins Brothers, "From Palace to Palace," Sioux City *Daily Journal*, September 25, 1891, p. 5.
81. Perkins Brothers, "Plankinton Grain Palace," Sioux City *Daily Journal*, September 30, 1891, p. 3.
82. Perkins Brothers, "Two Grand Concerts Given," Sioux City *Daily Journal*, October 4, 1891, p. 6.
83. Perkins Brothers, "Not A Very Large Crowd," Sioux City *Daily Journal*, October 21, 1891, p. 3.
84. Perkins Brothers, "The Carnival Is Ended," Sioux City *Daily Journal*, October 26, 1891, p. 5.
85. Perkins Brothers, "Not A Very Large Crowd," Sioux City *Daily Journal*, October 21, 1891, p. 3.
86. John W. Carey, "Fifty Years Ago," Sioux City *Daily Journal*, June 2, 1942.

(Courtesy of Iowa's Union County Historical Society)

Creston Blue Grass Palace 1889

Section 1 ❖ Iowa
CHAPTER 2

After watching Sioux City host two successful Corn Palace Expositions in 1887 and 1888, the town of Creston, Iowa, determined it was time to promote southwestern Iowa's Blue Grass Region in a manner similar to northwestern Iowa's Corn Belt. It was decided to test the waters in 1889 with a modest but attractive structure decorated with locally grown blue grass.[1] But that was practically the only decision that came easily. When a local newspaper headline referred to the proposed structure as the "Harmony Palace," the editor was making an attempt at sarcasm, for there was considerable dissention in the community concerning the name of the palace, the location, and the cost.[2]

The most amusing and often reported debate occurred between two rival newspapers concerning the naming of the palace. The editor of the Creston *Advertiser* wanted the structure called the Hay Palace to encompass all of the grasses in the area, but the editor of the Creston *Gazette,* W.T. Foster, said "such a name is absurd,

Creston Daily Gazette

Wednesday, August 21, 1889

THE PALACE

EVERYTHING NOW READY FOR A GLORI-
OUS OPENING TO-MORROW.

———

The Blue Grass Counties Magnificently
Represented

(Newspaper courtesy of
State Historical Society of Iowa)

ridiculous, and no man with any refinement of sentiment would suggest such."[3]

Foster preferred Blue Grass Palace, but said he supported the *Advertiser's* first suggestion of Grass Palace. The editor of the *Advertiser* then fired back that he had "never suggested anything but a Hay Palace, constructed of baled hay, embellished with dried grasses and other products of the country, as an appropriate advertisement of the blue grass section of Iowa as the greatest stock raising and general farming country in the world. Neither did the *Gazette* 'endorse' the *Advertiser's* suggestion, though we are sorry it did not, as reference to its files will show that after two months of silence its first utterance on the subject was an ill natured snarl about the proposed name, devoid of the slightest vestige of 'endorsement' or even ordinary courtesy."[4]

After further exchanges between the two newspapers, the Advertiser editor finally gave in to the Blue Grass Palace concept, but not before firing off a particularly vitriolic salvo. "We care not what it may be named so long as it be a 'hay palace' and accomplishes the mission for which it should be designed. We are perfectly willing, neighbor, if it will broaden the diameter of your jealous, shriveled little soul, that you should call it the 'Blue Grass Palace,' the 'Gazette Palace,' the 'Senator Harsh Palace,' the 'Tornado-Cyclone-Drought-Weather-Bureau Palace' or any other high-sounding name that will influence you to do something beside finding fault with everybody else."[5]

The editor of the *Advertiser* had no shortage of opinions, and one of his ideas which received some support was to construct the palace of baled hay, and

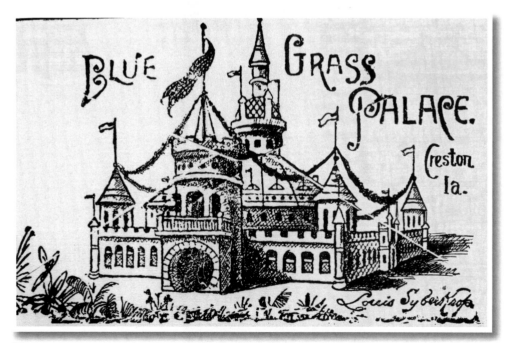

(Courtesy of Iowa's Union County Historical Society)

then at the end of the exposition, dismantle the palace and sell the bales throughout the country for advertising purposes. Each bale would be labeled with a sign indicating that it came "From the Walls of the Celebrated Hay Palace, Creston, Iowa. The Metropolis of the Blue Grass Garden Spot of Southwestern Iowa."[6]

Architects throughout the region were encouraged to submit designs for Creston's palace, and those of two architects drew the most attention. O.J. King of Omaha submitted plans for an 8,000-square-foot circular structure that had outer walls 19 feet high, and a center court 64 feet at its highest point. Louis Syberkrop apparently tried several designs before settling on one that could be either circular or octagonal. On June 12, the planning committee selected Syberkrop's general plan, but chose to go with a rectangular design 150 feet long, 100 feet wide, and 92 feet tall at its highest point. It would have the look of a fortified castle with a tall central dome reachable by a spiral staircase, and four large corner towers within the massive battlement walls.[7] A neighboring newspaper, the *Journalist,* described the palace as 100 feet by 100 feet and 120 feet high, and the August 8 issue of the Chicago *Daily News* mentioned the same measurements.[8]

On August, 21, 1889, reporters were allowed a sneak preview of what would be shown to the public on the following day. The Creston *Daily Gazette* stated the following: "Creston's Blue Grass Palace, as the flag above the massive tower over the main entrance to the palace informs the visitors, presented a gay and magnificent appearance this morning. The handsome and unique structure of Creston's pride could not present a better appearance, with the five big towers floating the national colors and hundreds of small flags, banners and streamers of bright colors fluttering in every breeze."[9]

The reporter thought the palace interior was just as stunning and complimented the contractor, Mr. Woodruff, and the Union County Ladies' Blue Grass League for the fine job of organizing and decorating. Each county that had a booth was mentioned, but not always in a positive manner, as in the case of Appanoose County, whose booth was initially empty because they didn't organize their display in time. Those receiving praise included

Pottawattamie County, which exhibited an Indian chief made entirely of apples; Adair County, which had a sheep made of oats; and Montgomery County, which was "great for tall things."[10]

When the Blue Grass Exposition formally opened on August, 22, 1889, Iowa's Senator Harsh, who was president of the Exposition, gave a few opening remarks and then turned the dais over to Governor Larrabee for the event's first speech. He said what was expected of a politician — a short history lesson followed by a flowery progress report, and of course a declaration that Iowa

---

"While, according to the tenth census, thirteen states show each more than a million acres mown, only one state, New York, produced in 1870 a greater number of tons of hay than Iowa, and it would not be at all surprising if the eleventh census should place Iowa at the head of the column of hay-producing states."

From Governor Larrabee's speech at the Creston Blue Grass Palace, August 22, 1889.

Creston Daily Gazette

Thursday, August 22, 1889

OFFICIALLY OPENED.

The Blue Grass Palace Formally Opened by the Governors of Iowa and Nebraska.

A Glorious Dedication for the Ninth Wonder of the World.

FORMAL OPENING

Creston's pride, her Blue Grass Palace, was formally opened at high noon to-day. The occasion was marked by great splendor, there being present Governor and Mrs. Larrabee and the governor's staff and Governor Thayor, of Nebraska, and staff.

Senator Harsh, as president of the exposition, called the large assembly together promptly at noon. A selection by the Council Bluffs band followed. Prayer was then offered by Rev. W.S. Hooker, of Creston. A selection by the Creston band followed and then Senator Harsh introduced Governor Larrabee, who was received with applause.

Creston Daily Gazette

Thursday, September 5, 1889

THE WORLD'S FAIR.

Resolutions by the Blue Grass Palace Gathering.

During to-day's proceedings at the Palace the following resolution was unanimously adopted:

WHEREAS, The United States is to be the site of the World's Exposition of 1892 and

WHEREAS, Chicago is more easily accessible to the people of all parts of the Nation than any other place therefore

Resolved, by the people of southwest Iowa assembled at the Blue Grass Palace in Creston Iowa this day that Chicago is a proper place for said World's Exposition to be held and we pledge ourselves to do all that lies in our power honorably to locate said Exposition at Chicago.

(Newspapers courtesy of State Historical Society of Iowa)

was "the grandest state in the Union."[11]

Both of Creston's newspapers declared the opening day a success, though it would be difficult to tell from the *Advertiser's* headline, which read "Gone to Grass."[12]

Each successive day honored a well-known individual who was expected to give a speech, and each day was named for a nearby county whose exhibit received special attention. The second day featured General James B. Weaver and Appanoose County,[13] and the third day focused on Senator J.G. Hutchison and two counties — Adair and Madison. Unfortunately, 60 residents of Adair County failed to make the journey to Creston because they missed the train, so not only did they fail to see the palace, but they also got cheated out of

(Courtesy of Iowa's Union County Historical Society)

the blue grass dances at the Pine Street Opera House.[14]

Visitors were invited to attend Sunday services at the palace, and those present were able to hear Reverend H.W. Thomas of Chicago exclaim, "Never did I feel that I stood in a pulpit more sacred than in this temple built from the new mown hay, the gathered grain and garnered corn. How much more pure and holy are lessons here taught from those that are learned in bloodstained cathedrals or churches built from forests or quarry."[15] The welcome mat was not out for everyone, though, as was made apparent by the local marshal's suggestion that city residents organize their own neighborhood watch programs to protect themselves from petty thieves.[16]

The Union County Fair opened on August 27, which brought even more people to the Blue Grass Palace and provided a larger audience for the day's main speaker, Iowa's Senator Allen. He gave a speech on protectionism, especially concerning agricultural products in competition with those of Australia, South America, India and Canada, and then went on to inform his audience why Iowa was better than all the other states. According to his theory, it was because Iowa had "such a moral, intelligent and Christian people, with a high regard for our laws and institutions." [17] His next statement may have caused a few people to scratch their heads: "Our future is safe for we have nothing of luxury or wealth to debauch our youth."[18] He probably didn't take into account how many of the state's youth might move elsewhere due to the lack of opportunities for wealth or debauchery when he predicted a future state population of more than 7,000,000. Had he lived long enough, he would have noticed that Iowa still hadn't reached half that number 100 years later, though it must be noted that he didn't set a specific date for the record number to be reached.[19]

August 28 honored veterans of the Mexican War and the Civil War (Union soldiers only),[20] and on August 30 a prettiest baby contest was held. There weren't as many babies entered as in previous years, but the fair administrators didn't mind so much because then there wouldn't be as many disappointed mothers.[21] C. B. & Q.

(Newspapers courtesy of
State Historical Society of Iowa)

(Courtesy of Iowa's Union County Historical Society)

Day (Chicago, Burlington & Quincy Railroad) on August 31 offered an interesting twist when 40 locomotives were brought to town, many decorated with grains and grasses. While it was without a doubt quite the attraction, "the screeching of whistles and ringing of bells was deafening."[22]

On September 2, the 10th day of the Blue Grass Exposition, festival-goers finally had to put up with rainy weather. Fair officials decided that "the weather clerk had been so good to us during fair week, we had not the heart to kick."[23] The day was dedicated to Clarke County, and its gimmick was for each of its 400 residents to carry a tall stalk of corn as a walking stick. The following sounds a bit like a Paul Bunyan story, but the newspaper claimed that local resident "Judge McDill tried to show the boys how he used to husk corn when he was a boy. He selected the shortest stalk on the Clarke County corn, on which were two big ears, to make his exhibition with, but lo and behold the ears were too high up and the Judge had to get a step ladder before he could grasp the ears."[24]

The following day it rained even harder,[25] but when it cleared up on September 5, ironically enough, the fire department put on a water demonstration.[26] The closing day speech praised Iowans for progressing far beyond their European ancestors, yet bemoaned the harsh treatment of the Native Americans in achieving that progress. The small crowds didn't come close to matching the 25,000-plus visitors of the previous week,[27] but the exposition still made an overall profit of $197. While not a huge amount, it was large enough to call the 1889 event a success, and encouraging enough to warrant the building of a new and bigger palace the following year.[28]

(Courtesy of Iowa's Union County Historical Society)

Creston
Blue Grass
Palace
1890-1892

Section 1 ❖ Iowa
CHAPTER 2

In 1890, the Blue Grass League of Southwestern Iowa, an organization consisting of 18 counties, united to build a palace three times the size of the 1889 palace. It was erected on the Creston fair grounds and measured 260 feet in length by 130 feet in width. The center tower was 120 feet tall, the tower over the entrance reached 100 feet, and the wing towers were 90 feet in height, both connected by a 12-foot-wide bridge. The two stories combined had nearly 32,000 square feet, and the south wing had an auditorium seating 2,000.[29] What was unusual about the 1890 Exposition was that participating counties took turns being in charge of each day's program, which not only divided the responsibilities, but also helped promote better programming as each county tried to outdo the others.[30]

"It costs money to get good attractions such as the managers of the Blue Grass Exposition proposes to have. The gentleman who owns the trotting moose charges $1,000 for a performance by his animal." —The Editor

Creston *Daily Gazette*
July 18, 1890

"I would advise that every organization in the league commence work at once to secure their exhibits, which should be far in advance of last year's, as to kind and design, as this year's palace building is ahead of the former one."

W.W. Ellis, President Blue Grass League of southwestern Iowa.

Creston *Daily Gazette*
July 18, 1890

Not ones to procrastinate, by July 7 the Ladies Blue Grass League of Union County was already organized for decorating the new building, and the ladies declared it their goal to "stimulate the formation of similar organizations in the counties of the region."[31] The 1890 palace was already up and declared "a magnificent structure of colossal proportions rivaling in size, architectural design and beauty of finish anything ever attempted in the palace line."[32] That quote may have made it sound as though there was competition among Sioux City, Creston and the

---

Creston Daily Gazette

Tuesday, July 22, 1889

PICK A POSITION.

League Vice Presidents Select Sites in the Palace.

A Good Representation and a Successful and Magnificent Exhibition Assured.

A General Line of Newsy Notes Gathered in All Portions of the City Regardless of Wet Weather.

Several counties sent letters authorizing the selection of booths but saying their representatives could not come.

---

new Coal Palace at Ottumwa, but that was not the way the editor of the Creston *Daily Gazette* viewed it. He stated that he wanted to see the coal counties of the Blue Grass Region go into the Coal Palace movement at Ottumwa. "That is a worthy enterprise and will but fittingly supplement and emphasize the work of the Blue Grass League and Palace."[33] And then he added that visitors would "see that the Corn Palace, the Blue Grass Palace and the Coal Palace have done more to bring Iowa and her advantages before the world than all other means hitherto employed combined."[34]

The value of the Blue Grass Festival was driven home during a meeting at City Hall on July 11, 1890. While visiting the Festival the previous year, a buggy manufacturer, Mr. W.M. Meyers, had become impressed with Creston's initiative and decided he wanted to move his Nelson Carriage Factory from Stuart, Iowa, to Creston. He offered to build a large, three-story structure that would require 40 or 50 men receiving wages averaging $2 per day.[35]

Concession privileges were granted in mid-July. They included exhibition rights for photography, jewelry and glassware, badges and souvenirs, ball-throwing games and score card privileges. On the expenditure side, administrators paid out $1,000 for a man to exhibit his trotting moose.[36]

THE BLUE GRASS PALACE

EXPOSITION

—AND—

CRESTON ❖ DISTRICT ❖ FAIR.

AUGUST 21 to 30, INCLUSIVE.

The Grandest Double Attraction of the Year!

$7,500 in the Speed Ring.

The opening meeting of the collosal central circle, embracing CRESTON, LINCOLN, TOPEKA and KANSAS CITY, will be held here, and with the largest purses of the circuit, with fresh horses and extra attractions the speed ring presents extraordinary attractions.

FINEST HALF-MILE TRACK IN THE STATE.

The three fastest heats trotted in Iowa in the season of 1889 were made on the Creston track.

The Blue Grass Palace of 1890!

The largest and most unique of palace wonders, will be three times larger than last year, and with its lofty towers, castelated walls, and superb decorations, will be at once the wonder and admiration of the observer, while the interior booths, filled with the

Exhibits of Eighteen Counties,

—COMPRISING THE—

Blue Grass League of Southwestern Iowa,

Will present a veritable panorama of the wealth of products and manufactures of this most wonderful agricultural, horticultural and stock raising district of the world.

GOV. BOIES will open the palace August 21, and ROGER Q. MILLS and other distinguished men of national reputation will be present from day to day. Excursions with one fare for round trip will be made on all railroads from Minnesota, Wisconsin, Illinois, Indiana and Missouri, and thousands should avail themselves of this opportunity of visiting this grandest of all expositions, combining

Novelty, Amusement, Instruction and Profit.

For premium lists, speed programs, descriptive circulars and all particulars, address

GEO. E. McELWAIN, Secy,
Creston, Iowa.

(Newspaper ad courtesy of State Historical Society of Iowa)

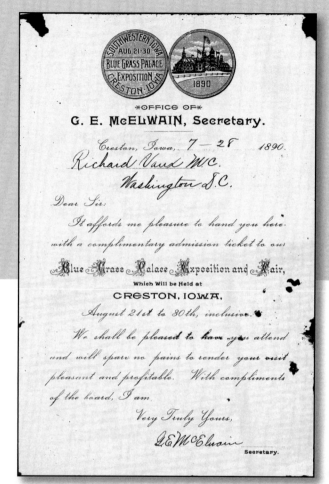

❋OFFICE OF❋
G. E. McELWAIN, Secretary.

Creston, Iowa, 7 — 28 1890.

Richard Vaux MC.

Washington S.C.

Dear Sir:

It affords me pleasure to hand you herewith a complimentary admission ticket to our

Blue Grass Palace Exposition and Fair,

Which Will be Held at

CRESTON, IOWA,

August 21st to 30th, inclusive.

We shall be pleased to have you attend and will spare no pains to render your visit pleasant and profitable. With compliments of the board, I am

Very Truly Yours,

G.E.McElwain
Secretary.

(Courtesy of Iowa's Union County Historical Society)

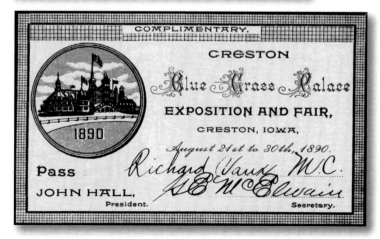

COMPLIMENTARY.

CRESTON
Blue Grass Palace
EXPOSITION AND FAIR,
CRESTON, IOWA,

August 21st to 30th, 1890.

Pass Richard Vaux MC.

G.E.McElwain

JOHN HALL,
President.

Secretary.

Exterior decorating of the Palace began on July 31, interior decorating began on Monday, August 4,[37] and on the following day it was announced that the Blue Grass Festival was being advertised in 700 newspapers. And for those who didn't read newspapers, men were sent to many surrounding towns to put up fliers, their progress being reported on a regular basis.[38]

By August 20, the day prior to the Exposition opening, the exterior decorating was completed, most exhibits had arrived, and lighted arches were being constructed at each intersection on Main Street. The only disappointments noted included businesses that were not being decorated to the extent expected by Exposition organizers and the rain that had fallen for the previous 12 hours.[39]

When the doors were thrown open to the public on August 21, those in attendance passed through the east entrance under a three-story tower. They entered a rotunda which was, in essence, the 1889 Palace, and which contained the same decorations in its dome as the previous year. Counties and businesses occupied most of the new north wing with their booths, while the new

(Courtesy of State Historical Society of Iowa Special Collection)

south wing contained a large auditorium and stage, behind which was a mural of the palace and "cherubs bearing banners on which were inscribed the names of each county represented in the Blue Grass League."[40]

While the Iowa governor was the main attraction on the opening day, a train was the center of attention on the second day. "On the pilot of the engine was a miniature palace of hay, and the smoke stack, cab, tender and all available space was decorated in a handsome manner. The first coach bore large banners inscribed 'Armour Cudahy Company,' while those on the second and third coaches were respectively 'George H. Hammond & Co.,' and the 'South Omaha Livestock Exchange.' All the cars were tastefully and handsomely decorated."[41] Oddly enough, the second day's write-up was the only Blue Grass Palace-related article to make the front page of the Creston *Daily Gazette* during the entire run of the Exposition.

Rain plagued the festivities on the third day, resulting in small crowds, but on the fourth day people flocked to the palace's north wing to see and hear a wonderful new invention — Edison's phonograph. According to the program, there were "instrumental and vocal music, recitations, etc."[42] The article went on to say, "the phonograph was on exhibition at the Ottumwa fair last week and out of the many attractions there, was pronounced the best of all. Visitors to the Blue Grass Palace should not miss hearing this wonderful machine."[43]

The most notable items in the August 25 write-ups were disgruntled remarks by the *Daily Gazette's* editor. Delegations from the Sioux City Corn Palace and the Ottumwa Coal Palace had been expected to arrive the previous day, but now there was some question whether they would show up at all. The editor also suggested that a roll call be taken for the Iowa State Band because it seemed to be diminishing in number each day, and then he went on to explain why. "The Iowa State band played just once in the amphitheatre yesterday. They were too busy to play, but enjoyed the races. One has to pay ten cents to hear them perform. Will the management have a cheap boy and a hand organ for the benefit of the visitors? It may not be as fine music, but it will be a good deal more appreciated than to have a high-toned band sitting around smoking cigarettes."[44]

The editor was in a much better mood later in the week thanks to the arrival of the Ottumwa delegation, and due to the fact that the Iowa State Band not only played several times during the day, but also performed in the palace auditorium at night to entertain the visitors from Ottumwa. He was especially pleased with Ole Oleson's Swedish dialect songs, which he thought "could draw crowds for a solid month."[45]

The Sioux City delegation showed up on August 29, helping boost the day's attendance to an estimated 15,000 to 20,000, though someone said that was only a drop in the bucket compared with the attendance the day before — which may have been stated to impress Sioux City. Everyone that day must have been on his best behavior because it was reported that there were no accidents, no fights and very little pickpocketing. The hack service

PALACE HACK!

During the Fair and Blue Grass Palace Exposition the

NEW PALACE HACK

will run from the PALACE to

Any Part of the City

With Passengers.

(Newspaper courtesy of State Historical Society of Iowa)

Creston Daily Gazette

Tuesday, August 19, 1890

GRASS GREATNESS.

The Arrangements for the Great Exposition Almost Finished.

A Magnificent Structure, Which Publishes Southwestern Iowa's Fertility to the World.

Creston Daily Gazette

Wednesday, August 20, 1890

OPEN SESAME.

Gov. Boies Will Speak the Magic Words To-morrow Afternoon.

Creston Daily Gazette

Thursday, August 21, 1890

GOVERNOR'S DAY.

The Blue Grass Palace Exposition of 1890 Opens Auspiciously.

(Newspapers courtesy of State Historical Society of Iowa)

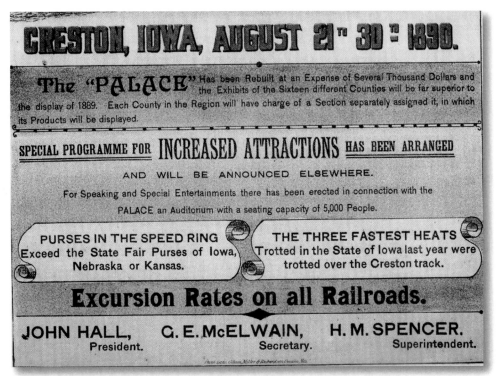

(Courtesy of Iowa's Union County Historical Society)

— the predecessor to the taxi — was even so honest that the drivers didn't try to charge anyone more than 10 cents for a ride.[46] On the next and final day, however, a jockey riding "Peanut" was fined $10 for disorderly conduct in the first heat. According to the *Gazette* editor, "It was a punishment richly merited, as he had acted in a ruffianly manner on the previous day also."[47] The editor's latter statement seems to contradict what he said about the absence of fighting on the previous day.

And with that, the 1890 Blue Grass Exposition came to a close. In spite of a few complaints, the final assessment was that the Exposition was a huge success. The editor exclaimed that "the citizens of Creston are to be congratulated, and all residents of the Blue Grass League of southwestern Iowa should feel proud of the record. The eye of the whole country has been drawn in this direction and the result will be felt in the increased demand for products of all kinds from this region."[48]

The Ottumwa *Weekly Democrat* reported that the 1890 Creston Blue Grass Palace made a profit of $10,000, which if true, was certainly a monumental increase over the previous year's net of $197. The paper also went on to say the palace was to be a permanent structure, but that statement would prove to be false soon enough.[49]

Very few changes were made for the 1891 Exposition other than repairs, redecorating and a new façade around the main entrance to provide a different look and make access easier. Inside, the palace's architect, Louis

---

Creston Daily Gazette

Tuesday, August 25, 1890

BEAUTY OF THE PALACE.

Being Viewed by Thousands To-day From all Sections.

The Exposition Attended by a Constantly In-creasing Throng of Visitors.

Creston Daily Gazette

Friday, August 28, 1890

MERRIMENT AND MUSIC.

Hold Full Sway, at Creston's Blue Grass Palace To-Day.

Delegations From Every Surrounding Town Hold High Carnival at the Palace.

(Newspapers courtesy of State Historical Society of Iowa)

Creston Daily Gazette

Saturday, August 29, 1890

NEARING THE CLOSE.

Blue Grass Palace Coning to Conclusion of a Successful Meeting.

Not an Accident Mars the Record of an Unprecedented Success in Every Respect.

Creston Daily Gazette

Monday, August 30, 1890

SATURDAY SUMMARY.

The Closing Hours of the Greatest Show on Earth.

The Creston Blue Grass Palace Exposition and Fair Comes to a Successful Finish To-Day.

Syberkrop, exhibited 100 of his own paintings depicting scenes in the surrounding Blue Grass League counties, and an elegant fountain was built in the center of the north wing. For entertainment, organizers hired an Italian orchestra and an "excellent band composed of twenty ladies."[50]

According to the Union County Historical Society's *Blue Grass Palaces,* 1891 was the final year for the Blue Grass Palace,[51] but *The Palimpsest* of the State Historical Society of Iowa states that in 1892, the Blue Grass Palace exterior was given a medieval castle look with a thatched roof and walls painted to resemble stone and brick. After that year, however, people in the area were looking for a new type of entertainment; the Creston Blue Grass Exposition died a quiet death, and there were no further attempts at resurrection.[52]

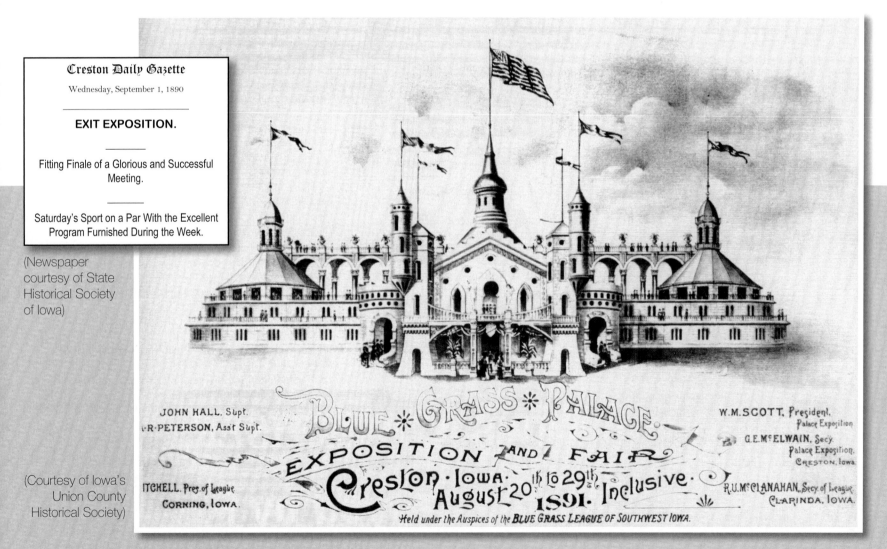

(Newspaper courtesy of State Historical Society of Iowa)

(Courtesy of Iowa's Union County Historical Society)

JOHN HALL, Supt.
R. PETERSON, Ass't Supt.

W.M. SCOTT, President, Palace Exposition

G.E. McELWAIN, Sec'y. Palace Exposition. Creston, Iowa.

BLUE GRASS PALACE.

EXPOSITION AND FAIR

Creston, Iowa. August 20th to 29th 1891. Inclusive.

ITCHELL, Pres. of League CORNING, IOWA.

R.U. McCLANAHAN, Sec'y. of League CLARINDA, IOWA.

Held under the Auspices of the *BLUE GRASS LEAGUE OF SOUTHWEST IOWA.*

Footnotes for the Creston Blue Grass Palace, 1889-1892

1. William J. Peterson, *The Palimpsest* (The State Historical Society of Iowa, December 1963), 563.

2. Alfred Lucas, *Blue Grass Palaces* (Union County Historical Society, Creston, Iowa, 1991), 16.

3. Ibid, 14-15.

4. Ibid.

5. Ibid, 15-16.

6. Ibid, 14.

7. Ibid, 17.

8. Ibid, 21.

9. W.T. Foster, "The Palace," Creston *Daily Gazette*, August 21, 1889, p. 3.

10. Ibid.

11. W.T. Foster, "Officially Opened," Creston *Daily Gazette*, August 22, 1889, p. 4.

12. Alfred Lucas, *Blue Grass Palaces* (Union County Historical Society, Creston, Iowa, 1991), 23.

13. W.T. Foster, "The Second Day," Creston *Daily Gazette*, August 23, 1889, p. 4.

14. W.T. Foster, "The Exposition," Creston *Daily Gazette*, August 24, 1889, p. 4.

15. Perkins Brothers, "The Blue Grass Palace," Sioux City *Journal*, August 27, 1889, p. 1.

16. W.T. Foster, "The Exposition," Creston *Daily Gazette*, August 24, 1889, p. 4.

17. W.T. Foster, "The Big Fair," Creston *Daily Gazette*, August 27, 1889, p. 4.

18. Ibid.

19. Ibid.

20. W.T. Foster, "Old Soldiers' Day," Creston *Daily Gazette*, August 28, 1889, p. 4.

21. W.T. Foster, "Montgomery's Day," Creston *Daily Gazette*, August 30, 1889, p. 4.

22. W.T. Foster, "C. B. & Q. Day," Creston *Daily Gazette*, August 31, 1889, p. 4.

23. W.T. Foster, "Clarke County's Day," Creston *Daily Gazette*, September 2, 1889, p. 4.

24. Ibid.

25. W.T. Foster, "Mills County's Day," Creston *Daily Gazette*, September 4, 1889, p. 4.

26. W.T. Foster, "Exposition," Creston *Daily Gazette*, September 5, 1889, p. 4.

27. W.T. Foster, "At the Palace," Creston *Daily Gazette*, September 9, 1889, p. 4.

8. Alfred Lucas, *Blue Grass Palaces* (Union County Historical Society, Creston, Iowa, 1991), 21.

29. Ibid, 53.

30. William J. Peterson, *The Palimpsest* (The State Historical Society of Iowa, December 1963), 563.

31. W.T. Foster, "Palace Notes," Creston *Daily Gazette*, July 7, 1890, p. 2.

32. Ibid.

33. W.T. Foster, "Area Notes," Creston *Daily Gazette*, July 7, 1890, p. 2.

34. Ibid.

35. W.T. Foster, "Carriage Council," Creston *Daily Gazette*, July 11, 1890, p. 3.

36. J.B. Harsh and Ed. H. Brewster, "Palace Notes," Creston *Daily Gazette*, July 18, 1890, p. 3.

37. J.B. Harsh and Ed. H. Brewster, "Palace Notes," Creston *Daily Gazette*, August 1, 1890, p. 2.

38. J.B. Harsh and Ed. H. Brewster, "Waking Up," Creston *Daily Gazette*, August 2, 1890, p. 2.

39. J.B. Harsh and Ed. H. Brewster, "Open Sesame," Creston *Daily Gazette*, August 20, 1890, p. 3.

40. J.B. Harsh and Ed. H. Brewster, "Governor's Day," Creston *Daily Gazette*, August 21, 1890, p. 3.

41. J.B. Harsh and Ed. H. Brewster, "Roger's Rhetoric," Creston *Daily Gazette*, August 22, 1890, p. 1.

42. J.B. Harsh and Ed. H. Brewster, "Crowds Congregate," Creston *Daily Gazette*, August 24, 1890, p. 3.

43. Ibid.

44. J.B. Harsh and Ed. H. Brewster, "Palace Small Talk," Creston *Daily Gazette*, August 25, 1890, p. 3.

45. J.B. Harsh and Ed. H. Brewster, "Merriment and Music," Creston *Daily Gazette*, August 28, 1890, p. 3.

46. J.B. Harsh and Ed. H. Brewster, "Palace Notes," Creston *Daily Gazette*, August 29, 1890, p. 3.

47. J.B. Harsh and Ed. H. Brewster, "Saturday Summary," Creston *Daily Gazette*, August 30, 1890, p. 3.

48. J.B. Harsh and Ed. H. Brewster, "Exit Exposition," Creston *Daily Gazette*, September 1, 1890, p. 3.

49. Robert H. Moore, "The Democrat," Ottumwa *Weekly Democrat*, September 5, 1890, p. 1.

50. Alfred Lucas, *Blue Grass Palaces* (Union County Historical Society, Creston, Iowa, 1991), 58.

51. Ibid.

52. William J. Peterson, *The Palimpsest* (The State Historical Society of Iowa, December 1963), 571.

1891

This photo may have been taken in 1890 rather than 1891, as marked. Other 1891 photos show decorative designs on the roof of the palace buildings. (Courtesy of Ruth Leibrand and Carol Whiteis)

Forest City Flax Palace 1890

Section 1 ❖ Iowa
CHAPTER 3

The Burlington, Cedar Rapids and Northern railways sent out a notice in September 1890 that all passengers would get a round-trip ticket for the price of a one-way fare to the Forest City Flax Palace Festival, which they claimed was "the most unique and interesting ever held in the northwest."[1] Whether the Flax Palace was the most interesting palace in the northwest might have been debated by three other Iowa cities, but it was certainly unique, being the first and only palace made chiefly of flax at that time. It would not, however, be the last. It was reported in Forest City's *Centennial Sketches* that the Flax Palace idea was inspired by South Dakota's Corn Palace, but it was more likely inspired by Sioux City's Corn Place since South Dakota's first Corn Palace, in Mitchell, wasn't built until 1892.[2]

Forest City, founded in 1855, was basically a farming community that began hosting an agricultural fair in 1887. When flax was introduced into the area, it was decided to promote the crop in a big way, and thus the Flax Palace idea was conceived.[3]

To make sure the idea was taken to the next step, the local editor harangued his readers into action by stating: "To make this a success we must have the hearty cooperation of every individual interested. Let the older heads promulgate the plans (for experience has been their teacher) and let the young blood course through our veins with renewed activity, as we rush to execute them, and woe to the sluggard, for the finger of scorn and derision is pointed at him."[4]

The editor apparently made his point, for on July 16, 1890, businessmen met at the courthouse to organize a cooperative effort with the Agricultural Society in the construction of a Flax Palace in conjunction with the annual county fair.[5] The joint meeting was held two weeks later,[6] and by August 7, a dozen committees were in place and requested to begin work immediately. It's interesting to speculate why the flax committee shared the fewest members (six), along with the oats and rye committees, while the wheat committee had eight members, the corn and sorghum committees had 10, and the grass committee boasted 16 members.[7] They were, after all, building a Flax Palace.

Plans were submitted the following week to build an octagonal structure 44 feet away from a similar one already on the fairgrounds, and then connect the two eight-sided buildings with a two-story main building, making the entire structure approximately 130 feet long. The plans were approved on the condition that they could be altered as deemed necessary by the building committee.[8]

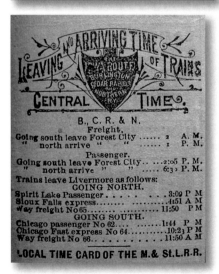

Newspaper ads and articles from 1890 issues of the Winnebago *Summit* (Courtesy of Forest City *Summit* Newspaper)

Logo for Forest City's weekly newspaper in the 1890s, the Winnebago *Summit*

(Courtesy of Forest City Winnebago *Summit*)

Octagon structure built prior to 1890 (Courtesy of Ruth Leibrand and Carol Whiteis)

The alteration clause proved very fortuitous, as the building ended up being a three-story building 158 feet in length, with one octagon 36 feet in diameter and the other 24 feet.[9] C.H. Lackore was awarded the contract for the palace's construction, and G.H. Hurst from Chicago was hired to do the decorating, using a combination of 12 weaving machines and several young boys to make decorative bundles out of the straw and heads. The boys were paid three cents a yard, and presumably were assisted by the 68 men assigned to the committee on outside decorations. Other grains also were used to enhance designs and add color.[10]

By August 21, the Ladies Flax Palace Organization had committees in place for interior decorations, organized by townships within Winnebago County. The north wing was designated specifically for an art gallery, and all women were encouraged to display their handiwork. The Art Gallery Committee was first in importance and size, consisting of 75 women, most of whom were married. The single women throughout the county were assigned to the smaller, lesser committees, such as the Pressed Flowers Committee, the Paintings and Artificial Flowers Committee, the Fancy Work of Any Kind Committee, the Pressed Flowers and Ferns

Committee, and the Grasses and Cat Tails Committee.[11] One could only hope no serious altercations would arise from overlapping assignments, especially between the 18-member Pressed Flowers Committee and the badly outnumbered 11-member Pressed Flowers and Ferns Committee.

By September 4, the nearly completed palace already was declared a wonder and a delight, and Mr. Hurst was hailed as a creative genius. The public was anxiously awaiting the September 15 opening for the opportunity to view the rock fountain, the second-floor auditorium and, most of all, the 75-foot-high grand promenade at the top of the palace where visitors could look out upon the town, the Pilot Mound and the winding Red Cedar River.[12]

With admission only 25 cents (one source says 35 cents), people flocked to the palace in droves, and one-day gate receipts reportedly totaled $3,900, which, if accurate, means more than 11,000 people passed through the doors, an astounding number for a community of only 1,000 residents (one source says 1,700).[13] Whatever the numbers, they were impressive enough to ensure that the festival would continue for at least another year.

OLSON'S PALACE STORE

Ad from December 11, 1890, issue of the Winnebago *Summit*
(Courtesy of Forest City *Summit* Newspaper)

Interior of 1890 Forest City Flax Palace
(Courtesy of Ruth Leibrand and Carol Whiteis)

FLAX PALACE and WINNEBAGO COUNTY FAIR,
Forest City, Iowa, September 8th to 12th Inclusive, 1891.

Newspaper advertisement from the April 23, 1891, issue of the Winnebago *Summit* (Courtesy of Forest City *Summit* Newspaper)

Forest City Flax Palace 1891

Section 1 ❖ Iowa
CHAPTER 3

While Forest City residents no doubt spent the early months of 1891 planning for the fall's activities, the Winnebago *Summit* gave the most extensive coverage to two exciting crazes that were sweeping across the country — bicycling and hot air ballooning. Bicycling had long been popular as a spectator sport as fans cheered on their favorite big-wheel riders at fairground racetracks across the country, but the invention of the safety (or "goat") bicycle made cycling an exciting participatory sport for both men and women once there was no longer "the constant fear of a broken nose."[14]

On August 6, 1891, the Winnebago *Summit* announced that "F.N. Pitkin, that prince of decorators, has commenced decorating the Palace for the next annual exposition (September 8 to 12) and is doing a fine job."[15] There was also mention that a balloonist/ parachutist was being lined up, that the fair edition of the *Flax Palace Facts* was being distributed, and that G.R. Maben had donated an acre of timothy grass for decorating the Flax Palace.[16]

A week later, editor Mahoney reported, "The Flax Palace is at present a busy

scene. About fifty hands are employed at the building. Thirty-five weavers are preparing flax, wheat, oats, and rye for thatching. Carpenters are arranging the booths, painters are painting the roof and decks and the artists are laying out designs for decorations inside that will be a surprise for all."[17] During the final week of August, the downhill street to the depot (where the Flax Palace stood) was being leveled for both buggy and pedestrian traffic, and Flax Palace Cigars were selling like hotcakes.[18]

The exposition was declared a success, and if there was an issue of concern, it was merely determining the highlight of the event. Vying for consideration were the speech of Senator Allison that drew an audience of more than 5,000; The Young Ladies Brigade that gave a fine marching exhibition while armed with flax brooms; Professor Jones' balloon ascension and subsequent parachute jump that landed him only 100 feet away from his target; and record-breaking gate receipts far surpassing expectations. If there was little agreement on the ranking of the above items, there was consensus that the 1891 event's success was sufficient to warrant yet another festival in 1892.[19]

While Forest City was basking in the sunlight of its success, prospects for Creston's Blue Grass Palace were not so bright, as was reported by the Sioux City *Journal*. "Recent meetings of the blue grass palace directors have developed the fact that the institution, in spite of its series

Winnebago Summit

May 21, 1891

A POPULAR RECREATION

ASTONISHING GROWTH OF THE BICYCLE FAD.

Between 250,000 and 300,000 Wheels in the Country at the Present Time—Will the Bike Catch Up With the Trotting Horse?

"The English Bicycling News says that a ladies' college debated the question whether wheeling was a proper sport for women. Afterward the women voted on it, thirty-two favoring the sport, fourteen denouncing it, and seven 'hedging.' It is difficult to see why any one should wish to negative such a question, provided the woman has time, money, and strength. But no; time and money alone are necessary. The strength comes by using it."

Winnebago *Summit*
May 21, 1891

LADIES' SAFETY.

THE NEW STEAM TRICYCLE.

"The safety or 'goat' bicycle is the universal favorite nowadays with men and women alike. Even in racing the safety is only about five seconds to the mile behind the big wheel."

"Robert Bonner says the bicycle rider will never catch up with the trotting horse for a single mile, but Mr. Bonner is a prejudiced witness and apt to be mistaken."

Winnebago *Summit*
May 21, 1891

of successful expositions, is $6,000 in the hole. Although the palace association has over $2,000 on deposit at the First National bank here, the banker refused to cash checks, claiming they owe the bank the full amount now on deposit. It is believed, however, that matters may be satisfactorily adjusted soon and all obligations paid in full."[20]

It may have seemed to some that Forest City was rubbing salt in Creston's wounds when a later newspaper article appeared extolling the virtues of the Flax Palace. The local Farmer's Institute claimed that although the Flax Palace was younger than the original palaces of Sioux City, Ottumwa and Creston, the Flax Palace had established itself as being the most wonderful. That claim was based on the fact that the Flax Palace was the most interesting, was financed locally, was designed by a local architect, and was built and decorated by a community of fewer than 1,200 inhabitants.[21] The writer was apparently unaware that Ottumwa's Coal Palace was also built in 1890, and that Forest City's decorator for their 1890 exposition was from Chicago.

Ads from 1891 issues of the Winnebago *Summit*

(Courtesy of Forest City *Summit* Newspaper)

I Should Say!

That it is most time for the Opening of the

Flax Palace

BUT

O. A. OLSON

Has Already Opened up his Large Stock of New Fall and Winter Goods at the

Palace Double Store.

The Ladies' Home Journal

Mailed to any address from now TO

Jan. 1, '92
(BALANCE OF THIS YEAR)
On Receipt of only

50 Cents

"Where are you going, my pretty maid?"
"I'm going to Olson's, kind sir, to trade."

FLAX PALACE AND FAIR,
FOREST CITY, IOWA.

PROGRAM.
WEDNESDAY, SEPT. 9th.

Opening Address, - - - T. P. BYRNES.
————MUSIC.————
Ladies Rifle Club Tournament, Prizes Gold and Silver Medals.
Base Ball.
Ladies Brigade Drill, - - Sixty Young Ladies.

THURSDAY, SEPT. 10th.
SENATOR ALLISON'S DAY.

Address, - - SENATOR WM. B. ALLISON.
Music, - - BRUNDIN'S BAND.
Umbrella Brigade Drill.
Three Minute Trotting Race, - Purse $100 00
Farm Trotting Race, - - Purse 20 00
Farm Running Race, - - Purse 20 00

FRIDAY, SEPT. 11th.
LADIES' DAY.

Address, - - - T. P. BYRNES.
Music, - - BRUNDIN'S BAND.
Address, "Flax Industries," EUGENE BOSSE, U. S. Government Expert.
Ladies Brigade Drill.
Grand Balloon and Parachute Leap, PROF. W. W. JONES
Three-year-old Trotting Race, - Purse $ 50 00
Three Minute Stallion Race, - Purse 100 00
Two-forty Class Trotting Race, - Purse 100 00

SATURDAY, SEPT. 12th.

Address, L. L. KLINEFELTER, Editor, "Farmers Institute.
Music by Brundan's Band.
Free for all Trotting Race, - Purse $200 00
Free for all Pacing Race, - Purse 100 00
Running Race, - - Purse 100 00

SUNDAY, SEPT. 13th.
Address,
Sacred Concert.

Various other attractions are being arranged for and will take place on each day during the progress of the exposition.
Excursion Rates on Railroads.

"FLAX PALACE"
FOREST CITY IOWA

1891

"BROOM BRIGADE"

(Courtesy of State Historical Society of Iowa, Special Collections)

1891 Flax Palace "Broom Brigade"
(Courtesy of State Historical Society of Iowa, Special Collections)

View from the top of the 1891 Flax Palace
(Courtesy of State Historical Society of Iowa, Special Collections)

(Courtesy of Ruth Leibrand and Carol Whiteis)

Forest City
Flax Palace
1892-1893

Section 1 ❖ Iowa
CHAPTER 3

(Courtesy of Ruth Leibrand and Carol Whiteis)

No local newspapers from 1892 have been found to detail the events of that year's Flax Palace Festival, but the 1893 event promised a lady balloonist taking a daring flight through "the fenceless fields of air."[22] Organizers also guaranteed eloquent speakers, excellent racing and toe-tapping music for the five-day event running from September 12 through September 16. And as a testimonial to the newfound popularity of cycling, both men's and ladies' bicycle races were to be held, with a $20 purse for the men … and a $25 purse for the ladies! It must have shocked the men's ego to suddenly be on the lower end of the totem pole.[23]

While 100 volunteers were at work on palace decorations, the newspaper editor was traveling by both freight and passenger trains to neighboring towns, plastering them with lithographic advertising bills for the Flax Palace. Several other residents were visiting Chicago, presumably attending the World's Fair, though perhaps they journeyed to the Windy City after Chicago detectives reported that burglars were leaving for more lucrative rural communities due to the large number of people who had removed their money from banks and were hording it instead in mattresses.[24]

The *Summit* reported that opening day receipts for 1893 were better than those of the corresponding date in 1892 and urged its readers to visit all of the booths in the Flax Palace, including its own, undecorated though it might be. But folks were especially encouraged to visit Barth's booth, which contained a convex mirror, because "it may take some of the conceit out of you."[25]

Looking east, a view of the 1892 Forest City Flax Palace behind the railroad depot. Note the wooden sidewalk extending from the Forest City business district.
(Courtesy of Ruth Leibrand and Carol Whiteis)

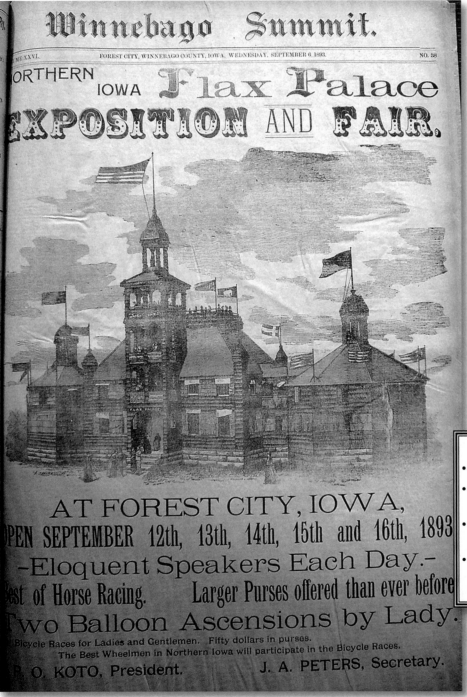

Winnebago Summit.

VOLUME XXVI.   FOREST CITY, WINNEBAGO COUNTY, IOWA, WEDNESDAY, SEPTEMBER 6, 1893.   NO. 38

NORTHERN IOWA **Flax Palace**

EXPOSITION AND FAIR.

AT FOREST CITY, IOWA,

OPEN SEPTEMBER 12th, 13th, 14th, 15th and 16th, 1893

-Eloquent Speakers Each Day.-

Best of Horse Racing.   Larger Purses offered than ever before

Two Balloon Ascensions by Lady.

Bicycle Races for Ladies and Gentlemen. Fifty dollars in purses.
The Best Wheelmen in Northern Iowa will participate in the Bicycle Races.

R. O. KOTO, President.   J. A. PETERS, Secretary.

It's doubtful the convex mirror was a reason, but an undetermined combination of other factors caused Forest City's "palace fever" to die out, and the doors closed prematurely after the 1893 exposition. There is some question about how long the building remained standing, with one report claiming the palace was torn down in 1932 to make room for the new highway east of town, while others say part of the building remained standing as late as 1940.[26]

During the next century, the community continued to grow even without its Flax Palace, boasting approximately 4,500 citizens, but it continued to search for the next unique idea that would once again put the town back on the map.[27] Interestingly enough, one event almost stole Forest City's notoriety a few months before the Flax Palace was even built. On May 2, 1890, a meteor entered the atmosphere, disintegrated, and showered a nearby area eight miles square with fragments weighing up to 81 pounds. Fortunately, both the city and the fragments can still be viewed today.[28]

PALACE POINTERS

• The balloon ascensions will take place on Friday and Saturday.

• The usual number of museums, merry-go-rounds and catering tents are pitched upon the grounds.

• There are no empty booths upon the first floor and those on the second floor are nearly all occupied at this wiring.

• The first day of the fair closed more auspiciously than did the same day last year and the gate receipts were larger than for the first day last year.

From the September 13, 1893, issue of the Winnebago *Summit*

"The Washburn-Crosby exhibit embraces models of their whole plant in Minneapolis upon a large and extensive scale. Including all of their mills, elevators, warehouses, truck and switching facilities, etc. It is the largest flour exhibit here and embraces many novel features. For instance, the company has constructed a large barrel containing 10,000 small barrels 2 by 2 1/2 inches, representing their output of flour in one day. They are also furnishing an unlimited number of these small barrels as a memento of the Columbian exposition to visitors. They are made hollow with a removable cap, so that they furnish an excellent receptacle for small articles.

The exhibit contains a large painting on a field on the farm of Dairymple of North Dakota containing 2,500 acres of standing wheat, which is being harvested by self-binders. It requires that this field be cut in one day and the wheat threshed to supply the mills of this company with sufficient wheat for one day's grinding."

Many small newspapers included illustrations of the 1893 Chicago World's Fair, but very few had illustrations of their local expositions. Was there a shortage of talented artists in small communities?

Illustration and article of the Chicago World's Fair from the September 27, 1893, issue of the Winnebago *Summit*

(Courtesy of Winnebago *Summit* Newspaper)

Minnesota Flour Exhibit.

Footnotes for the Forest City Flax Palace, 1890-1893

1. Charles M. Day, "Flax Palace," Sioux Falls *Argus Leader*, September 22, 1890, p. 3

2. Forest City Centennial Committee, *Centennial Sketches*, Forest City, IA: 1855-1955 (Forest City: Forest City Centennial Inc., 1955), 49.

3. Ibid.

4. A.H. Chase, "The Proposed Flax Palace," Winnebago *Summit*, July 24, 1890, p. 1

5. Ibid.

6. A.H. Chase, "Special Meeting," Winnebago *Summit*, July 31, 1890, p. 3

7. A.H. Chase, "Flax Palace Announcement," Winnebago *Summit*, August 7, 1890, p. 3

8. A.H. Chase, "Flax Palace Meeting," Winnebago *Summit*, August 14, 1890, p. 3

9. Forest City Centennial Committee, *Centennial Sketches*, Forest City, IA: 1855-1955 (Forest City: Forest City Centennial Inc., 1955), 49.

10. A.H. Chase, "The Flax Palace," Winnebago *Summit*, August 26, 1890, p. 3

11. A.H. Chase, "Ladies' Committees," Winnebago *Summit*, August 21, 1890, p. 3

12. A.H. Chase, "Palace Notes," Winnebago *Summit*, September 4, 1890, p. 3

13. Ibid.

14. J.W. Mahoney, "A Popular Recreation," Winnebago *Summit*, May 21, 1891, p. 1

15. J.W. Mahoney, "Local Record," Winnebago *Summit*, August 6, 1891, p. 3

16. Ibid.

17. J.W. Mahoney, "Local Record," Winnebago *Summit*, August 13, 1891, p. 3

18. J.W. Mahoney, "Local Record," Winnebago *Summit*, August 27, 1891, p. 3

19. J.W. Mahoney, "The Flax Palace and Fair," Winnebago *Summit*, September 17, 1891, p. 3

20. J.W. Mahoney, "Blue Grass Palace Failure," Winnebago *Summit*, October 1, 1891, p. 3

21. J.W. Mahoney, "The Forest City Flax Palace," Winnebago *Summit*, October 8, 1891, p. 3

22. S.C. Platt, "Local Brevities," Winnebago *Summit*, August 23, 1893, p. 5

23. S.C. Platt, "Northern Iowa Flax Palace Exposition and Fair," Winnebago *Summit*, August 30, 1893, p. 1

24. S.C. Platt, "Local Brevities," Winnebago *Summit*, August 30, 1893, p. 5

25. S.C. Platt, "Palace Pointers," Winnebago *Summit*, September 13, 1893, p. 5

26. Forest City Centennial Committee, *Centennial Sketches*, Forest City, IA: 1855-1955 (Forest City: Forest City Centennial Inc., 1955), 49.

27. State Historical Society of Iowa, *The Goldfinch* (Iowa City: State Historical Society Press, 1984), 1.

28. Forest City Centennial Committee, *Centennial Sketches*, Forest City, IA: 1855-1955 (Forest City: Forest City Centennial Inc., 1955), 64.

1890 Ottumwa Coal Palace
(Courtesy of Wapello County Historical Society)

Ottumwa Coal Palace 1890-1891

Section 1 ❖ Iowa
CHAPTER 4

On August 8, 1888, an article appeared in the Ottumwa *Weekly Courier* describing Ottumwa, Iowa, as well as the surrounding countryside. It was written as if an anonymous young woman were first setting eyes upon the city, though for being new to the area, she was extremely knowledgeable of its history, geography, industry and economy. She also seemed exceptionally willing to share her latest discovery with those who had the misfortune of living elsewhere.

She described that particular part of the Des Moines River Valley as the most prosperous and productive in the entire state; the hills, valleys, lakes and streams as the most beautiful; and its resources the most bountiful. She knew about the five railways that converged at Ottumwa, its paved streets with modern sewer lines running underneath, the modern electric lights that illuminated those streets, and the industries that provided for the moral and educational needs of its 14,000 citizens. However, she was unsure whether the city had two or three lines of horse cars.[1]

OTTUMWA WEEKLY DEMOCRAT

Wednesday, January 29, 1890

THE COMMERCIAL CLUB

The Meeting Last Night.

The Council Chamber was filled last night with business men who met there to complete the organization of a commercial club to advance our material and social interests.

OTTUMWA WEEKLY DEMOCRAT

Wednesday, February 5, 1890

THE PALACE IS A GO.

A LARGE AND ENTHUSIASTIC COAL PALACE MEETING LAST NIGHT.

A Grand Interest Manifested—

Everybody in Favor of It.

(Newspapers courtesy of State Historical Society of Iowa)

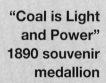

"Coal is Light and Power" 1890 souvenir medallion

(Courtesy of Wapello County Historical Society)

Courtesy of Wapello County Historical Society

Had she traveled to the city the following year, she would have had even more to report, for on August 7, 1889, the Ottumwa city council voted to increase the number of street lights from 22 to 77, and citizens were ready to throw a party.[2] Three of the city's prominent men tried to organize a Coal Palace Exposition that fall and, after a rough beginning, they finally sold enough shares in a stock company during the winter to get the project off the ground. The Ottumwa Commercial Club met on January 28, 1890, elected a slate of officers for the coming year, and called for the appointment of a committee to attend a meeting the following Friday concerning a proposed coal palace.[3] The meeting was held on February 4, and the February 5 headlines announced "The Palace is a Go."[4] The article reported that the courthouse was filled with enthusiastic businessmen who thought "a Coal Palace would be a grand thing, and be a valuable and wonderful enterprise for Ottumwa."[5] A committee drew up a resolution recognizing Iowa's benefits from Sioux City's Corn Palaces and Creston's Blue Grass Palace, and noted that Ottumwa would be providing a unique service to the state by promoting its manufacturing interests. The organizers expected at least eight surrounding counties to not only participate in a coal exposition but help fund it as well.[6]

On February 12, 1890, the Ottumwa *Weekly Democrat* reiterated that, "The coal palace at Ottumwa is a sure go. It will cost $30,000."[7] At the end of the paragraph was the good news that seed money in the amount of $5,000 was being donated by the Chicago, Burlington and Quincy Railroad.[8]

By the 16th of March, $22,000 in pledges had been raised — $4,400 by the retail committee, $450 by the professional men's committee, $1,500 by the bankers' committee, $250 by the traveling men's committee, $1,300 by the packing house committee and $100 by the hotel committee. The Phillips Coal Company had pledged another $400, but Col. Ballingall, a major ramrod of most public enterprises in Ottumwa, urged the committees to work harder by stating, "We dare not, can not, must not, shall not let this project fail."[9]

When several pledges were uncollected five weeks later, a special meeting was held at the home of Col. Ballingall. A committee headed by the host was formed to collect outstanding pledges, as the unanimous sentiment was "to build the coal palace at all hazards."[10] The following week the colonel reported that notes had been secured for $22,480, and that he'd soon have more than $25,000. Minutes later he was elected permanent president of the Ottumwa Coal Palace Company.[11]

The *Weekly Democrat* drummed up further interest in the Commercial Club's project by declaring 1890 as the Year of the Palaces, describing in detail not only the Coal Palace, but also the Sioux City Corn Palace and Creston Blue Grass Palace. It stated, "America, with its scarcity of those royal beings who

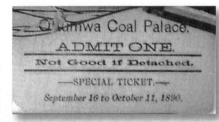

OTTUMWA WEEKLY DEMOCRAT

Sunday, March 16, 1890

IT WILL BE BUILT.

OTTUMWA'S COAL PALACE AN ASSURED SUCCESS.

Over $22,000.00 Has Already Been Subscribed.

(Newspapers courtesy of State Historical Society of Iowa)

1890 souvenir items

(Courtesy of Wapello County Historical Society)

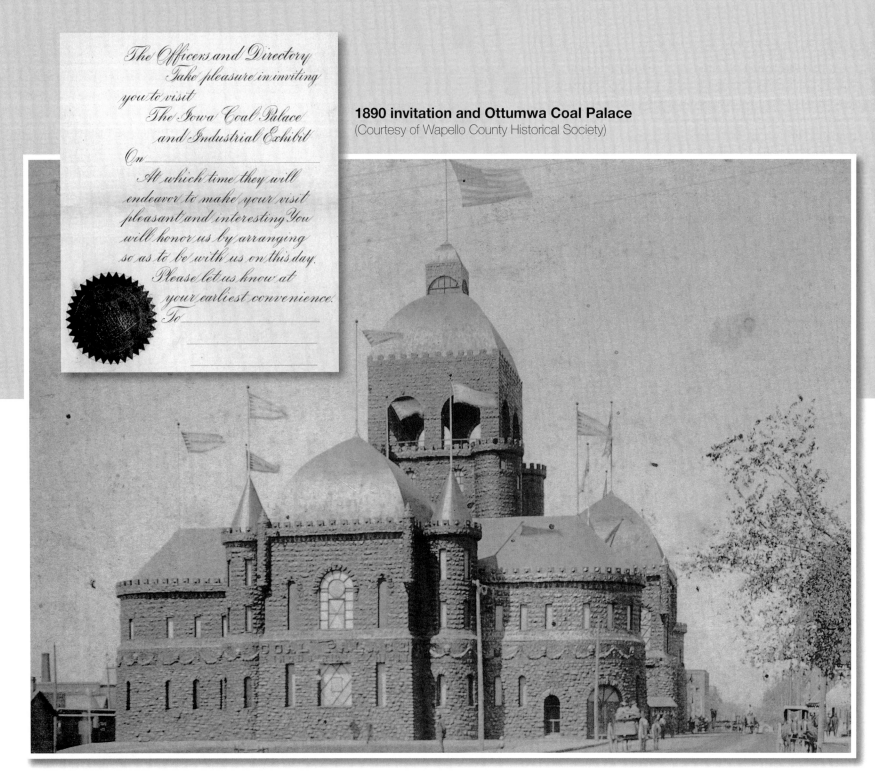

The Officers and Directory Take pleasure in inviting you to visit The Iowa Coal Palace and Industrial Exhibit On_____ At which time they will endeavor to make your visit pleasant and interesting You will honor us by arranging so as to be with us on this day. Please let us know at your earliest convenience. To_____ _____

1890 invitation and Ottumwa Coal Palace
(Courtesy of Wapello County Historical Society)

must have such luxurious surroundings, would not seem to be a very promising field for the erection of palaces, but, nevertheless, some structures have gone up of late years that for beauty and magnificence would compare favorably with some of the permanent abodes of royalty on the other side of the water."[12]

During the summer of 1890, in the city's Sunken Park, construction began on a large mediaeval-looking fortress that was to be approximately 230 feet long and 150 feet wide, with a central tower rising 200 feet in the air. It was to have all the turrets and battlements that a good feudalistic structure should have.[13] When the general superintendent of construction, George Withall, was asked on July 31 if the building would be done on time, he declared that it would be without a doubt. The first floor was about to be veneered with block coal, and the second story was receiving a veneering of fine coal, which involved a three-part process. Withall explained, "First a rough coat of plaster is put on, and then the fine coal is dashed into it, after which a coat of jet black composition is applied with brushes, giving it a very attractive appearance."[14] Workers were to begin on the roof as soon as materials arrived, and they were expected any day.[15]

On September 4, 1890, the Ottumwa *Weekly Democrat* reprinted an article from the Des Moines *News,* which claimed Ottumwa as Des Moines' favorite neighboring city. The editor of the *News,* Robert Moore, was happy to see a revival of life and business in the smaller city and advocated sending a large delegation to the Coal Palace Exposition. He then went on to state that "Des Moines and Ottumwa are the two northern centers of railroads, water power, population and agriculture which have coal at home and which are therefore especially adapted to manufacturers. If either succeeds, both will; if either fails, both must. But in the bright lexicon of the sister cities of the Des Moines valley, there is no such word as fail; and the outlook of Ottumwa is as bright with omens of future growth as that of the capital city."[16]

While the Ottumwa *Weekly Democrat* editor expressed his delight with matters within the state, he railed against those on a national level. He considered Harrison's presidency a failure; it was also evident he was

less than enthusiastic about Congress when he stated, "It is said that congress will adjourn in a few days. What a pity. Those congressmen are more out of the way where they are than they would be at home. Stay where you are until your time expires. It were better for the country."[17]

When a *Weekly Democrat* reporter crawled under the scaffolding on September 5 to note the palace's progress, he was met by Mr. Clark, the junior member of the decorating committee. Mr. Clark stopped the reporter before he could utter a word and declared, "I'll be hanged if I haven't been interviewed by about forty newspapermen in the last few days. Now, don't ask me if we'll be through by the time specified in the contract, or I'll brain you with a corn cob."[18] It wasn't that Mr. Clark feared being done on time, or that he was concerned with the quality of the work, for it was quickly evident to the reporter that progress was being made at a satisfactory pace, and that the work was "being done as only women can do it — clean, neat and artistic."[19]

A spectacular waterfall was being built inside the building, sod was ready to be laid in the sunken park in front of the palace, and Ottumwa's citizens were urged to start decorating the streets and businesses. Urged? Perhaps shamed, admonished or scolded would be a better way of putting it. Editor Moore sharpened his quill and wrote, "A suitable display will redound to the credit of the whole city, and we cannot fail to put on a gala attire in honor of the thousands of strangers who will crowd our streets. Any city that ever had an exposition within its limits, no matter how small an affair it may have been, always did its best in the matter of decorating, and if the city of Ottumwa, the site of what promises to be the greatest exhibit ever held in Iowa, cannot at least guarantee a few arches of colored lights to be thrown over its streets, then our citizens should shut up shop and our town rest under the accusation of a lack of public spirit that even eclipses the city of Philadelphia."[20] One would have to assume that at least a few guilty souls were moved to action.

A long meeting was held on September 10 to hammer out the program for the first day of the festival, which wasn't adopted until nearly midnight. It was concluded

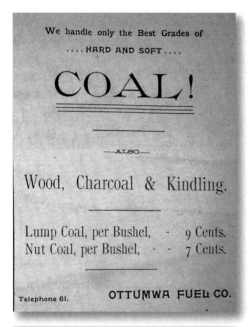

We handle only the Best Grades of

.... HARD AND SOFT ....

COAL!

—ALSO—

Wood, Charcoal & Kindling.

Lump Coal, per Bushel, - 9 Cents.
Nut Coal, per Bushel, - - 7 Cents.

Telephone 81.   OTTUMWA FUEL CO.

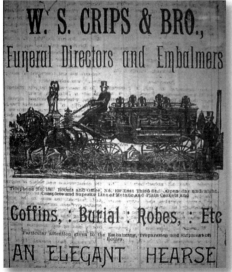

W. S. CRIPS & BRO.,
Funeral Directors and Embalmers

Telephone No. 161.   Booms and Office, No. 100 East Third St. Open day and night.
Complete and superior Line of Metalic and Plain Caskets and
...

Coffins, : Burial : Robes, : Etc

Particular attention given to the Embalming, Preparation and Shipment of Bodies.

AN ELEGANT HEARSE

"Coal" advertisement and W.S. Crips newspaper advertisement
(Courtesy of State Historical Society of Iowa)

that admission would be 50 cents for adults and 25 cents for children from 6 to 12, Iowa's Governor Boies would be the main speaker, the Iowa State Band would be the main entertainment along with a chorus 150 strong, and the musical selections would include Mozart's "Gloria," "Lullaby" and "Down in the Coal Mine," which would be sung by the chorus and the audience.[21]

Three days before the opening, men were still sodding the sunken park while others were constructing the flowing fountain in its middle. Large trees were being shipped in by rail to be planted in the park and, under Col. Ballingall's leadership, a large number of men were working underground "amid the slime and the rats"[22] to construct a replica of a working mine for the benefit of visitors. According to the local editor, it was "darker than the Republican party's hopes at the next election down underneath the palace floor," and the mining exhibition would be "in close proximity to that sulphur region that never freezes over, and where overcoats are unknown."[23]

In spite of the fact that a few odds and ends were left unfinished, on the morning of September 16, 1890, the Iowa State Band was ready to lead the public down Main Street to the imposing edifice of the Ottumwa Coal Palace.[24]

The words "Coal Palace" stood out above the main entrance, and two pictures adorned the main tower — one depicting the carboniferous age, and the other a modern coal mine. Ottumwa's major industries were represented in murals below the battlements, and an observation platform/dance floor 150 feet above the ground provided a

Interior of Ottumwa Coal Palace
(Courtesy of State Historical Society of Iowa, Special Collections)

spectacular view of the city and beyond.[25]

The inside provided more variety in color due to the use of several grains for decorative purposes. Adorning the walls were panels of corn "symbolical of agriculture, industry, mechanics, music, art, literature, geography, and commerce."[26] Behind the speakers' platform was painted an outdoor scene that included a real waterfall, which ingeniously blended into the painted background. The Blue Grass League was represented, as well as several other organizations and counties.[27]

The most entertaining feature of the Coal Palace was no doubt the working miniature coal mine where visitors could ride in a half-dozen coal cars pulled by a small mule named Maud S., but the biggest single-day draw was without a doubt the visit by President Benjamin Harrison on October 9. Following a parade down Main Street, the president spoke to a standing-room-only crowd and said, "If I should attempt to interpret the lesson of this structure, I should say that it was an illustration of how much that is artistic and graceful is to be found in the common things of life, and if I should make an application of the lesson, it would be to suggest that we might profitably carry into all our homes and into all neighborly intercourse the same transforming spirit."[28]

1890 commemorative coin, front and back

Coal Palace interior (Courtesy of Wapello County Historical Society)

(Newspapers courtesy of State Historical Society of Iowa)

It makes one wonder how many people in the audience actually understood what the president was trying to say, but most of them returned to the palace again in the evening for the privilege of shaking his hand. With large crowds and substantial profits, everyone was already looking forward to the next Festival.[29]

One of the first steps in planning the 1891 Coal Palace Festival was getting area communities to participate. Representatives were sent to surrounding towns and, by July 24, Ottumwa had received positive responses from the counties of Ringgold and Lucas, plus the town of Creston. A representative from Creston came to Ottumwa to pick out one of the best spots in the Coal Palace for a Blue Grass Palace exhibit, that being "immediately in front of the main entrance."[30] Lucas County would transfer its exhibit to the Coal Palace soon after the Creston Blue Grass Festival.[31]

Shares of stock were sold to finance the building and operation of the 1890 Coal Palace, and when a profit was realized after its first year, shareholders were given a dividend of 20 percent. The payout was no doubt a public relations ploy to build public confidence in the project in hopes of even greater investments in the future. Some investors criticized the directors for paying out dividends when the money most certainly would be needed for the following year, but the directors quickly pointed out that they easily could ask for the money to be reinvested — which they did. They sent out letters stating: "For the honor and credit of our city, we ask for that dividend to decorate the Palace. If we made a mistake in paying it to you, please pay it back that we may push the Palace to the front."[32]

The Coal Palace directors decided that a major renovation was necessary for the 1891 exposition, which included tearing off the old, deteriorated slabs of coal and replacing them with new pieces directly from the mine. Hundreds of men were employed to lay 60 tons of coal per day. A gold color was to be used for decorative accents, but experiments showed that the color faded too quickly, so an "unpretentious red" was used for the decorations and for the roof.[33]

Skilled decorators and professional artists created mosaics and other designs on the inside under the supervision of Mr. D.S. Clark and Professor De Long. Grains, grasses and other minerals were used alongside "King Karbon" to make colors richer and more harmonious than the previous year. In all, 1,800 tons of coal were required for the project, which filled 100 railroad cars of the largest capacity allowed by law. Two large skylights were placed to enhance the view of the palace's main attraction — a three-tiered waterfall 65 feet high and 60 feet wide. It was boasted that the water used in the fall could supply the city of 14,000 for 48 hours.[34]

There was apparently some concern that organizers were forgetting agriculture was still the number one industry in Iowa, and it was acknowledged that "many times the objection is made, and too often justly so, that the farmers are not given their share of attention. But whatever may have been the oversight in former years, certain it is that this year they are being well cared for by the management in many ways."[35]

On August 13, as renovations were nearing completion, a tornado (or cyclone, as they were then more commonly called) tore through the city of Ottumwa. According to the local newspaper, "Large buildings were unroofed, dwellings shaken on their foundations, trees blown down and life endangered. The Coal Palace, too, was in the track and from the lantern on the summit of the topmost tower the windows were torn. The large, portable scaffold that had been used on the outside was blown down and as its timbers were thrown in every direction, some struck the building and knocked off portions of the carved coal. The damage done to the Coal Palace is estimated at about $150."[36]

Repairs were made in time for the opening, but the festival failed to achieve the success of the preceding year. Perhaps it would have helped if a crystal ball

1891 Ottumwa Coal Palace
(Courtesy of Wapello County Historical Society)

had been available to foretell that one of the speakers, Representative William McKinley, would become president of the United States in a mere five years, but as it was, the lack of public enthusiasm in 1891 meant the end of the Coal Palace Festivals for the city of Ottumwa. Due to the rapidly deteriorating quality of coal, the palace soon was torn down before it became unsafe, becoming merely an interesting footnote in the city's history.[37]

Ottumwa Coal Palace model

(Courtesy of Wapello County Historical Society & Museum)

1891 Ottumwa Coal Palace, back view, and commemorative coin

(Courtesy of Wapello County Historical Society)

According to dates written on Coal Palace photos, there has been some confusion over which photographs date from 1890 and which date from 1891. Close inspection reveals obvious differences as evident in the decorative elements between the two stories and even more evident in the trees planted for the 1891 Coal Palace Exposition.

Footnotes for the Ottumwa Coal Palace, 1890-1891

1. A.H. Hamilton, "Modern Ottumwa," Ottumwa *Weekly Courier,* August 8, 1888, p. 2.

2. A.H. Hamilton, "Council Proceedings," Ottumwa *Weekly Courier,* August 7, 1889, p. 3.

3. Robert H. Moore, "The Commercial Club," Ottumwa *Weekly Democrat,* January 29, 1890, p. 1.

4. Robert H. Moore, "The Palace Is A Go," Ottumwa *Weekly Democrat,* February 5, 1890, p. 1.

5. Ibid.

6. Ibid.

7. Robert H. Moore, "The Democrat," Ottumwa *Weekly Democrat,* February 12, 1890, p. 1.

8. Ibid.

9. Robert H. Moore, "It Will Be Built," Ottumwa *Weekly Democrat,* March 16, 1890, p. 3.

10. Robert H. Moore, "The Diamond Palace," Ottumwa *Weekly Democrat,* April 23, 1890, p. 3.

11. Robert H. Moore, "Vice President Flagler," Ottumwa *Weekly Democrat,* April 30, 1890, p. 1.

12. Robert H. Moore, "The Three Palaces," Ottumwa *Weekly Democrat,* July 30, 1890, p. 7.

13. William J. Peterson, *The Palimpsest* Vol XLIV (The State Historical Society of Iowa, 1963) 572-573.

14. Robert H. Moore, "The Diamond Palace," Ottumwa *Weekly Democrat,* July 31, 1890, p. 5.

15. Ibid.

16. Robert H. Moore, "Ottumwa's Revival," Ottumwa *Weekly Democrat,* September 4, 1890, p. 1.

17. Robert H. Moore, "The Democrat," Ottumwa *Weekly Democrat,* September 5, 1890, p. 1.

18. Robert H. Moore, "The Palace Artists," Ottumwa *Weekly Democrat,* September 6, 1890, p. 5.

19. Ibid.

20. Ibid.

21. Robert H. Moore, "The First Program," Ottumwa *Weekly Democrat,* September 11, 1890, p. 4.

22. Robert H. Moore, "Palace Pencilings," Ottumwa *Weekly Democrat,* September 13, 1890, p. 4

23. Ibid.

24. William J. Peterson, *The Palimpsest* Vol XLIV (The State Historical Society of Iowa, 1963) 572-573.

25. William J. Peterson, *The Palimpsest* Vol XLIV (The State Historical Society of Iowa, 1963) 574.

26. William J. Peterson, *The Palimpsest* Vol XLIV (The State Historical Society of Iowa, 1963) 575.

27. Ibid.

28. William J. Peterson, *The Palimpsest* Vol XLIV (The State Historical Society of Iowa, 1963) 577.

29. William J. Peterson, *The Palimpsest* Vol XLIV (The State Historical Society of Iowa, 1963) 578.

30. A.H. Hamilton, "Coming Our Way," Ottumwa *Weekly Courier,* July 30, 1891, p. 3.

31. Ibid.

32. Ibid.

33. A.H. Hamilton, "The Castle of Coal," Ottumwa *Weekly Courier,* August 6, 1891, p. 1.

34. Ibid.

35. A.H. Hamilton, "The Farmers Take a Deep Interest," Ottumwa *Weekly Courier,* August 6, 1891, p. 1.

36. A.H. Hamilton, "Struck by a Cyclone," Ottumwa *Weekly Courier,* August 13, 1891, p. 3.

37. William J. Peterson, *The Palimpsest* (The State Historical Society of Iowa, December 1963), 578.

South Dakota

(Courtesy of South Dakota Mail Newspaper
and Aurora County Historical Society)

Plankinton
Grain Palace
1891

Section 2 ❖ South Dakota
CHAPTER 1

The Aberdeen *Weekly News* issued the following note of congratulations on September 11, 1891: "The News is in receipt of complimentaries to the Plankinton Grain Palace, which promises to be a unique and attractive affair. The managers say 'it will be the greatest display of grain ever shown by any country.' There is no doubt of its success. It will be open from Sept. 29th to Oct. 3d. All should see it."[1]

And so it was on September 29, 1891, that residents of Plankinton opened the first "palace" in South Dakota to be decorated in grain. It was modest in size, being 80 feet square and somewhat plain in appearance, perhaps resembling a barn more than a palace, but it brought the community together toward a common goal and provided a sense of pride for accomplishing something unique to South Dakota.[2]

The building sat on the north end of Main Street, where it was in plain view of anyone entering town from the south. Under one grain-covered gable were the words, "Dakota Feeds the World," which was hyperbole typical of the times, as was the following statement made by the editor of the Aurora County *Standard:* "No other city on earth of its size has so many public spirited citizens with a faith in their country, state and city that finds instantaneous expression in work as well as in the words as Plankinton has."[3]

Plankinton was not alone in its endeavor, as White River residents assisted in the construction of the palace. Thirty-five residents of Sioux City attended the opening, one of whom provided the following description: "It is, in its exterior decoration, distinctly symbolic

(Newspaper courtesy of State Historical Society of Iowa)

of grain, corn occupying no conspicuous place, but ranking in its order. The tasty building adorned with gable, tower and minaret, makes an attractive heading for the principal street. … The wheat, flax and other small grain specimens win the admiration of all. The Plankinton schools occupy a handsomely arrayed corner, including art pieces worthy of the best efforts of older hands and heads. Three specimens of genuine art in decoration challenge attention. Mrs. John Rogers, assisted by Mrs. M.W. Egan, has produced an elk, with head upraised as if suddenly startled, which would rank with the best efforts that have yet been exhibited by the west. The splendid blending of color is produced with differing shades of corn silks, while the spreading antlers are composed of wheat and flax grains. The whole effect is beautiful and the general design thoroughly artistic. Opposite this picture is one by Mrs. H.C. Holmes, representing sheep in the field. The wool on the animals, perfect in appearance, is composed of clematis. The third piece is a South Dakota farm house, field and buildings, taken from nature and done in cornstalks."[4]

Mitchell residents felt it was a very generous gesture for a large city such as Sioux City to send a delegation to a small town such as Plankinton. On the other side of the coin, they felt that Sioux Falls, which was hosting the State Fair, also should have been represented and clearly made their point with the following statement: "Sioux Falls, which aspires to be the metropolis of South Dakota, might learn some valuable lessons from the farsightedness of the Sioux City rustlers, who not only sent a train load

The Lennox band in front of the 1891 Plankinton Grain Palace
(Courtesy of South Dakota Mail Newspaper and Aurora County Historical Society)

of people to the State Fair, but also went to the trouble and expense of being largely represented at the less pretentious Grain Palace in Plankinton."[5]

To drive their point home even further, Mitchell sent an even bigger delegation on October 1 and proudly described the experience. "About two hundred people gathered at the depot Friday morning in response to the invitation of Plankinton's citizens to spend a day at their Grain Palace. Two extra coaches and a combination car were filled and many had to stand throughout the trip. The University and High school was each represented by a party of forty or fifty students, the rest of the party being composed of business men and their families. The train left Mitchell at eight o'clock, a short stop being made at Mt. Vernon while the K. P. band gave them a tune. As the train pulled into Plankinton the Lennox band, which furnishes the music for the Grain Palace, played a lively air and the citizens welcomed the excursionists. A parade was formed on lower Main street, headed by the two bands. The students who came next in the procession carried a large silk flag

on which was a neat motto in gold letters, and following these was a long line of citizens of both towns. The parade passed up Main street to the Grain Palace, where the bands formed in open order and furnished music while the people entered."[6]

Following several speeches, the visitors were let back outside to watch the "University boys" defeat Hooper Township in a baseball game, as well as a horse race that was decided by inches. At 5 p.m., the K. P. band escorted the Mitchell delegation back to the railroad depot and then gave another short performance. What followed was "a general chat winding up in three rousing cheers for Plankinton and the Grain Palace by the Mitchellites, which were as heartily returned by the Plankintonians."[7]

A few days later the Plankinton *Herald* praised Mitchell with the following article: "The band and a large delegation of citizens accompanied our guests to the train and it is safe to say that the prevailing opinion was one of the warmest friendship toward Mitchell after the demonstration of yesterday. The first man who defames Mitchell should be promptly set down upon — be he editor or private citizen. 'Rah for Mitchell.'"[8]

There appears to be no record who that first man was to defame Mitchell, but it happened only a few months later when Mitchell decided to build a Corn Palace. When Mitchell was criticized a second time, the Plankinton *Standard* editor came to Mitchell's rescue. "The City of Mitchell should not be damned and held responsible for the mouthings of its idiots and cranks, for even Plankinton has a few of this kind of cattle who in no manner represent the sentiment of the people in their foolish talk and action. This accounts for some of the wild ravings we have read lately about Plankinton people boycotting the Exposition."[9]

MITCHELL DAILY REPUBLICAN

Sunday, October 4, 1891

AT THE GRAIN PALACE.

Two Hundred Mitchellites Visit
Plankinton's Exposition.

(Newspaper courtesy of
Mitchell Public Library)

(Courtesy of Aurora
County Historical Society)

(Courtesy of South Dakota Mail Newspaper)

Plankinton
Grain Palace
1892

Section 2 ❖ South Dakota
CHAPTER 1

Whether spurred on by feelings of competition or camaraderie, Plankinton prepared to build a bigger and better palace for the following year. The Aurora County *Standard* dedicated much of its September 8, 1892, issue to the second annual Grain Palace Exposition. An elaborate sketch of the new palace covered most of the front page, and it announced that the $14,000 building "will be 86x120 feet in size and 100 feet to the top of the tallest tower. Gables, towers, minarets, and spires will largely enter into the architectural beauty of the upper part of the building, and the handsome decorations on the sides and approaches will make the building one of rare beauty."[10]

The Mitchell *Daily Republican* was more specific in its description of Plankinton's exterior decorations. "On one side of the building the artists have arranged pictures showing the wheat crop from the seeding time until it is threshed, and on the other side a complete train is shown loaded with wheat. It must be remembered that this work was done by deft hands with wheat and grain. Plenty of attractions have been arranged for and all who see the palace will have a large time."[11]

The September 8, 1892, Aurora County *Standard* also had several articles about Aurora County, one of which told visitors "don't think for a moment that you are coming to a cold, bleak, blizzardy country." Another proudly announced that "there are easy, shiftless farmers who have succeeded in a measure in this country."[12]

Taking a broader view, the editor wrote that western hospitality was the greatest in the nation, that land would soon reach $50 an acre, that soon all land would be in private hands, and that "the best investment today is the cheap farm lands of the Northwest. It is better than a savings bank; surer than life insurance; safer than even government bonds and more profitable than a gold mine."[13] His views on the value of land, however, should not lead one to believe that he had anything against mining, for he went on to say: "The mineral wealth of South Dakota is unequalled. In gold production she exceeds California. In silver she is richer than Nevada. In lead she is the peer of Wisconsin and Missouri. Her coal fields are greater in extent than those of Iowa and Illinois. Her

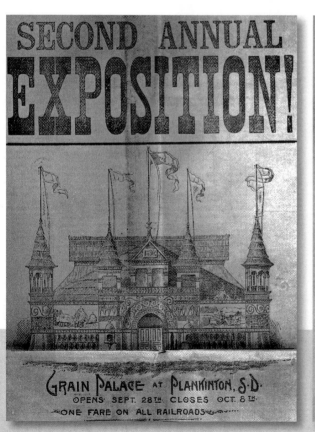

(Courtesy of South Dakota Mail Newspaper)

tin mines are richer than England's. ..."[14] In other words, welcome to paradise.

1892 Schedule of Events

September 28 ...... Opening Day
September 29 ...... Sioux City's Day
September 30 ...... From Palace to Palace
October 1 .... Farmer's Day
October 3 .... Traveling Men's Day'
October 4 .... Republicans Day
October 5 .... Democrats Day
October 7 .... From Palace to Palace

On September 10, 1892, a drawing of Plankinton's new Grain Palace accompanied the following article found in the Aberdeen *Daily News:* "The second annual exposition of the Plankinton, S.D., Grain Palace will open on Sept. 28th and continue to Oct. 8th. Plankinton is the original Grain Palace city of the state, having erected the first one last year which proved a grand success. This year the palace will in every particular exceed the former one which in itself was no small advertisement to South Dakota's progress. Special features have been prepared for each day, notably a political tournament, at which the leading parties will be represented by the leading orators of the day. One fare for the round trip has been made and it will pay all who can to visit this grand harvest festival of rejoicing."[15]

The Watertown *Public Opinion* called Plankinton "a bright little city. Her people are first water diamonds and it will do us all good to visit the Grain Palace this year."[16] And to sum it all up, the Mitchell *Capital* stated, "The Plankinton Grain Palace is completed and from all reports, it is an honor to the citizens of that town and Aurora county. The opening day was on Wednesday and fully a thousand people were present."[17]

Despite such high praise, when 1893 rolled around, the citizens of Plankinton decided that their community no longer could support a Grain Palace, and no doubt a few of them blamed their failure on Mitchell's success. When a representative of Mitchell visited Plankinton in September 1893 to advertise the Mitchell Corn Palace, the editor of the Plankinton Herald wrote: "Plankinton people do not

GRAIN PALACE AT PLANKINTON, S.D.
OPENS SEPT. 28TH CLOSES OCT. 8TH
ONE FARE ON ALL RAILROADS

"Hospitality is one of the predominant traits of western character."

Aurora County *Standard*
Thursday, September 8, 1892

On September 30, an eight-coach train transported 500 citizens from Plankinton to visit the Mitchell Corn Palace.

On October 7, a seven-coach train transported 500 citizens from Mitchell to visit the Plankinton Grain Palace.

take a great deal of interest in her neighbor's enterprise."[18] But the Mitchell *Daily Republican* editor tried to smooth things over by saying, "Oh yes they do, and they will be down here by hundreds to enjoy an Exposition which will benefit Plankinton and Aurora county just as much in the long run as it does Mitchell."[19]

The Plankinton Grain Palace eventually was torn down and rebuilt as a barn a few miles outside of Plankinton. When the barn was demolished many years later, a painted board was saved by family members, but the writing is difficult to distinguish. Another painted sign that survived advertised the dates of the 1892 Grain Palace Exposition and probably stood at the southern entrance to Plankinton. It now hangs on a wall of the local museum.[20]

GRAIN PALACE CITY
Sept. 28. To Oct. 8 1892.

(Courtesy of Aurora County Historical Society)

Footnotes for the Plankinton Grain Palace, 1891-92

1. H.C. Sessions, "Area News," Aberdeen *Weekly News*, September 11, 1891, p. 3.
2. A.M. Andrews, "Plankinton Grain Palace," Aurora County *Standard*, September 8, 1892, p. 2.
3. "The Grain Palace at Plankinton," South Dakota Mail, June 4, 1981, p. 3.
4. R.W. Wheelock, "At the Grain Palace," Mitchell *Daily Republican*, October 4, 1891, p. 4.
5. R.W. Wheelock, "Notes," Mitchell *Daily Republican*, September 30, 1891, p. 1.
6. R.W. Wheelock, "At the Grain Palace," Mitchell *Daily Republican*, October 4, 1891, p. 4.
7. Ibid.
8. R.W. Wheelock, "Mitchell at Plankinton," Mitchell *Daily Republican*, October 6, 1891, p. 2.
9. R.W. Wheelock, "This Accounts for It," Mitchell *Daily Republican*, September 26, 1893, p. 2.
10. A.M. Andrews, "Plankinton Grain Palace," Aurora County *Standard*, September 8, 1892, p. 2.
11. R.W. Wheelock, "Grain Palace," Mitchell *Daily Republican*, September 25, 1892, p. 9.
12. A.M. Andrews, "Notes," Aurora County *Standard*, September 8, 1892, p. 2.
13. A.M. Andrews, "Hints to Home Seekers," Aurora County *Standard*, September 8, 1892, p. 1.
14. A.M. Andrews, "South Dakota and Her Resources," Aurora County *Standard*, September 8, 1892, p. 3.
15. H.C. Sessions, "Plankinton, S.D. Grain Palace," Aberdeen *Daily News*, September 10, 1892, p. 3.
16. A.M. Andrews, "Watertown Public Opinion," Aurora County *Standard*, September 8, 1892, p. 2.
17. R.W. Wheelock, "The Plankinton Grain Palace," Mitchell *Capital*, September 30, 1892, p. 3.
18. R.W. Wheelock, "The Corn Belt Exposition," Mitchell *Daily Republican*, September 14, 1893, p. 2.
19. Ibid.
20. John Paul Studeny and Gayle A. Van Genderen, interview by author, Plankinton, South Dakota, August 24, 2007.

Mitchell
Corn Palace
1892

1892 Mitchell Corn Palace
(Courtesy of Mitchell Area Historical Society)

Some of the most notable newspaper headlines in the Mitchell *Daily Republican* during the summer of 1892 included the following: preparations for the Chicago World's Fair, both nationally and locally; plans in Eastern cities to replace the smoke, heat and cinders from city steam engines on elevated railways with pollution-free electric motors — an idea that seemed a bit far-fetched at the time;[1] and statistics showing that males outnumbered females in the United States, Canada, and Australia, but females outnumbered males in most of Europe.[2] But the main topic of discussion seemed to be the decline in railroad building in the previous five years, not to mention that a turn-around in the following year did not look promising. Many argued that communities could not look to the railroad to increase prosperity and therefore should develop new opportunities.[3]

A 15-county organization called the Real Estate Corn Belt Association was doing just that. The southeastern South Dakota organization, which was trying to increase corn production and demand throughout the region, held one of its regular meetings in Mitchell on Wednesday, July 27, 1892. One purpose was to determine if the citizens of Mitchell would like to host a Corn Belt Exposition that fall, and another purpose was to select a town to host the association on a permanent basis. Mitchell was eager to secure the exposition and to host the association permanently.[4]

At 10 a.m. on Thursday, July 28, several members of the city met with the association "to discuss the feasibility of holding a Corn Belt exposition."[5] The association quickly passed a resolution "to do everything in their power to further the undertaking."[6] And at another meeting held that evening, a five-member committee was appointed to help the city of Mitchell make the Corn Belt Exposition a reality.[7]

Within the next three days, two Mitchell businessmen, who were not members of the association or of the five-member committee, came up with an idea to take matters a step further. L.O. Gale and Louis Beckwith, while out for an evening stroll, ruminated on the fact that Sioux City was no longer building Corn Palaces, and that the small town of Plankinton had built a Grain Palace the previous year and was planning to build a bigger and better one that fall. The men felt embarrassed that Plankinton appeared more progressive than Mitchell and decided that having the Real Estate Corn Belt Association in town was the perfect time for Mitchell to propose building a Corn Palace of its own in conjunction with the Corn Belt Exposition.[8]

The next day Gale and Beckwith canvassed Mitchell's businesses to determine whether their idea had the support of the community, and by that evening, they not only had the support but also numerous pledges for the project in the amount of $3,700.[9]

On August 2, a formal decision was made to build a Corn Palace, to make L.O. Gale permanent chairman of the Corn Belt Exposition, and to send him along with Louis Beckwith to Sioux City to learn as much as possible

A yearly harvest exposition was held before the Corn Palace was built.

(Newspapers courtesy of Mitchell Public Library)

L. O. GALE,
DRUGGIST, JEWELER, BOOKSELLER.

HEADQUARTERS FOR

Window Shades

ALL KINDS PAINTS ALL KINDS.

(Newspapers courtesy of State Historical
Society of Iowa)

HATS! HATS!

HATS!

HATS!

HATS!

The boy is father of the man, and when the
boy dons the man's hat he is **"Out of
Sight."** These boys are **"Right in it"**
and have old heads on young shoulders. No
boy in this town need wear his **"Grandfather's Hat"** if his doting parent will
trot him around to

SMITH & CONYES.

had learned a great deal.[13] The
next day two sets of plans arrived
from Mr. C.P. Brown, a Sioux City
architect who had designed the
last Corn Palace in 1891. One plan
had the proposed Corn Palace
extending halfway across Main
Street, while the other didn't.[14]

A call quickly went out
stating, "Every man, woman
and child in Davidson county
must donate, not only part of
his choicest productions, but a
certain proportion of his talent,
time and energy in the erection
and decoration of our exposition
building if we expect to make
this great enterprise a success.
The citizens of Mitchell will
contribute six thousand dollars
in cash, besides their services in
this undertaking. It is but right that the farmers should
each contribute and bring to town, free gratis, oats, corn,
barley, rye, flax and all varieties of grasses (wild and
tame) with which to ornament and decorate the building.
Remember to preserve the straw as long as possible
and cure the small grains and grasses in the shade."[15] In
addition, townships, organizations, and individuals were

about constructing and decorating such a building. The
committee wanted its new Corn Palace to be located on
Main Street, most likely on Fourth Street or Fifth Street.[10]

Things were moving so quickly that by the following
day, Gale and Beckwith were on their way to Sioux
City and a building site was selected — a vacant lot
on Fourth Street west of Mr. Beckwith's residence that
"will extend about thirty feet on Main street, so that a
portion of the building will be visible from both depots."[11]
Press releases were sent out to numerous newspapers,
and the people were urged to "commence now and
talk exposition until the opening day. Don't miss an
opportunity to say something about the exposition in your
correspondence."[12]

Mr. Gale and Mr. Beckwith reported to the committee
on August 7 that they had interviewed every man in Sioux
City who had anything to do with its Corn Palace and

(Newspaper courtesy of
Mitchell Public Library)

Andrew Jackson Kings, head carpenter of the 1892 Corn Palace, and the tools he used to build the structure

(Courtesy of Mitchell Area Historical Society)

1892 Mitchell Corn Palace

(Courtesy of Mitchell Area Historical Society)

(Newspapers of courtesy Mitchell Public Library)

"There ought to be more of the old time chivalry among the male portion of Mitchell. The ladies are devoting every spare moment to help beautify the interior of the building, but there is even some work a woman can't do, such as climbing ladders, driving nails, etc., and they would be very glad indeed if several more gentlemen would lend their services in the same manner."

Mitchell *Daily Republican*
September 13, 1892

asked to make an exhibit that would impress both investors and thousands of visitors.[16]

The architect's plans were in place and ground was broken by August 10, though construction beyond the foundation had to be put on hold until the decorator's plans arrived. A. Rohe of Lawrence, Kansas, who had been in charge of decorations for the Sioux City Corn Palaces, was hired to be in charge of the decorating and had not yet had time to create Mitchell's design.[17]

At about this time, some friction was generated between Mitchell and Sioux Falls because of rumors that the Queen City (in reference to the Queen Bee Mill located next to the Falls) was considering the possibility of building a competing Corn Palace. The rumor was denied, and Sioux Falls assured its neighbors to the west that it was content to concentrate on the State Fair, which it hoped to hold on a permanent basis. Mitchell's

concern about the possible competition was a little ironic considering that it was competing with Plankinton, at least in the eyes of some citizens in the smaller city. An article originally from the Plankinton *Herald* was reprinted in the Mitchell *Daily Republican* on August 12, and it stated: "Any one of our citizens buying a bill of goods at Mitchell hereafter should be boycotted at home by all citizens having an interest in the prosperity of our city. A Grain Palace city is as good as a Corn Palace city."[18]

The Corn Palace foundation was nearly completed by August 14, but work could not proceed further because Mr. Rohe's plans still had not arrived.[19] In the meantime, committee members were out searching for the best produce samples available, and a stalk of corn was found near Scotland, South Dakota, that measured 14 feet in height.[20]

The decoration plans arrived on August 17, and a large work force was expected to begin constructing the framework while the women, under the leadership of Mrs. Beckwith, organized to plan the interior decorations.[21] Perhaps it seemed imperative to get the building up as quickly as possible because of rumors that both Pierre and Aberdeen were discussing plans to build palaces of one kind or another. The editor of the Iroquois *Chief* believed the more grain palaces the better, stating, "That's the right spirit."[22]

By August 19, the framework was finished on the first story, and carpenters were starting on the second. An interior problem also was solved at this time when the Electric Light Company made a generous offer to donate lights free of charge if the Exposition committee would provide a man to string the lights and run the engine.[23]

"The hearts of the executive committee were made glad Wednesday by the receipt of a letter from S.D. Cook saying that Sioux City would take possession of Mitchell and her corn palace at least one day. It is the intention to bring a trainload of Sioux Citians on the day they select. Sioux City will have no demonstration this year but will throw her strength for Mitchell."

Mitchell *Daily Republican*
Thursday, August 25, 1892

(Newspapers courtesy of
Mitchell Public Library)

An announcement was made on August 24 that a $25 chamber suite would be awarded to a couple willing to be married at the Corn Belt Exposition — no prior engagement necessary. Also on that day, the Madison *Leader* stated that Aberdeen had indeed been planning to build a Grain Palace, but had abandoned the idea for the time being.[24]

By Monday, August 29, the Corn Palace roof was being shingled, the flooring was being laid, and 150 bushels of red corn were delivered to join other grains and grasses already in storage. A total of 1,000 bushels eventually would be used. Decoration of the interior was expected to begin that week, and booths were being organized to accommodate the 19 counties that had pledged to set up exhibits.[25]

The promotional campaign was off and running as 35,000 advertising stickers were delivered the following day, and the Chicago Tribune agreed to run an article on the Exposition, complete with a sketch of the building. The C.M. & St. Paul and Northwestern railroads had already agreed to charge a low round-trip rate in any direction within 200 miles of Mitchell, and arrangements had been made with the Mystic Shrine to bring 200 members as well as a caravan of camels and elephants to enhance the "splendor of their pageantry."[26]

Several bushels of red, white and yellow corn had been soaking in water for several days, so when the chief decorator, Mr. Rohe, arrived in Mitchell the first week of September, it was time to start making the Corn Palace a thing of beauty.[27] Wheat and flax were also ready, thanks to about 50 boys and girls who had been sorting and tying the grain into small bundles,[28] and work quickly started on the second story with an attractive design of corn and wheat against a blue background.[29] Mr. Rohe's reputation was further enhanced that same week when he was notified that he had been elected to decorate the Kansas exhibit at the Chicago World's Fair.[30]

On September 9, the flag staff was raised on the center tower, and the ladies were busy decorating the second story interior, using wheat straw and sugar cane in many of the designs. The Electric Light Company installed two arc lights so the ladies could work into the night if necessary.[31] There was apparently some feeling that the women were doing more work than the men, so the newspaper editor put out an appeal to Mitchell's male population to display a little more chivalry. "The ladies are devoting every spare moment to help beautify the interior of the building, but there is even some work a woman can't do, such as climbing ladders, driving nails, etc., and they would be very glad indeed if several more gentlemen would lend their services in the same manner."[32]

He also suggested that a large delegation from Mitchell should attend the State Fair in Sioux Falls, especially considering that Sioux Falls was planning to send a large group to the Corn Belt Exposition.[33]

Three days later, the editor's call was heeded as 100 Mitchellites made the train trip to Sioux Falls. The Sioux Falls *Argus Leader* counted even more, and noted its appreciation. "The Corn Palace city did itself proud today. One hundred and seventy-five of Mitchell's first citizens, decorated with Corn Palace badges and corn husk neckties, came in on the Omaha special. They were met at the station by the Sioux Falls band and a big crowd and escorted up Phillips avenue. They were all in high spirits and full of the mutual friendship which unites the two towns."[34]

By September 16, exterior decorating on the nine towers was nearly complete and widely admired. The southwest corner tower was considered the best designed, where the words "Corn Belt Exposition" were worked into the south wall with different colors of corn that gave off a shaded appearance.[35]

On Sunday, September 25, with the Exposition nearly ready to open, a detailed description of the Corn Palace was first shared with the public. "The exposition building has a total frontage of about 200 feet on Main and Fourth streets. Nine circular towers, which project half their diameter beyond the walls of the building, rise from the foundation and run up above the roof fifteen or twenty feet, and are roofed in the Japanese style of architecture, and each surmounted with a tall flag pole with the Stars and Stripes unfurled to the breeze. Around the base of the building sugar cane has been used and made into handsome Mosaic designs. Above this various colored corn has been worked into figures most intricate, the colors being made to blend in harmony, the effect of which heightens its beauty to a great extent. In the center of the south wall the words 'Corn Belt Exposition' has been worked in different shades, the whole enclosed with a Grecian border. On the two roof gables pretty designs are made with wheat straws, forming tasty scroll work, and the American Eagle made of straw stands out in bold relief over a scarlet background. On two of the gables on the west side appear the crop estimates for the state of South Dakota in 1892. No. 1 shows a sheaf of wheat in the centre and worked in letters of grains and straw on a scarlet background in the legend, wheat 41,711,000 bushels. No. 2 shows a most perfect imitation of a bushel basket full to overflowing with ear corn and beneath it the figures and words 47,110,000 bushels.

"The tower in the center of the roof rises fully 25 feet above and is surmounted with a flag staff on which has been placed a mammoth ear of corn. The decorations on this tower are a work of art and form a striking and beautiful top piece for the building.

"Entering the building the eye is dazzled with a scene of brilliancy and beauty that is almost beyond description. The four walls enclose a floor space of 20,000 square feet, and in the second story of the building is a wide gallery on the sides with about 10,000 feet more of space, so that in both stories combined there will be ample room to accommodate a very large number of people without any crowding or inconvenience. The lower floor will be devoted to county exhibits and every available space will be consumed by them. At least fifteen counties have made application and been assigned space. In the northeast corner is the electric light plant where the power is furnished for lighting the building day and night.

"A large semi-circular stage at the east end of the building will make pleasant quarters for the Iowa State Band, which will give concerts daily while the Exposition lasts, and that the people may have the full benefit of the music and be able to hear without effort any speeches that are made, the entire back and sides of the stage has been enclosed like a large sea shell with the mouth towards the audience. This is lathed and plastered and

1892 Mitchell Corn Palace entrance

(Courtesy of Mitchell Area Historical Society)

when decorated and lighted by several electric arc lamps one can easily imagine what a beautiful and effective picture it will present to the eye."[36]

Men and women worked furiously right up to the opening at 2:30 on Wednesday afternoon, September 28, when the assembly was called to order and the speeches began. The ceiling centerpiece, in the design of a star made of wheat, was greatly admired, but "perhaps the handsomest piece of work done in corn was the design over the proscenium arch. In a large half circle the word 'Welcome' had been wrought in various colored corns, making the effect elaborate, and below it a Grecian border, the large scroll work at the end setting the piece off to perfection."[37]

Thursday was Sioux City's Day, Friday was Plankinton's Day, and the rest of the run was dedicated to farmers, Shriners and others. The town of 3,500 people was proud of its accomplishments, with visitors doubling the town's population on one day and tripling it on another. The neighboring towns were lavish in their praise.[38] Two days after the Corn Belt Exposition closed, Mitchell residents filled seven coaches for a visit to Plankinton's Grain Palace. The spirit of cooperation was back in full bloom.[39]

With subscriptions totaling $5,268, ticket sales reaching $6,379, and a balance of $1,736.70 after expenses, there was no doubt that Mitchell would host another Corn Belt Exposition in 1893.

THE CORN BELT EXPOSITION

Will be held in Mitchell September 27th to October 6th, inclusive.

Bigger and more attractive than before.

One Thousand Dollars in county prizes—$500 to first; $250 to second; $150 to third; $100 to fourth.

(Newspaper courtesy of Mitchell Public Library)

(Ribbon courtesy of Mitchell Area Historical Society)

There was also no serious debate about tearing down the existing building and constructing a new one, as did Plankinton once, and Sioux City five times in five years.[40]

The first newspaper ad for the 1893 Exposition appeared on the front page of the August 2 edition of the Mitchell *Daily Republican* with a very impressive cut of the Corn Palace. It announced the dates as September 27 to October 6 and promised to be "bigger and more attractive than before."[41] The building itself was definitely bigger due to a 42- by 100-foot addition on the north side.[42]

The Exposition committee again hired Mr. Rohe and promised more beautiful designs, bigger prizes, better lighting — 20 arc lights and 40 incandescents, vs. 13 arc lights and no incandescents in 1892 — new uniforms for the Corn Palace Band, a Native American wedding, and a more equitable work distribution for the women.[43] There appeared to be more of an emphasis on music than in the previous year, with entertainment provided by a 24-piece Mitchell Exposition Band; a 28-piece Iowa State Juvenile Band (made up of players from 6 to 16 years of age); an enlarged Santee Indian Band; and a 50-piece Massachusetts Regimental Band that cost $5,000.[44]

The 1893 Exposition also branched out to include more special interests by adding Corn Belter's Day, Old

Soldiers' Day, Chamberlain's Day, German Day, Woman's Day, Bicycle Day, and Cement City (Yankton) Day.[45] Perhaps because of the added lighting, there were also added precautions against fire: additional fire escapes and a three-inch pipe connecting the building with the street hydrant. [46]

Exterior decorating was completed on Saturday, September 23, and decorator Rohe was praised at length for his accomplishments. "The eye is first attracted by the great southwestern tower rising seventy-two feet above the base against a background of brilliant and varied colors, and surrounded by a cluster of spires with waving pennants. The Saracenic style of architecture predominates here and the decoration of this part is one of the most striking pieces of the entire structure. The upper portion of the tower is open and the columns and

1893 Mitchell Corn Palace (Courtesy of Mitchell Area Historical Society)

1893 Mitchell Corn Palace, left to right: south gable, west gable and one of the main entrances
(Courtesy of Mitchell Area Historical Society)

brackets supporting the dome are beautifully trimmed in grains. Surrounding the open space is a balustrade and beneath this a handsome Grecian border in oats and corn relieves the more solid work of the lower portion, which is an excellent imitation of brick work, done in red corn with the husks interwoven as mortar, and producing an effect so natural as to completely deceive any but a close observer. At the base of the lower corner are two handsome panels in ear corn which display some beautifully shaded scroll work.

"The front of the Palace, which faces south, presents a scene of surpassing splendor — a vast and varied expanse of form and color which conforms to no single style of art or architecture, but utilizes all which have in them the elements of beauty. On this side are four circular towers jutting from the walks of the building, and between the two more central ones rises the large southern gable, which projects several feet beyond the towers and on its broad façade is a tasteful design in corn and flax.

"In the center a circular border of flax six feet in diameter contains a large star in corn and straw, above and on either side of which is a rare piece of scroll work, the whole showing up beautifully against a rich background of red corn. At the base of the gable the words

"Corn Belt Exposition" are worked in yellow corn on a blue ground.

"Beneath the gable is a spacious balcony with a wickered balustrade of cane and corn, the whole supported by neat brackets with pendants of flax and a mosaic panel of cane and corn filling the spaces between the supports and extending down to the neat and serviceable wainscoting of cane which surrounds the entire building at the base.

"On either side of the central gable at a distance of several feet a smaller gable is situated directly above the main entrances. The general design of the decoration on these two gables is similar, the one being worked in corn and flax, and the other in corn and cane. In the arch of the entrances and extending across the space immediately above are handsome mosaic borders of various grains, and above these the ground of blue corn sets off in bright contrast a neat design in yellow and white corn in the center of which are the figures '1893.' The smaller towers are prettily ornamented with zigzag rows of corn, borders, and bands of varied colors, and the cones are neatly thatched with oats and flax.

"Passing to the west side of the Palace the scene is as dazzling as the one we have just left, and he must have a fine discrimination who presumes to judge between the two. For convenience in description we may divide the side at the central tower, first looking at the south half in the center of which rises the big western gable. At the height of twenty feet from the base is a circular balcony extending between the central and corner towers, with a pretty balustrade of cane and neatly fringed with oats and flax. Beneath the balcony are some artistic pieces of panel work. Three windows open on the balcony, the panels between them being worked in red and blue corn on a yellow background. In the broad space above the windows is some of the finest work on the building."[47]

South Dakota's Governor Sheldon opened the 1893 Exposition, but the second day created more interest thanks to the Native American wedding. The Santee Band participated in the Sioux ceremony by forming a semicircle around the bride and groom. The bride was described as resplendent in her red horse blanket and jewelry, but the groom was more modest in appearance with his $11 suit. "The bride looked at the groom with a sort of 'I-got-you-now' expression, and the groom looked back at her as much as to say, 'There's no string on me yet,' while the members of the tribe danced a wedding breakdown that brought down the house. This closed the exercises and as the wedding party left the house they were wildly cheered, while two drays backed up to the door to carry off their numerous wedding presents."[48]

What was not known, except by a select few, was that the entire ceremony was staged. One day prior to the event, Mr. T.C. Burns, who was in charge of the wedding, received word without explanation that the bride, groom and

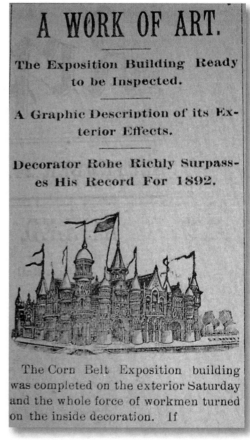

A WORK OF ART.

The Exposition Building Ready to be Inspected.

A Graphic Description of its Exterior Effects.

Decorator Rohe Richly Surpasses His Record For 1892.

The Corn Belt Exposition building was completed on the exterior Saturday and the whole force of workmen turned on the inside decoration. If

(Newspapers courtesy of Mitchell Public Library)

Mitchell Daily Republican

Sunday, August 27, 1893

EXPOSITION MATTERS

An Indian Wedding Arranged For.

The Exposition committee is arranging for a novelty in the line of attractions for Wedding Day, it being an Indian marriage ceremony which will be performed by an Indian preacher.

Mitchell Daily Republican

September 28, 1893

THE SECOND DAY

A Big Crowd Witnesses the Native American Wedding.

Another Splendid Concert Program by the Lynn Band

(Newspaper courtesy of
Mitchell Public Library)

officiating minister were not going to show up. Mr. Burns was not about to disappoint the Exposition visitors, so he rounded up replacements, including a fake minister who could not speak English. As the above newspaper quotes indicate, no one was the wiser, including the editor, and it wasn't until several years later that the truth came out.[49]

The 1893 Exposition was considered a resounding success, not necessarily in the sense that more people attended than the previous year, but that visitors came from a broader area, thereby generating new business that might be repeated in the future. There was unanimous sentiment that the Exposition should be held again the next year and every year following,[50] but that was before an economic recession and drought hit the country. In spite of a favorable balance of $1,034.88, the Exposition Committee voted in August 1894 to cancel that year's festival. Conditions during the next five years were no better, so the building sat empty except for an occasional convention, wedding, or other special event. In 1898, the grain decorations were removed and the building was given a coat of paint, but two years later it was time to decorate once again so the building could return to its original splendor.[51]

In August 1900, it was decided to hold another Corn Belt Exposition, and Mr. Gale and Mr. Beckwith were again put in charge. Two-time presidential candidate William Jennings Bryan was the headliner and the building again needed to be enlarged to handle the growing crowds. The exposition committee paid investors 11 percent interest and still realized a $1,384 profit, but no exposition was organized for 1901, probably because Mr. Gale and Mr. Beckwith were being spread too thin and refused to head the event.[52]

In 1902, the Corn Belt Exposition got back on track essentially because many prominent Mitchell citizens wanted the state capital located in their city. They were sure that a thriving Corn Palace would give them an advantage over other cities, especially since Aberdeen's Grain Palace had burned down earlier that year, leaving Mitchell with the only palace of any kind still standing. Mr. Gale again was persuaded to be in charge, but Beckwith begged off and was replaced by Dr. R.F. Dundas. The building again had to be remodeled, enlarged, and redecorated, and Mr. Rohe again was put in charge of the

1902 Mitchell Corn Palace
(Courtesy of Mitchell Area Historical Society)

latter task. The event was successful enough that articles of incorporation were filed to make the Exposition a permanent institution.[53]

The 1903 Exposition was similar to previous ones except that the featured musical entertainment was an Italian band, which didn't draw the attention of 1904's musical legend, John Philip Sousa. Even though the palace was enlarged even further in 1904, people had to be turned away at the door.[54] According to a popular story, there was, however, one moment of trepidation.

1900 Mitchell Corn Palace (Courtesy of Mitchell Area Historical Society)

1903 Mitchell Corn Palace (below) and interior (left)
(Courtesy of Mitchell Area Historical Society)

John Phillip Sousa.

(Newspaper article courtesy of Mitchell Public Library)

After taking one good look at Mitchell's muddy Main Street, Sousa demanded to be paid his $7,000 in full before he'd step one foot off the train. The demand was met, the event was a success, and promoters realized a larger structure would be necessary for the success of future expositions.[55] The newspaper article to the left indicates that the story was probably a fabrication.

1904 Mitchell Corn Palace
(Courtesy of Mitchell Area Historical Society)

OFFICIAL PROGRAMME
Corn Belt Exposition
Mitchell, South Dakota

THURSDAY AFTERNOON, SEPT. 29, 1904

For Comfort and Pleasure of All, Ladies are Requested to Remove their Hats

Grand Concert by Sousa and his Band

JOHN PHILIP SOUSA, Conductor

ESTELLE LIEBLING, Soprano.
LEO ZIMMERMAN, Trombone
HERBERT L. CLARKE, Cornet

Left: John Philip Sousa on stage during 1904 Exposition

Below: Note harp still on stage during demolition

(All photos and program courtesy of Mitchell Area Historical Society)

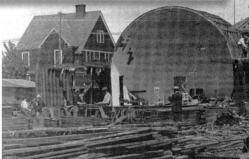

Far left: 1904 crowds

Left: Sousa's band in front of 1904 Corn Palace

Mitchell Corn Palace 1905

1905 Mitchell Corn Palace
(Courtesy of Mitchell Area Historical Society)

Section 2 ❖ South Dakota
CHAPTER 2

In 1905, a new palace measuring 125 by 142 feet was constructed on Fifth and Main, and the name was officially changed from the Corn Belt Exposition to the Corn Palace. The name change was an easy matter, but the new building was not. Promoters found it difficult to raise enough funds for the structure, and construction could not begin until the railroads agreed to wave freight charges on lumber and the lumberyards agreed to allow payments to be made after the Exposition was over. Even at that, the $15,000 Corn Palace left the committee $7,500 in debt, and local banks had to step in to ensure that festivals would continue in the future.[56]

Scottish bagpipers were the featured entertainment in 1906, and John Philip Sousa made a return appearance in 1907, which happened to be the only year the Exposition ended in the red. The loss was blamed on poor advertising and not on Mr. Sousa. Three major presidential candidates — William Jennings Bryan, William Taft, and E.W. Chafin — brought large enough crowds to Mitchell in 1908 to allow the Corn Palace Committee to nearly pay off the mortgage on the new building, and in 1909, the Palace was decorated by someone other than Mr. Rohe — a local man by the name of Floyd Gillis, who was only 21 years old. Gillis had worked under Mr. Rohe in previous years and remained in charge of decorating for several years thereafter.[57]

The 1912 Exposition proved to be a benchmark simply because the Corn Palace Committee decided to stop selling photography rights as a concession. The fact that anyone with a camera could now take pictures of the Corn Palace inside and out proved to be one of the best advertising strategies ever employed. Photographs of the Palace soon found their way all over the world.[58]

1921 Mitchell Corn Palace
(Courtesy of Mitchell Area Historical Society)

Mitchell
Corn Palace
1921

Section 2 ❖ South Dakota
CHAPTER 2

In 1921, the third palace was built on Sixth and Main with flat rooflines at a cost of $275,000 plus $10,000 to decorate.[59] Because of drought conditions in the early 1930s, there wasn't always enough corn to complete all of the decorations, but then 1937 saw an abundance of grain plus the addition of Moorish style minarets and turrets to the building's roof. During the World War II years of 1943 and 1944, painted murals replaced the grains as part of the war effort to practice conservation of resources.[60]

An arsonist seriously damaged the Corn Palace in 1979 but failed to prevent the Exposition from proceeding on schedule, and the previous year's decorations were mostly left in place for the 1980 Exposition because of local drought conditions. No matter what problems have arisen, Mitchell residents have dealt with them, keeping thousands of visitors flocking to the city each year.[61]

1937 Mitchell Corn Palace program
(Courtesy of Mitchell Area Historical Society)

Footnotes for the Mitchell Corn Palace, 1892-Present

1. R.W.Wheelock,"World News," Mitchell *Daily Republican*, July 24, 1892, p. 8.
2. Ibid.
3. R.W.Wheelock,"Railroad Building in 1892," Mitchell *Daily Republican*, July 24, 1892, p. 2.
4. R.W.Wheelock,"Corn Belt Association," Mitchell *Daily Republican*, July 26, 1892, p. 2.
5. R.W.Wheelock,"Thursday Morning's Session," Mitchell *Daily Republican*, July 28, 1892, p. 2.
6. Ibid.
7. R.W.Wheelock,"The Evening Session," Mitchell *Daily Republican*, July 28, 1892, p. 2.
8. N.J.Dunham, History of Mitchell Corn Palace (Mitchell: *The Mitchell Gazette*, 1914), 3.
9. Ibid.
10. R.W.Wheelock,"Corn Belt Exposition," Mitchell *Daily Republican*, August 2, 1892, p. 2.
11. R.W.Wheelock,"Exposition Doings," Mitchell *Daily Republican*, August 3, 1892, p. 2.
12. C.W.Downey,"Local and Personal," Mitchell *Daily Republican*, August 4, 1892, p. 2.
13. R.W.Wheelock,"What They Learned in Sioux City," Mitchell *Daily Republican*, August 7, 1892, p. 4.
14. R.W.Wheelock,"Have Received Their Plans," Mitchell *Daily Republican*, August 8, 1892, p. 3.
15. R.W.Wheelock,"Davidson County Farmers," Mitchell *Daily Republican*, August 9, 1892, p. 3.
16. Ibid.
17. R.W.Wheelock,"Corn Belt Exposition," Mitchell *Daily Republican*, August 10, 1892, p. 3.
18. R.W.Wheelock,"Outside Comment," Mitchell *Daily Republican*, August 12, 1892, p. 2.
19. R.W.Wheelock,"The Corn Belt Exposition," Mitchell *Daily Republican*, August 15, 1892, p. 2.
20. R.W.Wheelock,"Attractions of Interest," Mitchell *Daily Republican*, August 15, 1892, p. 2.
21. R.W.Wheelock,"The Corn Belt Exposition," Mitchell *Daily Republican*, August 17, 1892, p. 2.
22. R.W.Wheelock,"Outside Comment," Mitchell *Daily Republican*, August 18, 1892, p. 2.
23. R.W.Wheelock,"The Corn Belt Exposition," Mitchell *Daily Republican*, August 19, 1892, p. 2.
24. R.W.Wheelock,"A Flattering Offer," Mitchell *Daily Republican*, August 24, 1892, p. 3.

1937 Mitchell Corn Palace (Courtesy of Mitchell Area Historical Society)

25. R.W.Wheelock,"The Corn Belt Exposition," Mitchell *Daily Republican*, August 29, 1892, p. 2.

26. R.W.Wheelock,"The Mystic Shrine Coming," Mitchell *Daily Republican*, August 30, 1892, p. 2.

27. R.W.Wheelock,"The Corn Belt Exposition," Mitchell *Daily Republican*, September 2, 1892, p. 2.

28. R.W.Wheelock,"Exposition Notes," Mitchell *Daily Republican*, September 4, 1892, p. 4.

29. R.W.Wheelock,"Exposition Notes," Mitchell *Daily Republican*, September 5, 1892, p. 2.

30. R.W.Wheelock,"Exposition Notes," Mitchell *Daily Republican*, September 7, 1892, p. 2.

31. R.W.Wheelock,"The Corn Belt Exposition," Mitchell *Daily Republican*, September 9, 1892, p. 2.

32. R.W.Wheelock,"Exposition Notes," Mitchell *Daily Republican*, September 13, 1892, p. 2.

33. R.W.Wheelock,"Exposition Notes," Mitchell *Daily Republican*, September 12, 1892, p. 3.

34. R.W.Wheelock,"Mitchell at Sioux Falls," Mitchell *Daily Republican*, September 16, 1892, p. 2.

35. Ibid.

36. R.W.Wheelock,"The Exposition Nearly Ready," Mitchell *Daily Republican*, September 25, 1892, p. 4.

37. R.W.Wheelock,"A Brilliant Success," Mitchell *Daily Republican*, September 29, 1892, p. 2.

38. R.W.Wheelock,"The Exposition Reviewed," Mitchell *Daily Republican*, October 9, 1892, p. 1.

39. R.W.Wheelock,"Mitchell to Plankinton," Mitchell *Daily Republican*, October 9, 1892, p. 4.

40. N.J.Dunham, History of Mitchell Corn Palace (Mitchell: *The Mitchell Gazette*, 1914), 46.

41. R.W.Wheelock,"The Corn Belt Exposition," Mitchell *Daily Republican*, August 2, 1893, p. 1.

42. N.J.Dunham, History of Mitchell Corn Palace (Mitchell: *The Mitchell Gazette*, 1914), 11.

43. R.W.Wheelock,"Exposition Matters," Mitchell *Daily Republican*, August 27, 1893, p. 4.

44. R.W.Wheelock,"A Great Program," Mitchell *Daily Republican*, September 20, 1893, p. 3.

45. Ibid.

46. R.W.Wheelock,"Palace Notes," Mitchell *Capital*, September 23, 1893, p. 2.

47. R.W.Wheelock,"A Work of Art," Mitchell *Daily Republican*, September 24, 1893, p. 4.

48. R.W.Wheelock,"The Indian Wedding," Mitchell *Daily Republican*, September 28, 1893, p. 2.

49. N.J.Dunham, History of Mitchell Corn Palace (Mitchell: *The Mitchell Gazette*, 1914), 14.

50. R.W.Wheelock,"Exposition Results," Mitchell *Daily Republican*, October 9, 1893, p. 2.

51. N.J.Dunham, History of Mitchell Corn Palace (Mitchell: *The Mitchell Gazette*, 1914), 14.

52. Ibid, 16.

53. Ibid, 18.

54. Ibid, 22.

55. Herbert T. Hoover and John E. Miller, *A New South Dakota History* (Sioux Falls: The Center for Western Studies, 2007), 408.

56. N.J.Dunham, History of Mitchell Corn Palace (Mitchell: *The Mitchell Gazette*, 1914), 24.

57. Ibid, 26-33.

58. Ibid, 42.

59. *A Chronological History of the World's Only Corn Palace* (Mitchell, South Dakota, 2001), 1-7.

60. Ibid, 8.

61. Ibid, 16.

1893 Aberdeen Grain Palace
(Courtesy Aberdeen's Alexander Mitchell Library)

Aberdeen
Grain Palace
1893-1902

Section 2 ❖ South Dakota
CHAPTER 3

berdeen had been looking upon Sioux City's five corn palaces with a sense of awe and envy,[1] but there was no sign of Aberdeen trying to jump on the palace band wagon until the following one-sentence statement was issued: "The corn belt association of South Dakota has decided to hold a corn belt exposition at Mitchell, sometime during the autumn."[2] That announcement, which appeared in the Aberdeen *Daily News* on August 2, 1892, sent a shock wave through Aberdeen that neither the Sioux City Corn Palaces nor the Plankinton Grain Palaces could send. Sioux City was probably too big to be viewed as direct competition, and Plankinton perhaps too small, but Mitchell was "just right," and as far as H.C. Sessions, editor of the Aberdeen *Daily News,* was concerned, his city was not going to be outdone by an equal competitor if he had anything to say about it — and he had plenty to say.

In the same issue as the Mitchell announcement, Sessions proposed that Aberdeen should start a Wheat Festival. He reminded townsmen and farmers alike of the projected bountiful harvests and how it would be good to show off the abundant crops in the northern part of the state. He also asked a simple question: "Shall the Hub City Invite the People to Come and Rejoice?"[3]

The editor quoted several businessmen who supported the idea and then finished with, "The *News* has started the ball rolling, now let the people do the rest and not allow the matter to go to sleep. Considerable work will have to be done and it is not too early to begin."[4]

A committee was set up, meetings were held, and a program was outlined for a two-day event at an estimated cost of $1,000. Details about the structure were very vague, with the only clue being, "It will be in the nature of a grain palace."[5]

At a following meeting, there was discussion of erecting a temporary building or perhaps just moving a building from the fairgrounds to Main Street and converting it into a grain palace of a modest nature. When that idea didn't catch fire, someone suggested decorating a railroad car with various grains and sending it around the country. With ideas getting smaller instead of grander, the *News* editor and the mayor told Aberdeen to "wake up!"[6] However, Aberdeen didn't wake up and, within a few days, it was obvious that the Wheat Festival idea was not going to reach fruition in 1892. On August 19, 1892, the editor wrote, "That harvest festival matter, which everybody endorsed as so good a thing, seems a little slow in materializing. There is a hitch somewhere. Can the people of Aberdeen, the county seat of the banner county of South Dakota, afford to let this matter drop with out at least some strong effort to bring out a result?"[7]

Apparently they could, and Sessions had to admit defeat for the 1892 Exposition, but the editor wasn't about to be defeated a second time. Mr. Sessions made it clear that "organization could be perfected and proper literature covering the wheat belt district prepared and distributed in the east during the coming fall, winter and spring, to be followed with a festival next year."[8] He was determined to promote his city and he spelled out in detail how his plan would work. "By means of the festival they will secure reduced rates to home seekers from other states to come to the state, and hundreds by means of

---

ABERDEEN DAILY NEWS

August 2, 1892

WHEAT FESTIVAL

Shall the Hub City Invite the People to Come and Rejoice?

What the People of Aberdeen Have to Say About It.

Will a festival be of benefit? Let's see. Every city in the west that has made any forward strides in the march of progress has not allowed a single opportunity to pass when the attention of the outside world could be attracted to it. We have here a staunch, thriving, agricultural city with such ample transportation facilities as to bring it in close proximity with every section of the country. There are many avenues still open for the investment of capital in diverse enterprises. Communities cannot expect people to come flocking to them without some efforts on their part.

ABERDEEN DAILY NEWS

August 3, 1892

THE FESTIVAL

Citizens Meet to Discuss Plans for a Rousing Harvest Festival.

An Executive Committee Appointed to Canvass the City.

Neighboring counties desire to join hands with Brown county in the formation of a wheat belt association.

(Newspapers courtesy of Aberdeen's Alexander Mitchell Library)

the low rates and judicious advertising will be induced to come to South Dakota and view for themselves the desirability of South Dakota as a place of investment or a home. ... For, to view our beautiful and productive land is to be convinced of its desirability as a home."[9]

Aberdeen apparently wasn't the only desirable place on earth for Mr. Sessions because within a few months, he pulled up stakes and moved to Sioux Falls.[10] By the next spring, the Aberdeen *Daily News* had a new editor, C.J. McLeod, who had been publishing the Warner *Sun* 11 miles south of Aberdeen.[11] Though McLeod shared Session's enthusiasm for a harvest exposition, instead of scolding and cajoling his readers, he used a much gentler approach. On March 27, 1893, he reported that a meeting would be held to discuss hosting the State Fair and to secure a tow mill for the budding flax industry, but he intentionally failed to specifically mention a grain palace. Instead, he created a sense of mystery around the topic by stating "business of vital importance will come up for discussion which at this time must be acted upon with care and conservatism. It is of such a nature and character that every business man is directly interested, and his presence is therefore urged."[12]

Perhaps McLeod's subtle approach worked, as plans for an exposition progressed very rapidly. A meeting was held on March 28, 1893, and was reported to be the "most enthusiastic and largely attended of any held."[13] A five-member committee was appointed to organize a corporation for the Inter-State Grain Palace Association, which it did that very evening. The committee decided to build a wheat palace, make it a joint effort between North and South Dakota, construct it in Aberdeen, and open it during September in conjunction with the State Fair.[14] State Fair? That had to come as a surprise announcement to most people because the State Fair Commission had decided in February to forego a State Fair in 1893.[15]

The State Fair phenomenon had been most interesting since its inception, with intrigue and turmoil around every corner. The first State Fair was held in 1885, four years before South Dakota acquired statehood. Many of the major towns wanted to host the Fair, so it was moved from city to city, depending on who wanted it,

(Newspapers courtesy of Aberdeen's Alexander Mitchell Library)

who could come up with a bond, who was aligned with the current political climate, and who could give the best sales pitch. Huron captured the prize the first two years, and then it moved on to Mitchell in 1887-1888, to Aberdeen in 1889-1890 and to Sioux Falls in 1891-1892.[16] The first sign of trouble was in 1891, when Sioux Falls had difficulty raising the bond required by the Legislature. Aberdeen was quick to offer "assistance" by announcing, "Sioux Falls seems to have considerable trouble in raising the pledged funds for the state fair. It is not too late to transfer the whole matter to Aberdeen. The citizens here can take care of the state fair in good shape. The grounds are all ready and a few scrapes of the pen would settle the matter."[17]

Sioux Falls leaders managed to come up with the bond money but perhaps wished they hadn't. The State

"Great State Fair" advertisement from the September 24, 1891, issue of the Sioux Falls *Argus Leader*

(Courtesy of Sioux Falls Public Library)

Chicago, Milwaukee and St. Paul Railroad depot and train, 1892
(Courtesy of Aberdeen's Dacotah Prairie Museum)

Fairs had been profitable up until 1891, but the combined Fairs of 1891 and 1892 resulted in losses amounting to a whopping $4,084.65 — big money in those days. As a result, the 1893 Fair was cancelled, and the Legislature agreed to help defray up to $2,500 of the losses so the institution could get back on its feet enough to have another State Fair in 1894.[18]

In spite of the February decision, Aberdeen felt it needed a State Fair to help draw crowds to its proposed grain exposition. The city was no doubt confident of its ability to produce another successful event, based on record profits of $1,403.59 when it hosted the 1890 State Fair.[19] The city lobbied hard to get the State Fair approved for 1893, and its efforts paid off. The day *after* Aberdeen announced that it would hold a Grain Palace Exposition in conjunction with the State Fair, there was an official announcement declaring that Aberdeen had defeated Mitchell and Sioux Falls for the right to host the state event — with the stipulation that it raise $1,500 and repair the present fair buildings. The article also mentioned that Aberdeen would be the headquarters for all State Fair business, which, according to the Aberdeen *Daily News* editor, was "an indication that ere long the Hub city will, and by right ought to, secure the permanent location of South Dakota's fair."[20] Aberdeen's future appeared promising indeed.

The following day, on March 31, Aberdeen's *News* editor suggested that 1893 would go down as a memorable year in the city's history, thanks to the upcoming Exposition and State Fair, thanks to its having the best railroad facilities of any city in the northwest, and thanks to the city's citizens who had finally woken up and were ready to leave "nothing undone to foster the growth of their favorite town."[21]

On April 4, 1893, the *News* printed excerpts of congratulatory remarks extended from other cities, including Pierre, Mitchell, Volga, Ellendale, Lake Preston, Frederick and even Sioux Falls. Although the latter city didn't comment on Aberdeen's getting the State Fair, it did say that its planned grain exposition was "a laudable enterprise."[22]

Eight days later, an immigration meeting was held at Eureka to secure "as large a percentage of the influx of settlers as possible."[23] Five counties were represented at the meeting — Edmunds, McPherson, Campbell, Walworth and Brown — and they resolved to "most heartily endorse the plan of holding a grain exposition at Aberdeen this fall and cordially fall in with the plans of the Interstate Grain Palace Association, and look upon the enterprise as one of the means of advancing the interstate of our meeting today by attracting settlers to our wonderful country."[24]

It's interesting to note that there was no specific mention of a wheat palace at the Eureka meeting, especially considering that Eureka billed itself as the "Wheat Capital of the World" in 1892, when the area was producing and shipping nearly 4,000,000 bushels of wheat, more than any area in the Midwest.[25] It was probably fortunate that the committee members didn't concentrate on wheat because the area farms needed to diversify, and some farmers wanted the northern part of the state to be recognized for its ability to grow corn and other crops. Mr. Sutherland from Mound City sent a letter to the Aberdeen *Daily News* editor asking that the city go with the Grain Palace moniker so corn could be included, saying people in his area "will want to exhibit our corn as well as our wheat."[26] The farmer got his wish. An article in the April 6th edition of the Aberdeen *Daily News* gave reference to a wheat palace, but a day later the *News* reported, "It will not be a wheat palace or a corn palace, but will embrace both productions and all others of a similar nature that may add to the attraction or profit."[27]

Why did the north-central counties of South Dakota think they could hold a successful harvest exposition when it included the expenses involved with building a grain palace? Why such optimism? Didn't these rural communities know the country was going through a depression? In fact, weren't they aware that the South and rural states in general were supposed to have been in a serious recession since the late 1880s?[28] Didn't they think the end of the Sioux City Corn Palace epoch in 1891, followed by termination of the Plankinton Grain Palace projects in 1892, should have been construed as dark omens?

There's little question that the economy was of serious concern, but the Aberdeen *Daily News* was quick to deny that its city would be adversely affected. On April 1, 1893, it stated, "Notwithstanding the general financial depression of 1890 and 1891, Aberdeen kept right along growing. Today the population is greater than it ever was before, vacant residences are unknown, and every business building is filled from cellar to garret."[29]

Sioux Falls had been denying economic hardship since 1891, as evidenced by a retaliatory reply to a charge made by a smaller Aberdeen newspaper, the *Star*. "It may be that the farmers of Brown County cannot pay their taxes, as the Aberdeen *Star* says, and that the list of farm lands advertised for sale for taxes is larger than ever before in the history of that county, but the Star makes a great mistake in supposing that the whole of South Dakota is like Brown county. The tax list of this county is not yet printed, but it may be stated, authoritatively, that fewer farm lands will be sold for taxes this year than ever before, and that very few mortgages are being foreclosed on Minnehaha farms. Agricultural land in this county has increased in value by 25 percent since last year. The farmers are prosperous and very many of them have good fat bank accounts."[30] Perhaps most South Dakotans subscribed to the theory that "you're only in a recession if you think you are." If so, then it appeared that South Dakota's economy should have been booming.

One reason Aberdeen was so optimistic is that it caught World's Fair Fever thanks to Chicago's Columbian Exposition, also being held in 1893. Probably for the first

> The northern part of the state, which for some years back has received but little advertising, will have in the state fair and grain palace an excellent opportunity to place itself on dress parade before the world.
>
> Aberdeen *Daily News*
> April 1, 1893

(Newspapers courtesy of Aberdeen's Alexander Mitchell Library)

South Dakota's building at the World's Fair, from the July 22, 1893, issue of the Edmunds County *Democrat*

(Courtesy of Ipswich *Tribune*)

a 100-by-60-foot building of Yankton cement, with the exterior finished to give it the appearance of cut stone.[34]

World's Fairs had been capturing attention since 1851, when London hosted the first exposition. The focus was mainly on architecture, and its Crystal Palace was the most spectacular structure of the modern world. From then on, it was the dream of the nearly 30 succeeding World's Fair hosts to match or top London's achievement. Paris perhaps succeeded with the Eiffel Tower in 1889, and Chicago did its best with a monstrous Ferris Wheel in 1893.[35]

While smaller Midwestern cities had no chance to compete on that scale, they still caught the World's Fair spirit and did what they could to draw attention to themselves in the form of an Exposition. And as World's Fair hosts invited other countries to participate, Exposition hosts did the same for surrounding counties and states.

So what was the Grain Palace for Aberdeen's Exposition supposed to be? Judging from Aberdeen architect E.W. Van Meter's drawing, it was to be a beautifully decorated building somewhat resembling a mixture of the Main Building of the Philadelphia Centennial Exposition of 1876, the Main Building of the Melbourne Exposition of 1880, and the Manufactures and Liberal Arts Building of the Chicago Columbian Exposition of 1893.[36] They were among the more attractive and functional of the World's Fair buildings, and it was hoped that visitors would associate Aberdeen's Grain Palace with the worldwide expositions.

Aberdeen may have had the design, but what it needed was the lumber, which only eight weeks prior to the exposition's opening was still sitting at the lumber mill. There was some question whether it would arrive in time, but it eventually did, and committees were organized quickly.[37]

Everything soon appeared to be set for the upcoming Grain Palace Exposition. A carpenter from nearby Ipswich, D.M. Birdseye, was hired to foreman a crew of local male volunteers to put up the basic structure of the building. Two women from Minneapolis, the Misses Purvis, who most recently had decorated the Minnesota

time ever, Aberdonians considered Chicago to be in their own backyard, and instead of thinking of the Windy City as competition, the Aberdeen *Daily News* said, "Thousands will come west from the World's Fair, and the great majority of them must be attracted in this direction. The opportunity is a grand one and should be made the most of. Now is the time to make preparation for the exhibit. Every farmer should take it upon himself to produce something that will astonish the world."[31]

The *News* advertised the train schedules to Chicago and their reduced rates, and made note of the local citizens who took advantage of those fares. One of the more interesting notes read, "Gilgallon left for Chicago this morning to meet Susan B. Anthony and discuss with her the equal suffrage question on the World's Fair ground. That's his word for it anyhow."[32] The city also stood behind the state's attempt to raise $80,000 by subscription apportioned pro rata among the counties for the construction and maintenance of a South Dakota building at the Chicago exposition.[33] The plan was to build

THIS IS OUR **INTER-STATE · GRAIN · PALACE ·**
ABERDEEN, SOUTH DAKOTA.

You are coming, of course.

Exposition and Harvest Festival
SEPTEMBER 11-23, 1893.

(Courtesy of Aberdeen's Dacotah Prairie Museum)

and North Dakota state buildings at the Chicago World's Fair, were hired on August 8th to be in charge of the Grain Palace interior and supervise the female volunteers. The father of the decorators, George Purvis, was appraiser of lands for the Great Northern Railway.[38]

The Aberdeen Grain Palace was constructed at 502 South Main Street, and though it was at that time the most spectacular building in Aberdeen's short history, it did not turn out to be nearly as spectacular as originally envisioned. The building came in slightly under budget[39] but only because very little money was expended to decorate the exterior. Only the trim boards were covered with grains and grasses, and the rest of the building was simply painted white. The *News* glossed over the sparse exterior decorations by stating, "The beautiful building stands before you. It is the plan of the architect to make it resemble the World's Fair buildings in color, with enough grain decorations to indicate its character. While the entire outside could have been covered with grain, this plan was thought appropriate for this Columbian year. So it is Aberdeen's World's Fair building."[40]

While it's true that the Chicago World's Fair buildings, known as "The White City," were indeed white,[41] it should be noted that the Aberdeen Grain Palace exterior never received further decorations in subsequent years, and never did rival in beauty the Mitchell or Sioux City Corn Palaces.

Figures vary on the size of Aberdeen's palace. An early report put the length at 150 feet and the width at 108 feet,[42] but another article listed the interior length at 116 feet, the width at 64 feet, the walls 32 feet high, the corner towers 40 feet high and the center tower 60 feet high.[43]

What the men failed to decorate on the outside, the women made up for on the inside, and the *News* duly reported, "The interior decorations, completed under the immediate supervision and direction of the Misses Purvis, are of great beauty and appropriateness."[44] The paper also reported, "The county exhibits are extensive and beautiful, but it should be understood that every kernel and bit of decoration on the outside or in is the product of Brown County soil and most of it grown within five miles of Aberdeen."[45] The editor of the Edmunds *County Democrat* later disputed that claim, noting that some of the grain was gathered in Edmunds County.[46] If the Grain Palace Exposition was still intended to be a joint effort with the surrounding counties, it seems strange that the *News* editor would even want to make such a claim, and stranger still that the Grain Palace Committee would not make an effort to include grain from several surrounding counties.

There were no doubt many frayed nerves as the Grain Palace Exposition prepared to open on the evening of September 11, 1893, as evidenced by one sentence in that day's *Daily News:* "The Grain Palace is practically completed and will be opened this evening with appropriate ceremonies."[47]

Regardless of what "practically completed" meant, the exposition opened with pomp and ceremony. "The Festivities were presided over by the Grain Lady known as the Queen of Aberdeen. She was wholly garbed in grains and grasses, on her head a crown of the same. Her left hand held flowers and upon her wrist was poised a live pigeon."[48] There was no mention of any accidents with the live pigeon, but not everything went according to plan. The weather was described as "annoying and harassing,"[49] North Dakota's Governor Shortridge canceled his appearance at the last minute, South Dakota's governor, C.H. Sheldon, arrived two hours late, and officials from the city of Aberdeen failed to showed up at all — without explanation.[50]

Nightly admission to the palace was 50 cents, and

attendance estimates varied from 700 to 1,000, yet the newspaper said the building's seating capacity was taxed. Some of the county exhibits were still incomplete (Clay, Sully, and Potter were mentioned by name), but there was no mention whether the blame rested with the counties or with the "practically completed" Grain Palace. Due praise was given to Edmunds, Campbell, and Walworth counties, whose displays adorned the west side of the first floor, and to Lake County on the east side. Mr. Parmley and Mr. Lewellyn of Edmunds County were specifically singled out for their county map that was intricately designed in grains and grasses.[51]

Only months after aluminum had been introduced to the American public at the Chicago World's Fair, Mrs. Helen Leslie Gage, who owned a variety store on Aberdeen's Main Street, displayed the first aluminum products ever seen in Aberdeen.[52] She acquired her business by default after her brother-in-law L. Frank Baum, who had rented the building from her, went broke while trying to operate Baum's Bazaar just two years earlier. That was Baum's first of two business failures during his short, two-year stay in Aberdeen, and it resulted in his moving to Chicago, where he reversed his fortunes and gained fame with *The Wonderful Wizard of Oz* a few years later.

Had Baum remained in the city a couple more years, perhaps Aberdeen's Grain Palace would have become world renowned, having been described in detail as the Wizard's palace. After all, many speculate that happenings during Baum's stay in Aberdeen contributed to several of his stories: for example, the cyclone (tornado) he wrote about in 1890; balloon ascensions he witnessed at the State Fairs held in Aberdeen in 1889 and 1890; and Dorothy, who many believe was based on Baum's niece, Matilda Gage, who lived next door to him on Aberdeen's Kline Street.[53]

By the Exposition's fourth day, which was billed as Sioux Falls Day, the State Fair and the Exposition combined pulled in an estimated 8,000 to 10,000 visitors, which was double the number from the previous day. Attendance was reported picking up to the point that "hotel accommodations, usually adequate, failed, and

Aberdeen Grain Palace interior
(Courtesy of Aberdeen's Dacotah Prairie Museum)

hundreds had to seek lodging and board at private residences."[54] Among the additional guests were pickpockets, who relieved one woman of $30 and another of $5 and some valuable papers. There were bands, baseball games, horse races, and bicycle races, though the *News* reported that "the pneumatic bicycle tire does not appear to be altogether a success. Accidents have been frequent, and in one instance nearly the whole tire was stripped from the wheel, necessitating the abandonment of the heat and race by the driver and owner."[55]

Admission was reduced to 25 cents just in time for "Woman's Day,"[56] and then a fine reception was held at the close of the fair with guests of honor Count Rostovtzof of Russia and H.W. Pearson of Great Britain, agricultural commissioners in their respective countries. The closing of the exposition was not so fine. Cold temperatures required the Grain Palace to be heated with oil stoves, and one young man received an even chillier reception. The Exposition was to culminate with a wedding to be performed on the main stage. The local paper reported the arrival of the young couple from Westport, but when it came time for the ceremony, the bride was nowhere to be found. No explanation was ever given, but the Exposition was declared a success anyway.[57] Perhaps part of the success was due to the last evening's performance of the romantic war drama, *The Veteran of 1812,* which elicited the following statement: "Mr. Lawson's goatee was on its good behavior and never once dropped from his chin although the audience patiently waited for such catastrophe."[58]

All in all, the State Fair failed to pull in as many entries as in previous years, which was said to be no big surprise, as "this is very much an off-year for state and local fairs and expositions all over the country."[59] There was no mention whether that might be due to the fact that neither games of chance nor alcohol were allowed on the grounds.

By the end of September 1893, the Aberdeen Grain Palace Commission no doubt felt the year's business at an end, but Edmunds County viewed things differently. Its exhibit had won first place in the county competition, but the Commission had failed to cough up the award money. That led to cries of foul play, beginning with, "How about the $300 prize due Edmunds county?"[60] That was followed two weeks later by, "The three hundred dollar premium due Edmunds county from Aberdeen Grain Palace is still unpaid. Pass the hat boys and remove this little blot."[61] The last complaint stated, "We are now informed, that owing to the fact there are other bills to pay, Edmunds county need not expect any money. If Aberdeen ever expects to have another interstate grain palace she is making a serious mistake in attempting to repudiate lawful debts at this time."[62] Thus far, no articles have been found indicating that the payment was ever made or that legal action was taken.

Perhaps the Panic of 1893 contributed to the unpaid debt, and if that wasn't bad enough, the crops harvested in 1894 were the worst ever since settlers came to Dakota. It's not surprising then that by 1894, Aberdeen was the only city left in the Midwest with a palace exposition.[63] Perhaps that's the reason the *Daily News* reported, "Aberdeen is receiving the highest compliments from every quarter of the state, and from the entire northwest for that matter, for her enterprise in pushing the Grain Palace project this year. People everywhere are talking about Aberdeen's pluck and commending Aberdeen's enterprise."[64]

The Grain Palace Association must have been looking beyond 1894 because it bought 40 gallons of paint and gave the palace two coats, which certainly should be interpreted as a positive view toward the future. The State Fair didn't begin on such a promising note, being

ABERDEEN DAILY NEWS

September 14, 1893

BEST DAY OF ALL.

———

Eight Thousand People Visit the City and the Various Attractions Provided.

———

Splendid Attendance and Superb Entertainment at the Grain Palace.

———

ENTHUSED AND DELIGHTED.

ABERDEEN DAILY NEWS

September 15, 1893

FAIR AND PALACE.

———

The Largest Throng of the Exposition Session Crowds and Packs the Palace.

———

World's Fair Commissioners from Russia and Great Britain Arrive at Last.

———

Last Day of the Fair Marred by Windy Weather.

(Newspapers courtesy of Aberdeen's Alexander Mitchell Library)

described as "all right — a trifle shy perhaps on some exhibits but still very complete and satisfactory in a general way."[65] But as for the Exposition, the *Daily News* reported, "All previous records for attendance and general interest at the Grain Palace were eclipsed last evening. The crowds kept pushing their way in until stairways, booths, display apartments, portions of the stage, and every foot of available space in the huge building were occupied by a crowding mass of humanity, which must have numbered all of 2,000 persons — perhaps more.[66] Improvements for 1894 included a new exit cut in the west side of the second floor, a large banana tree placed inside the building, a team of elk hitched to a carriage and driven about the grounds, and electric fountains that "worked beautifully and shed various colored mellow lights with great prodigality."[67]

The only negative mention, other than the weather on the closing day, involved Professor Ward, a balloonist who "gave the people their first disappointment. Just as he was about to launch into space, his assistants in some manner permitted the canvas to come in contact with the fire used to inflate the huge balloon and in an instant almost all of the bag was in flames in a number of places and speedily collapsed. An ascension of course for the day was out of the question. The professor fell a number of feet and suffered slight injuries to his hips. As he is paid only when he makes a trip through the air the loss is considerable to him. He will make an effort, however, to repair the balloon and carry out his part of the program tomorrow."[68]

At the opening of the 1895 Exposition, the *Daily News* allowed itself a moment of honest reflection while giving the community a hearty pat on the back when it stated, "Success has never been wanting, although industrial conditions have been disappointing and the Exposition has encountered many trying obstacles. The exhibits of '93 and '94 gave additional

(Newspapers courtesy of Aberdeen's Alexander Mitchell Library)

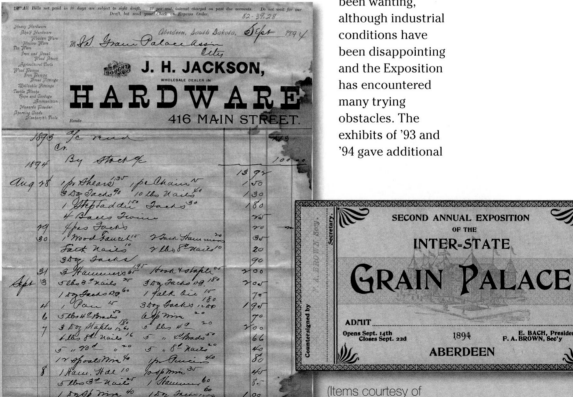

(Items courtesy of Aberdeen's Dacotah Prairie Museum)

(Newspaper courtesy of Aberdeen's
Alexander Mitchell Library)

**"Use Electric Lights" ad from the
September 21, 1895, issue of the
Aberdeen *Daily News***

(Courtesy of Aberdeen's Alexander
Mitchell Library)

(Items
courtesy of
Aberdeen's
Dacotah
Prairie
Museum)

luster to the reputation acquired abroad and at home by
the enterprising business men and citizens of Aberdeen.
Other cities have abandoned similar projects when once
undertaken, or have lacked the courage and energy to
enter upon them. Aberdeen has never faltered, not even in
times of more than usual hardship and disaster."[69]

To provide extra space for exhibits, one of the State
Fair buildings was moved and attached to the west side of
the Grain Palace. "This building will largely be surrendered
to farm products of all kinds which have heretofore been
rather cramped for lack of room." More seating was also
added, increasing capacity by one-third, and additional
electric lighting enhanced the interior grain designs.[70]

One of the difficulties of holding an annual Grain
Palace Exposition was how to top the previous years. In
1896, Aberdeen tried to accomplish that by contracting
with the lighting company to install 250 incandescent
lights of various colors, plus 10 large arc lamps, including
"a revolving arc globe through which shine incandescents
of different hues, and which are automatic in action, one
color constantly succeeding another."[71] Over the east
entrance were lights of different colors spelling out "Grain
Palace." Radiators were also installed to keep the guests
warm in case the weather turned cold — which it did.[72]

A new attraction was to be a picture play, but alas,
the "apparatus designed for the presentation was not
properly equipped for the occasion." It was explained as
"an unfortunate circumstance beyond average human wisdom
and experience to guard against and thwart," and it was especially

(Newspaper courtesy
of Aberdeen's
Alexander Mitchell
Library)

frustrating when the apparatus malfunctioned "just as the people had become intensely interested in the novelty and great beauty of the performance."[73]

Another new attraction, whose merit and novelty were not generally understood, was called the Mystic Bridge. The *News* editor did his best to explain it to his readers in the following article: "Visitors are shown into a neatly papered little room, about twelve feet square, and are seated in a little car suspended by trunnions on opposite sides of the wall, so that in reality it is a big swing capable of carrying eight persons. 'First, we'll take a little swing back and forth,' says Mr. Gibson, as he steps into the car, casts off the gang plank and gives a shove with his foot. The car begins to swing back and forth, higher and higher, till it closely approaches the horizontal at each oscillation. The effect is startling in the extreme, but is nothing compared to what follows when Mr. Gibson says: 'Now, if you can stand it, we'll go clear over.' There is no exaggeration about it either, for as the order is given the car swings higher and higher, and the passengers have the novel experience of momentarily sitting on the ceiling and looking down at the floor. The sensation is indescribable. After it is all over the conductor informs his passengers that it's all a delusion and very simple at that, but the illusion is perfect—so perfect that even when one knows how it's done, the sensation is still very eerie."[74]

The 1896 Exposition was rounded out in dramatic fashion by the boy orator of the Platte, William Jennings Bryan, who was crisscrossing the country while making his first of three bids for the presidency. He immediately caught the crowd's curiosity when escorted to the Palace by several Sioux Indians from the Sisseton Reservation. They were given seats of honor upon Bryan's platform, which nearly put them in danger when audience members rushed the stage to shake Bryan's hand. "The crowd closed in upon and jostled

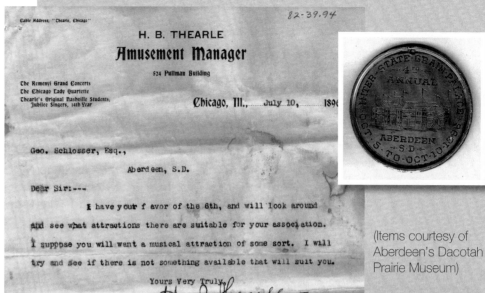

(Items courtesy of Aberdeen's Dacotah Prairie Museum)

BRYAN TONIGHT

He Will Reach the City and Address the People this Evening

WILLIAM JENNINGS BRYAN

him and his retinue very severely. Escape was finally made through a rear door."[75] Because of the large crowds anxious to hear Bryan, he gave another speech to 1,000 people at the Opera House, and another from the balcony of the Sherman House Hotel.

But even those crowds failed to make the Exposition a very profitable venture. On October 12, the *Daily News* headlines read, "The Grain Palace Likely to Little More Than Pay Out."[76]

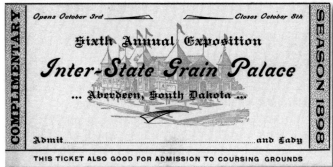

ABERDEEN DAILY NEWS.

ESTABLISHED JULY 1886.   ABERDEEN, SOUTH DAKOTA, THURSDAY EVENING, SEPTEMBER 30, 1897.   FIFTY CENTS A MONTH

THE FIFTH ANNUAL EXHIBITION

GRAIN ✶ PALACE

ABERDEEN, SOUTH DAKOTA

OCTOBER 4th to 9th, INCLUSIVE, 1897

SIX DAYS OF UNLIMITED ENJOYMENT, INSTRUCTION AND PLEASURE

GRAND HARVEST FESTIVAL

FINEST LIST OF ATTRACTIONS EVER PRESENTED IN THE STATE

Giffen-Neill Dramatic Company		Brookings Regimental Band
Twelve Performances		Grand Street Attractions
Two Daily		Agricultural and Art Exhibit
Afternoon and Evening		Live Stock Show

The Performances of the Giffen-Neill Company will be the Best Ever Seen in this Section of Country

MONDAY—All the Comforts of a Home
TUESDAY—Captain Swift
WEDNESDAY—Niobe
THURSDAY—The Fool of the Family
FRIDAY—Selwin's Night Off
SATURDAY—Incog.

THE BROOKINGS REGIMENTAL BAND

ENGAGED FOR THIS OCCASION, IS ONE OF THE BEST IN THE NORTHWEST

FREE STREET CONCERTS EACH DAY.

The management this year have prepared something entirely different from the attractions of previous years and it is confidently expected their enterprise will be rewarded by the largest attendance in the history of the association. Certainly a rare treat is in store for those who visit Aberdeen on those dates.

A Solid Week of Pleasure for Old and Young, You Shouldn't Miss It

You have but one life to live and you will not do yourself justice unless you attend this Great Entertainment. Enjoy yourself while you can; you will be a long time dead.

The year 1897 was a year of firsts. It was the first year an Exposition ad made the front page of the Aberdeen *Daily News,* the first time the city's population exceeded 4,000 citizens, the first time a moving picture was shown in the city, and the first time an automobile made its way down Main Street, which in turn gave the city its first car accident. A traveling salesman, from New York no less, was struck by the only automobile in town. The man was embarrassed but not

injured, and the car was smudged but not damaged, so the salesman went about his business and the car went about two more blocks to the Grain Palace, where it was put on public display.[77] The first Aberdeen residents to own an automobile were R.L. and F.A. Brown in 1900 — a Winton.[78]

On the closing day for the 1897 Exposition, the *Daily News* reported that "exterior and interior photographs of the Palace are on sale by the Ladies Guild of St. Mark's at the uniformly low price of 15 cents each. The Palace will be warmed by the steam heating apparatus tonight, so no one should remain away because of the falling temperature of the past twenty-four hours."[79]

The big draws for the 1898 Exposition were street fireworks; diving events, in which professionals dove from a 100-foot tower into a small tank of water; antique displays; the Andrews Opera Company; and free street

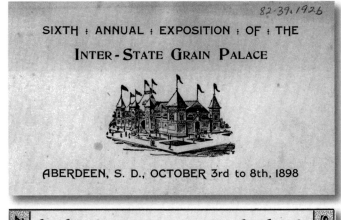

82-39.192b

SIXTH ⁚ ANNUAL ⁚ EXPOSITION ⁚ OF ⁚ THE

INTER-STATE GRAIN PALACE

ABERDEEN, S. D., OCTOBER 3rd to 8th, 1898

Opens October 3rd — *Closes October 8th*

COMPLIMENTARY

Sixth Annual Exposition

Inter-State Grain Palace

... Aberdeen, South Dakota ...

SEASON 1898

Admit _____ and Lady

THIS TICKET ALSO GOOD FOR ADMISSION TO COURSING GROUNDS

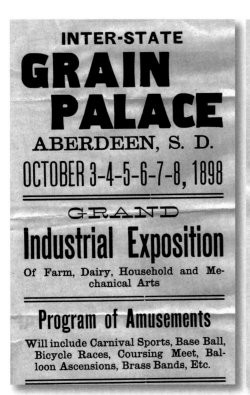

INTER-STATE
GRAIN PALACE
ABERDEEN, S. D.
OCTOBER 3-4-5-6-7-8, 1898

GRAND
Industrial Exposition
Of Farm, Dairy, Household and Mechanical Arts

Program of Amusements
Will include Carnival Sports, Base Ball, Bicycle Races, Coursing Meet, Balloon Ascensions, Brass Bands, Etc.

We Offer the Following Unequalled ... Attractions ...

ELLIS' HIGH DIVERS,
Including Prof. Clark, Champion High Diver of the World.

WATSON'S MILITARY BAND
of Minneapolis, Minn.

GRAND STREET ILLUMINATION,
and Thrilling Run by Fire Department each Evening.

LARGE EXHIBIT OF FARM AND HOUSEHOLD PRODUCTS.
LARGE EXHIBIT OF ART AND TEXTILE FABRICS.
The above are absolutely free.

THE FAMOUS ANDREWS OPERA CO.,
Consisting of 35 Artists will give one of their Matchless Operas every Afternoon and Evening in Auditorium of Grain Palace.

THREE DAYS COURSING MEET
The First Enclosed Coursing Meet ever Held in the West, will Occur During the week at the Fair Grounds.

(Items courtesy of Aberdeen's Dacotah Prairie Museum)

The two men quickly retreated from her heavy blows, and Mrs. Schlueter became not only the heroine of the day, but of the entire Exposition. Even with the day's receipts safe and secure, the Exposition ended with only $31.62 on hand, so Mrs. Schlueter was in a sense responsible for keeping the event in the black.[81]

How do you top diving people? Simple — bring in diving horses and elk! On October 4, 1899, Aberdonians read, "The big grand stand at Grain Palace Park was filled with people this afternoon to see Dr. Carver do his marvelous feats of shooting and

entertainment.[80] The event that garnered the most headlines, however, was extracurricular in nature and took place several blocks from the Grain Palace on October 5. The day's festivities were concluded, and city auditor J.A. Schlueter was walking home with his wife and daughter, as well as the day's box office receipts. He was carrying a weighted cane, which he handed to his wife as he stopped to light a cigar. She felt the weight of the cane and joked that she would use it to protect her husband if attacked.

The words were hardly out of her mouth when two men approached, blew a handful of red pepper into Mr. Schlueter's eyes, and prepared to strike him with a weapon. The hopeful robbers obviously forgot to take into consideration Mrs. Schlueter or the cane, and they suddenly found that the auditor's wife was true to her word.

Dr. Carver's diving horses (Courtesy of Aberdeen's Dacotah Prairie Museum)

to see the diving horses and elk perform. The doctor elicited warm applause, and the horses and elk made their plunges from the high tower without any delay. The animals did their work handsomely and were much admired. The horses went first, and Cupid varied the program by turning a somersault in the air."[82]

Festival-goers almost missed an opportunity to see the unusual antics of Dr. Carver's diving animals.

On January 20, 1899, stockholders of the Grain Palace Association met to discuss whether Aberdeen should continue with its annual expositions, and there was strong opposition against it. Several businessmen had failed to pay their assessment to the guaranty fund the previous year, so a double burden was falling upon the shoulders (and pocketbooks) of the other stockholders. It was decided to discuss the matter further at a later meeting.[83] Fortunately, the 1899 Exposition was revived at a board of directors meeting on May 10.[84]

As if the diving elk weren't enough, Aberdeen also brought in the president of the United States during the 1899 Exposition. President William McKinley welcomed home South Dakota's troops who had been fighting Spain in the Philippines since August 25, 1898. The war had become very unpopular, and it was time to do some damage control. The president's train left Washington on October 5, traveled to Chicago, St. Paul, Duluth, and then on to Fargo to review North Dakota's volunteers before traveling to South Dakota.[85]

The soldiers were coming from San Francisco, and the plan was to have them reach Aberdeen at about the same time as the McKinley delegation. The troops arrived at the appointed hour, and the *Daily News* reported that "the blue-coated heroes were welcomed with a thunderous tumult of cheers that could be heard for miles."[86] It went on to say that "never before in any city of 5,000 inhabitants in the United States was so large a crowd gathered as in Aberdeen today to welcome home the First Regiment South Dakota Volunteers and to greet President McKinley and members of the cabinet. It

> The Grain Palace windows were darkened and electric lights gave a very pleasing effect.
>
> Aberdeen *Daily News*
> October 3, 1899

> Tomorrow afternoon will be children's afternoon at the Palace, there being several numbers on the program especially for their pleasure.
>
> Aberdeen *Daily News*
> October 6, 1899

ABERDEEN DAILY NEWS

October 4, 1899

Grain Palace in Miniature.

Prominent among window attractions for carnival week is the model of the Grain Palace at Gallett's. This novel and appropriate window feature was designed and executed by Edwin Brandes, who is in the employ of D.G. Gallett, the jeweler and optician, and it is a marvel of beauty and graceful proportions. It is decorated with gold and silver jewelry, diamonds, opals, rubies, emeralds, almadines, and is of the most dazzling beauty. At one side, the Brownie Aberdeen band discourses music from tiny instruments, reminding one of the tin Gee Gee.

1899 Aberdeen Grain Palace festivities included a parade, which included President McKinley (below). The parade passed through an arch built especially for the occasion (left).

(Courtesy of Aberdeen's Dacotah Prairie Museum)

President McKinley speaks at the 1899 Aberdeen Grain Palace.

(Courtesy of Aberdeen's Dacotah Prairie Museum)

is well-nigh useless to attempt even an approximate estimate of the number of people in the city, the crowd is of such vast proportions."[87] Even though the newspaper only mentioned the First Regiment, the state "also furnished five troops of cavalry, officially known as the Third Regiment of the United States Volunteer Cavalry, but popularly designated Grigsby's Cowboys."[88] South Dakota's quota would have been about 850 men, but due to extreme patriotic fervor, the governor offered to send a full regiment of 1,000 men. Unfortunately, at the end of the war, the state had to raise $25,000 to pay for their return.[89]

Aberdeen Mayor Hute rode with the president in the carriage that led a parade from the train station to the Grain Palace. The dignitaries passed through a handsome arch built especially for the occasion, and it was reported that "President McKinley acknowledged rousing cheers of the populace by removing his hat and bowing repeatedly to the assemblage which packed the sides of the streets along the entire route. President McKinley has seen some big crowds on his tour of the west, but nothing he has heretofore encountered approached in magnitude the vast gathering in Aberdeen, when the population is considered. It took the utmost endeavors of the small army of marshals to keep the ground to be marched upon open for use."[90]

Vice President Garrett Hobart's death in November 1899 paved the way for another celebrity visit to Aberdeen in 1900 — that of Theodore Roosevelt. Campaigning vigorously between late June and early November, the vice presidential candidate traveled to 567 towns in 24 states, making 673 speeches to an estimated 3,000,000 people. From September 11-14, he hit 27 South Dakota communities and was told he'd receive one of his warmest welcomes in Aberdeen.[91]

With TR's arrival scheduled near the dates of Aberdeen's annual Grain Palace Exposition, it was decided to cancel the Exposition in favor of a "Carnival" to coincide with the vice presidential candidate's visit. The event was promoted heavily, but with a definite political slant. Since the vast majority of the citizens in Aberdeen were of the Republican persuasion, the effort met with little opposition.[92] In fact, all of the state's major

ABERDEEN *DAILY NEWS*

NOVEMBER 21, 1899

———

EXTRA

———

HOBART IS DEAD

———

The Vice President Passed Quietly Away at an Early Hour

———

Patterson, N.J., Nov. 21—Vice President Hobart died this morning at 8:30. His family and attending physicians were present. Death came quietly.

GARRET A. HOBART.

The Sioux Falls *Daily Argus-Leader* gave Roosevelt the front page during his visit, and boldly declared, *"Veni! Vidi! Vici!"*[59] (I came! I saw! I conquered!)

(Newspapers courtesy of Aberdeen's Alexander Mitchell Library)

ABERDEEN *DAILY NEWS*

SEPTEMBER 1, 1900

———

FOR TEDDY'S DAY

———

Committees Named and Arrangements Making for a Great Time

———

Greatest Reception He Will Have on His Trip in Northwest

———

Special Railroad Trains and Rates to Accommodate Visitors

ABERDEEN DAILY NEW

PUBLISHED JULY 1886   ABERDEEN, SOUTH DAKOTA, FRIDAY, AUGUST 31, 1900   EVENING

ROOSEVELT DAY IN ABERDEEN

THEODORE ROOSEVELT

YOU ARE INVITED TO BE PRESENT

YOU CAN'T AFFORD TO BE ABSENT

THURSDAY, SEPTEMBER 13, 1900

All March In Procession Thursday Night Torches for All

Turn out everybody and welcome the Gallant Rough Rider and next Vice-president

Interior of the 1900 Aberdeen Grain Palace

(Photos courtesy of Aberdeen's Dacotah Prairie Museum)

Theodore Roosevelt

(Newspaper courtesy of Aberdeen's Alexander Mitchell Library)

Theodore Roosevelt speaks at the 1900 Aberdeen Grain Palace Exposition.
(Courtesy of Aberdeen's Alexander Mitchell Library)

newspapers were Republican except the Vermillion *Plain Talk* and the Yankton *Press and Dakotan.* Six national newspapers sent reporters to travel with the Roosevelt contingent, and they came to be known as Camp No. 2 of the Roosevelt Rough Writers.[93]

The call went out for men to organize a Mounted Republican Club, and if the men didn't want to participate, they were asked to at least loan their horses and saddles for others to use upon Roosevelt's arrival. The horsemen were expected to drill for the Rough Rider Parade held during the day and the Torch Parade held at night.[94]

Expectations were met as Roosevelt's visit was without a doubt the second biggest event in the city's history, behind only President McKinley's visit the previous year, although William Jennings Bryan pulled in crowds that were nearly as large. But when it came to patriotic fervor, it would have been hard for anyone to compete with the leader of the Rough Riders. The parade included "700 torchbearers, 100 horsemen, and a long line of rough riders. The entire procession was six blocks in length with marchers moving six to ten abreast. Many wore McKinley and Roosevelt campaign buttons, which were advertised for sale ahead of the event by a local merchant."[95] The local newspaper estimated the number of men in the parade at 1,000 and claimed that Aberdeen provided the best reception of any city Roosevelt had traveled to thus far.[96]

It's safe to say that Aberdeen's 1901 Grain Palace Exposition — or "Carnival," as referred to in the paper — got off to a rocky start. President McKinley died on

Grain Palace

Traveling Men's Parade (or "White Hat and Bamboo Cane Parade") on September 21, 1901

(Courtesy of Aberdeen's Dacotah Prairie Museum)

September 14, just three days before the opening of the Carnival, and Aberdeen's mayor called for a period of mourning on the opening day. The weather was cold and windy, and the city chose September 17 to announce a huge increase in property taxes. Tents and other equipment didn't arrive on time for State Guard troops who were setting up camp, nor did events go well for

one of the visiting Native Americans. In one of the track races, he entered a horse that was not used to the crowd noise and, as a result, the animal "threw his rider over the fence and performed other antics that were not on the program."[97]

The 1901 Carnival ended as stormily as it began. On the night of September 22, as crowds were celebrating the festival closing with fireworks, dancing, and confetti throwing, Mother Nature decided when the festivities

THE LATE WILLIAM M'KINLEY

ABERDEEN DAILY NEWS

ESTABLISHED JULY 1886 · ABERDEEN, SOUTH DAKOTA, SATURDAY, SEPTEMBER 14, 1901 · EVENING EDITION

PRESIDENT M'KINLEY DEAD

Passed Peacefully Away at 2:15 This Morning After Being Unconscious for Several Hours

The Nation, the Whole World, Mourns the Death of Him Who Yesterday Was Its Greatest and Grandest Man

THE SAD, SAD STORY

Buffalo, Sept. 14.---President McKinley died this morning at 2:15 o'clock, after being unconscious from 7:50 o'clock.

Scenes at Dying President's Bedside

Buffalo, Sept. 14.—President McKinley died at 2:15 o'clock this morning. He had been unconscious since about 8 o'clock last evening. Before sinking into unconsciousness he bade his wife a tender farewell. Members of the cabinet took leave of their dying chief earlier in the evening. When death came, all members of the family, with the exception of the bereaved wife, were at the death bed. Mrs. McKinley was in an adjoining room. Dr. Rixey was the only physician present.

Exact Cause of President's Death

Buffalo, Sept. 14.—The exact cause of the president's death has not been fully determined. An autopsy will be held this afternoon. Undertakers who were called in were not permitted to embalm the body, because orders had been issued for a post mortem examination.

State Funeral at Washington

The state funeral will be held this afternoon. The body of the murdered president will be interred at Canton, his old home.

Date Set For the Funeral

Buffalo, Sept. 14.—The cabinet has decided that the president's body will be taken to Washington on Monday morning, where the corpse will lie in state. The interment will be at Canton on Thursday.

Earlier Reports of President's End

Buffalo, Sept. 13, 6:51 p. m.—The physicians to the president report that his condition is most serious. In spite of vigorous stimulants the depression continues and is profound.

WASHINGTON SHOCKED

Bad News From Buffalo Entirely Unexpected

Washington, Sept. 14.—The untoward news from the president's bedside came upon Washington with almost as great a shock as was caused by the first report of the murderous attack on him. Secretary Hay was among those first notified of the turn for the worse and he considered for a moment whether or not he should hasten to Buffalo. He decided not to do so but to remain on guard at the national capital ready to meet any emergency that might arise. This decision was in line with an understanding reached between the cabinet members in Buffalo when it was determined that the secretary of state should await a summons from his colleagues before returning to Buffalo.

"HERR MOST" ARRESTED

Locked Up by New York Police as "Suspicious Person"

New York, Sept. 14.—Johann Most, the most widely known of New York anarchists and editor of Freiheit, the organ of the anarchists, was arrested by Central Office Detectives Kuacb and Ferseleen. The arrest was made in a saloon over which are offices of the newspaper.

Mrs. McKinley in Serious State

Buffalo, Sept. 14.—Mrs. McKinley is prostrated and is under the care of Drs. Rixey and Warden, who are administering stimulants. Through the trying ordeal of the sorrowful parting at the bedside she bore up wonderfully. After the end was announced she swooned and has been very weak ever since.

Report of Collapse Denied

Buffalo, Sept. 14.—The rumor that Mrs. McKinley has suffered a collapse is not true. This statement is made on the authority of the chaplain of the United States navy. The chaplain says Mrs. McKinley has not suffered from collapse, but is bearing up bravely. She was informed of her husband's death shortly after it occurred. Naturally her grief is very great, but the rumors which say she is in a dangerous condition are not truthful.

Cabinet Meeting Held at Buffalo

Buffalo, Sept. 14.—Vice president Roosevelt has arrived. A cabinet meeting will be held today.

Roosevelt Takes Oath of Office

Buffalo, Sept. 14.—President Roosevelt, as he must hereafter be styled, arrived this afternoon of a 1:40 o'clock by special train. Admission to his private car was refused to newspaper men all along the route. He immediately repaired to the residence of Ansley Wilcox, where he took the oath of office as president of the United States. A meeting of the cabinet, with President Roosevelt presiding, is now being held.

ABERDEEN *DAILY NEWS*

SEPTEMBER 17, 1901

THE OPENING DAY

WEATHER BAD FOR FIRST
OF CARNIVAL

The weather is far from being pleasant for the opening of the carnival week in Aberdeen. The temperature is not very high and the wind, which comes from the northwest, is far from being conducive to a very spirited opening day. As is usual with the first day of a week given to a fair or entertainment, not much was expected, there not being many features on the program, and in consequence there has not been much of a turnout except among those who came in specially to see the horse racing, which began this afternoon at the fair ground. The aeronaut with his big balloon arrived this morning, but the wind prevented him from making any attempt to make an ascension today. The ascension will take place at the fair grounds every day hereafter at 1:30, if the weather permits.

ABERDEEN *DAILY NEWS*

SEPTEMBER 17, 1901

PROCLAMATION

In the death of President McKinley, the people of our nation have met a most grievous loss. No president since the birth of the nation so endeared himself to the hearts of his countrymen, as did our late chief executive. His character as a man was ideal. His loving devotion to his invalid wife presents a beautiful lesson. His statesmanship was characterized by firmness, integrity and patriotism. His splendid achievements in the Spanish American war will always be regarded as one of the greatest events in the world's history.

Therefore I, J.E. Adams, mayor of this city, as an expression of respect, desire that all citizens appropriately observe the day on which our late president's funeral will occur by uniting in public services at the Grain Palace at the hour of 2 p.m., refraining from all amusements and suspending business at least during the hours of the assemblage.

By the mayor

J.E. Adams

(Newspapers courtesy of Aberdeen's Alexander Mitchell Library)

would end. As reported in the next morning's paper, "It was late before the crowds broke up and it would have been later had not the wind begun blowing a strong gale, and dark clouds and lightning indicated a storm, which scattered people for their homes or their hotels."[98] Little did people know a bigger storm was brewing for the following year.

There was probably nobody in the city of Aberdeen who didn't already know the latest news, but the April 28, 1902, issue of the *Daily News* confirmed their worst fears when it reported, "Aberdeen's Inter-State Grain Palace was completely destroyed by fire this morning between 12 and 1 o'clock."[99] A pedestrian out for a late walk had smelled the smoke, discovered the fire, and reported it to firemen only two blocks away, but the building was quickly a mass of flames. The paper went on to say, "The origin of the fire is unknown, but it is alleged a number of young fellows were seen on the balcony on the Main street front of the building, some of them smoking. The theory is that some one dropped a cigar stump, which caused the fire."[100]

Once the fire reached the basement, no one could even come near the Grain Palace because most of the equipment of Company L of the South Dakota State Guard was stored there. It was all destroyed in the fire, including 2,000 rifle cartridges, which cleared the area when they began exploding.[101]

Aberdeen citizens must have been wondering how long the Grain Palace would have survived if it hadn't burned down in 1902. There was nearly an end to the expositions in 1899, and the 1900 and 1901 events were reduced to a "carnival" status. It's possible the 1899 and 1900 events were successful only because they were able to draw the big names — McKinley and Roosevelt. Otherwise, the Exposition had not found a way to reinvent itself, and there was a very limited supply of presidents and vice presidents. There was also no serious discussion of rebuilding, even though there was a shortage of public meeting places, especially when the Opera House burned only three days later. Investigators were quite certain the Opera House fire was the result of arson, so there's always a chance the fires were related.[102]

Whatever the future would have held for the Grain

ABERDEEN *DAILY NEWS*

MONDAY, APRIL 28, 1902

———

PALACE BURNED

———

THE INTER-STATE GRAIN PALACE DESTROYED BY FIRE

———

A House and Barn Go With It— Entire Business Section of City in Danger at One Time

———

Aberdeen's Inter-State Grain Palace was completely destroyed by fire this morning between 12 and 1 o'clock. The fire was discovered by a late pedestrian on Main street, who smelled smoke and made an investigation. He found the smoke coming from under the sidewalk and platform on the Main street side of the building. There was quite a volume of smoke and he looked no farther, but ran to the Sherman House two blocks away to turn in an alarm. As soon as he had done this he returned to the building, reaching there just as the firemen did.

At this time, less than three minutes after he had first seen the smoke, the flames were bursting out of the roof of the western part of what was known as the annex. Within a very brief period the roof of the main part was on fire and the entire interior was a mass of flames.

The origin of the fire is unknown, but it is alleged a number of young fellows were seen on the balcony on the Main street front of the building, some of them smoking. The theory is that some one dropped a cigar stump, which caused the fire.

Whole Business Section Endangered

The main building of the Palace and the annex on its west covered nearly the whole of a quarter block of ground, about 150 by 150 feet. Burning shingles and other pieces of wood were carried by the breeze for blocks, and for a time the entire business section of the city was threatened. Hundreds of people were out and scores of men made it their business to patrol the alleys and go between buildings to put out these burning embers and firebrands, and had they not done so the consequences would have been disastrous.

Most of the equipment of Company L of the S.D. State Guard was destroyed in the fire, including 2,000 rifle cartridges, which cleared the area when they began exploding.

(Newspapers courtesy of Aberdeen's Alexander Mitchell Library)

Palace, its problems could not have been blamed on the Aberdeen *Daily News,* for it continued promoting the Grain Palace and its expositions as much in the latter years as in the beginning, which was certainly not the case with some cities, including Sioux City. If there was an obvious strike against the continued success of Aberdeen's palace, it was undoubtedly the fact that the exterior simply wasn't spectacular enough. It was almost heresy for an Aberdeen citizen to admit that fact publicly, but at least one resident made mention of it in her diary, and photographs clearly show the palace was lacking when compared with Mitchell's Corn Palace.[103]

A letter sent out by the Brown County Circuit Court concerning the 1905 dissolution of the Inter-State Grain Palace Association. Stock value at that time was $3.75/share.

(Courtesy of Aberdeen's Dacotah Prairie Museum)

STATE OF SOUTH DAKOTA
Fifth Judicial Circuit

IN CIRCUIT COURT
COUNTY OF BROWN

In the Matter of the Inter-State Grain Palace Association, a Corporation, Dissolved.

$ 3 75

Received of *JAMES M. LAWSON, Trustee* of said Corporation, dissolved, the sum of _Three_ Dollars and _Seventy five_ Cents, in full payment of stockholder's dividend of $3.75 per share of capital stock, represented by Stock Certificates No. _60_ _1 sh._, which were duly issued to _C. L. Parkhurst_ by said Corporation, dissolved, and of which I am the lawful holder and owner, and which said Certificates are hereby surrendered to said Trustee in accordance with the order of the Court, duly made on the 4th day of December, 1905.

Dated at _____ this _____ day of _____ 190_.

In Presence of Two Witnesses

G. W. Wengell
Bessie M. Parkhurst

C. L. Parkhurst

Aberdeen, South Dakota, *December 4th, 1905.*

Dear Sir:

Please return this receipt duly executed, in presence of *'two* witnesses, together with stock certificates, and payment will be made at once

Yours truly,

JAMES M. LAWSON, *Trustee.*

An article that appeared after the 1901 carnival indicates that future expositions or carnivals were unlikely, stating "the promoters (B.B. Ward and R.E. Glass) of the carnival will lack much of making the receipts to pay the cost of entertaining the people of the city and the visitors, and they will be considerably out of pocket. They took the matter of the carnival up after the Grain Palace management had failed, and had it not been for their enterprise there would have been nothing doing in the way of amusement in Aberdeen this fall."[104]

Footnotes for the Aberdeen Grain Palace, 1893-1902

1. C.J. McLeod, "Inter-State," Aberdeen Daily News, March 29, 1893, p.3.
2. H.C. Sessions, "State News," Aberdeen Daily News, August 2, 1892, p.2.
3. H.C. Sessions, "Wheat Festival," Aberdeen Daily News, August 2, 1892, p.3.
4. Ibid.
5. H.C. Sessions, "The Executive Committee," Aberdeen Daily News, August 6, 1892, p.3.
6. H.C. Sessions, "The Festival," Aberdeen Daily News, August 6, 1892, p.3.
7. H.C. Sessions, "The Wheat Belt," Aberdeen Daily News, August 12, 1892, p.3.
8. H.C. Sessions, "The Festival Project," Aberdeen Daily News, August 19, 1892, p.3.
9. Ibid.
10. "Col. Sessions, Pioneer, Dies," Aberdeen American News, March 31, 1934, p.2.
11. "Early Aberdeen News Publisher Dies at 84," Aberdeen American News, , December 15, 1944, p.1.
12. C.J. McLeod, "Committees to Report," Aberdeen Daily News, March 27, 1893, p.5.
13. C.J. McLeod, "Interstate," Aberdeen Daily News, March 29, 1893, p.3.
14. Ibid.
15. H.C. Sessions, "State News," Aberdeen Daily News, February 27, 1893, p.3.
16. C.J. McLeod, "State Fair Receipts," Aberdeen Daily News, September 26, 1894, p.3.
17. H.C. Sessions, "Sioux Falls," Aberdeen Daily News, August 27, 1891, p.3.
18. C.J. McLeod, "State Fair Receipts," Aberdeen Daily News, September 26, 1894, p.3.
19. Ibid.
20. C.J. McLeod, "State Fair Notes," Aberdeen Daily News, March 30, 1893, p.3.
21. C.J. McLeod, "Aberdeen in 1893," Aberdeen Daily News, March 31, 1893, p.2.
22. C.J. McLeod, "Talking About Aberdeen," Aberdeen Daily News, April 4, 1893, p.3.
23. C.J. McLeod, "The Eureka Meeting," Aberdeen Daily News, April 13, 1893, p.3.
24. Ibid.
25. Elsie Heilman, Eureka: A Chronology of 100 Years, 1887-1987 (American Family Records Assn., 1987) 5-10.

26. A. Sutherland, "Editor News," Aberdeen Daily News, April 12, 1893, p. 6.

27. C.J. McLeod, "Local News," Aberdeen Daily News, April 7, 1893, p. 5.

28. Doane Robinson, History of South Dakota, Vol. I (B.F. Bowen & Co, 1904), 349.

29. C.J. McLeod, "State News," Aberdeen Daily News, April 1, 1893, p. 2.

30. Tomlinson & Day, "From Aberdeen," Sioux Falls Daily Argus-Leader, October 8, 1891, p. 5.

31. C.J. McLeod, "A Great Opportunity," Aberdeen Daily News, April 1, 1893, p. 3.

32. C.J. McLeod, "Local News," Aberdeen Daily News, August 14, 1893, p. 3.

33. H.C. Sessions, "World's Fair," Aberdeen Weekly News, October 1, 1891, p. 3.

34. F.J. Tracy, "South Dakota Exhibit," Edmunds County Democrat, October 21, 1893, p. 5.

35. Erik Mattie, World's Fairs (Princeton Architectural Press, 1998), 1-2.

36. Ibid. 32-100.

37. C.J. McLeod, "Open Tonight," Aberdeen Daily News, September 11, 1893, p. 3

38. Ibid.

39. C.J. McLeod, "Moving Right Along," Aberdeen Daily News, August 9, 1893, p. 3

40. C.J. McLeod, "Facts for the Public," Aberdeen Daily News, September 11, 1893, p. 3.

41. Erik Larson, The Devil in the White City (New York, Crown Publishers, 2003), 233.

42. A.M. Andrews, "The Dakota Grain Palace," Plankinton Hearld, August 10, 1983, p. 2.

43. Sue Gates, "A palace in Aberdeen once celebrated grain," Aberdeen American News, July 10, 2006, p. 6A.

44. C.J. McLeod, "Opens Tonight," Aberdeen Daily News, September 11, 1893, p. 3.

45. C.J. McLeod, "Facts for the Public," Aberdeen Daily News, September 11, 1893, p. 3.

46. F.J. Tracy, "That Premium," Edmunds County Democrat, October 21, 1893, p. 3.

47. C.J. McLeod, "Facts for the Public," Aberdeen Daily News, September 11, 1893, p. 3.

48. Brown County Territorial Pioneer Committee, Early History of Brown County South Dakota (Aberdeen, S.D., Brown County Territorial Pioneers, 1970) 54.

49. C.J. McLeod, "A Marked Success," Aberdeen Daily News, September 12, 1893, p. 3.

50. Ibid.

51. Ibid.

52. C.J. McLeod, "A Fine Event," Aberdeen Daily News, September 12, 1893, p. 3.

53. Louise Young, "L. Frank Baum: Over the Dakota Rainbow," Dakota West Vol. V, (Ft. Pierre, S.D., South Dakota Cowboy and Western Heritage Hall of Fame, Spring, 1979), 6-8.

54. C.J. McLeod, "Fourth Day of the Fair," Aberdeen Daily News, September 14, 1893, p. 3.

55. Ibid.

56. C.J. McLeod, "Exposition Echoes," Aberdeen Daily News, September 20, 1893, p. 3.

57. C.J. McLeod, "Beginning of the End," Aberdeen Daily News, September 15, 1893, p. 3.

58. C.J. McLeod, "Amateur Theatricals," Aberdeen Daily News, September 24, 1893, p. 3.

The Aberdeen Grain Palace replica built in 2003 by Richard and Matt Biegler of Biegler Construction (right). The 16-by-8-foot model was sponsored by South Dakota Wheat Growers, Campbell's Town & Country, Malchow's Furniture, and Biegler Construction and is sitting in front of the 1893 Grain Palace location at the northwest corner of Fifth Avenue and Main Street. Pictured left to right: Dale Locken (SDWG), Mark Malchow, Tom Malchow, Richard Biegler and Matt Biegler.

(Courtesy of Rod and Vicki Evans)

59. C.J.McLeod,"Picked Up on the Grounds," Aberdeen Daily News, September 14, 1893, p. 3.

60. F.J.Tracy,"First Prize," Edmunds County Democrat, October 1, 1893, p. 3.

61. F.J.Tracy,"Local News," Edmunds County Democrat, October 14, 1893, p. 3.

62. F.J.Tracy,"That Premium," Edmunds County Democrat, October 21, 1893, p. 3.

63. Doane Robinson, History of South Dakota, Vol. I (B.F.Bowen & Co, 1904), 353.

64. C.J.McLeod,"Local News," Aberdeen Daily News, August 27, 1894, p. 3.

65. C.J.McLeod,"State Fair Particulars," Aberdeen Daily News, September 18, 1896, p. 3.

66. C.J.McLeod,"A Big Evening," Aberdeen Daily News, September 20, 1894, p. 3.

67. C.J.McLeod,"Grain Palace Attractions," Aberdeen Daily News, September 18, 1894, p. 3.

68. C.J.McLeod,"On Midway," Aberdeen Daily News, September 20, 1894, p. 3.

69. C.J.McLeod,"Third Annual," Aberdeen Daily News, September 21, 1895, p. 1.

70. C.J.McLeod,"Opening Night," Aberdeen Daily News, September 30, 1895, p. 3.

71. C.J.McLeod,"Now for Palace," Aberdeen Daily News, October 3, 1896, p. 3.

72. C.J.McLeod,"Opening Night," Aberdeen Daily News, October 6, 1896, p. 3.

73. C.J.McLeod,"The Mystic Bridge," Aberdeen Daily News, October 6, 1896, p. 3.

74. C.J.McLeod,"Bryan in Hub," Aberdeen Daily News, October 10, 1896, p. 5.

75. C.J.McLeod,"Financially," Aberdeen Daily News, October 12, 1896, p. 3.

76. C.J.McLeod,"The First Night," Aberdeen Daily News, October 5, 1897, p. 3.

77. Ibid.

78. Brown County Territorial Pioneer Committee, Early History of Brown County South Dakota (Aberdeen, S.D., Brown County Territorial Pioneers, 1970) 58.

79. C.J.McLeod,"The Closing Day," Aberdeen Daily News, October 9, 1897, p. 3.

80. C.J.McLeod,"The Exposition," Aberdeen Daily News, October 1, 1898, p. 3.

81. C.J.McLeod,"Almost Murder," Aberdeen Daily News, October 7, 1898, p. 3.

82. C.J.McLeod,"A Great Success," Aberdeen Daily News, October 4, 1899, p. 3.

83. C.J.McLeod,"For No Exposition," Aberdeen Daily News, January 20, 1899, p. 3.

84. C.J.McLeod,"Monster Crowd," Aberdeen Daily News, May 10, 1899, p. 3.

85. C.J.McLeod,"President's Trip," Aberdeen Daily News, October 5, 1899, p. 3.

86. C.J.McLeod,"Our Brave Boys," Aberdeen Daily News, October 14, 1899, p. 3.

87. C.J.McLeod,"Vast Multitude," Aberdeen Daily News, October 14, 1899, p. 3.

88. Doane Robinson, History of South Dakota, Vol. I (B.F.Bowen & Co, 1904), 285.

89. History Committee, Brown County History (Aberdeen, SD, Brown Co. Museum and Historical Society, 1980) 488.

90. C.J.McLeod,"Vast Multitude," Aberdeen Daily News, October 14, 1899, p. 3.

91. John M. Hilpert, Ph.D.,"Thousands of Rough Riders and Monster Parades," (Ph.D. diss., University of Michigan, 1979), 271.

92. C.J.McLeod,"Monster Crowd," Aberdeen Daily News, September 10, 1900, p. 3.

93. John M. Hilpert, Ph.D.,"Thousands of Rough Riders and Monster Parades," (Ph.D. diss., University of Michigan, 1979), 272.

94. C.J.McLeod,"Rough Riders Attention," Aberdeen Daily News, September 7, 1900, p. 3.

95. John M. Hilpert, Ph.D.,"Thousands of Rough Riders and Monster Parades" (Ph.D. diss., University of Michigan, 1979), 280.

96. C.J.McLeod,"A Great Ovation," Aberdeen Daily News, September 14, 1900, p. 3.

97. C.J.McLeod,"The Opening Day," Aberdeen Daily News, September 17, 1901, p. 3.

98. C.J.McLeod,"Was Brilliant," Aberdeen Daily News, September 23, 1901, p. 3.

99. C.J.McLeod,"Palace Burned," Aberdeen Daily News, April 28, 1902, p. 3.

100. Ibid.

101. C.J.McLeod,"Military Equipment Burned," Aberdeen Daily News, April 28, 1902, p. 3.

102. C.J.McLeod,"Work of Firebug," Aberdeen Daily News, May 1, 1902, p. 3.

103. Meda Mason,"My Policeman: To whom I tell all my troubles" (Personal Diary, 1900)

104. C.J.McLeod,"Cost Projectors Much Money," Aberdeen Daily News, September 23, 1901, p. 3.

1909 Ipswich Corn Palace
(Courtesy of Parmley Museum and
Edmunds County Historical Society)

Ipswich
Corn Palace
1909

Section 2 ❖ South Dakota
CHAPTER 4

Each progressive community seems to have a handful of promoters who stand out from all the rest, and for Ipswich in the early 1900s, those men formed the Ipswich, South Dakota, Commercial Club. Four of the more prominent members of that club were Captain S.V. Arnold, Marcus P. Beebe, Joseph W. Parmley and F.J. Tracy.[1]

Captain Arnold was a prominent businessman who promoted the area's agriculture by decorating the interior of his business with attractive grain decorations. He also participated in endeavors to further the success of his community. Mrs. Arnold was credited with coining South Dakota's first motto, "The Sunshine State."[2]

Marcus Beebe started the Bank of Ipswich in 1883 and built up a 1,600-acre "Homewood Farm" with a beautiful grove of trees a mile east of town, which he opened to the public for picnics on any day but Sunday.[3] He helped finance the building of one of the most beautiful stone churches in the state, and his heirs built the city's library, which is named the Marcus P. Beebe Memorial Library.[4]

Captain S.V. Arnold's grain-decorated office in 1904

(Courtesy of Ipswich's Parmley Museum and Edmunds County Historical Society)

Marcus Beebe and the Bank of Ipswich

(Courtesy of Parmley Museum and
Edmunds County Historical Society)

M. P. Beebe, Pres.   W. K. Beebe, Vice-Pres.   Inez E. Beebe, Cashier

BANK OF IPSWICH

Ipswich, Edmunds County, S. D.

The Strongest
Bank of
South Dakota
In proportion to its
Capital and Resources

Capital Stock
$25,000.00

Surplus
$58,000.00

The Ipswich Auto Garage

Two-Cylinder Reo $1000

(Newspapers courtesy of Ipswich *Tribune*)

Joseph Parmley was a journalist, an educator, a public speaker, an advocate for peace through a United Nations-type organization before there was even a League of Nations, an attorney who never practiced law, a judge, a state legislator and an unsuccessful candidate for lieutenant governor who later decided he could better fight for causes as a private citizen than as a public official.[5]

Ipswich was a thriving town of around 1,000 citizens shortly after the turn of the 20th century, where farmers could sell their corn for 56 cents per bushel, wheat for 93 cents per bushel, hogs for 7 cents per pound and eggs for 25 cents per dozen.[6] While those prices may not seem very high, one could buy land for $25 an acre, a corset for 50 cents and a man's suit for less than $20, and stay in the local hotel for $2 a night.[7] The Ipswich Auto Garage sold two-cylinder Reo cars for $1,000 in 1909, which was an offer too good to pass up for Mr. Parmley, Mr. Beebe and others.[8]

The community was one of several trying to promote South Dakota as a corn state, and Parmley, Beebe and a few other members of the Ipswich Commercial Club

J.W. Parmley

(Photos courtesy of Parmley Museum and Edmunds County Historical Society)

Parmley's Ipswich office

(Photos courtesy of Parmley Museum and Edmunds County Historical Society; Newspapers courtesy Ipswich *Tribune*)

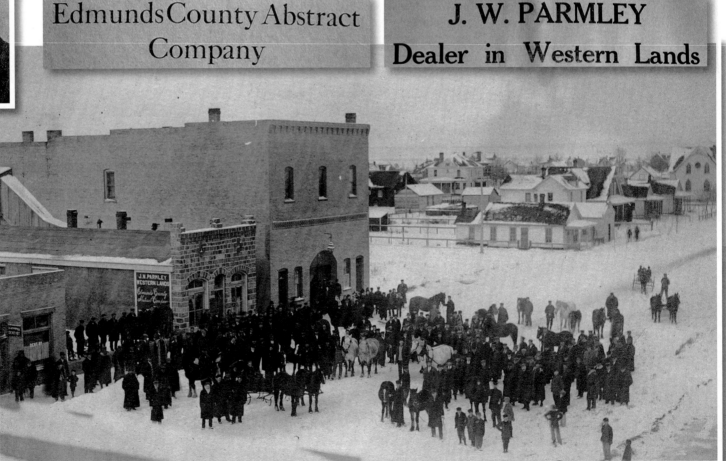

Edmunds County Abstract Company

J. W. PARMLEY
Dealer in Western Lands

knew just what the town needed — its own corn palace. They were very familiar with the Mitchell Corn Palace and the former Aberdeen Grain Palace, having led efforts to organize county agricultural displays for their expositions. In 1909, with Mitchell's palace the only one still in existence, Parmley in particular felt it was time for Ipswich to give it a try.[9]

The building was to be a modest enterprise, having no towers or turrets and measuring only 16 by 48 feet, although one of the local papers, the South Dakota *Tribune,* described the framework as being "mammoth." The article also stated that the structure would "hold

Future site of the Ipswich Corn Palace

(Courtesy of Parmley Museum and Edmunds County Historical Society)

Young men at the Edmunds County Fair display. The small photograph directly below the Edmunds County sign is of the Ipswich Corn Palace.

(Courtesy of Parmley Museum and Edmunds County Historical Society)

1917 Ipswich Corn Palace
(Courtesy of Parmley Museum and Edmunds County Historical Society)

close to 300 bushels of Edmunds county corn and other cereals." That figure obviously referred to the number of bushels needed to decorate the exterior, for a building that size would hold many more bushels in storage capacity.[10] The corn's purpose was more clearly stated in Ipswich's competing newspaper, the Edmunds County *Democrat,* whose editor was F.J. Tracy, uncle to Spencer Tracy, one of the biggest Hollywood film stars ever. The *Democrat's* article stated, "The boosters are busy advertising Edmunds county and Ipswich. About 300

bushels of corn has been worked into a fine display at the foot of Main Street near the depot where it can be seen by the crowds passing through here and will surely attract attention."[11] The crowds he was referring to were mainly new land seekers participating in the latest government lottery.

There was surprisingly little mention of the Ispwich Corn Palace in the local newspapers through the years. On September 19, 1912, Mr. Parmley placed a notice that stated, "It is intended to re-decorate the 'Corn Palace'

Machine Gun Company of the Fourth South Dakota Infantry ready to board the train for Camp Green, North Carolina, 1917
(Courtesy of Parmley Museum and Edmunds County Historical Society)

on the depot grounds and request is hereby made to all artistically inclined to submit designs to be worked out of white, yellow and different shades of red corn. The person whose design is adopted will be exempt from draft on decoration. All others are expected to respond on one day's notice."[12]

The few local residents who remember hearing of the Corn Palace believe the building survived until sometime in the 1920s. Surviving photographs indicate at least three different designs through the years, including a

1917 photograph showing the main theme changing from Edmunds County to Ipswich. The latter photo celebrates the Machine Gun Company of the Fourth South Dakota Infantry as it prepared to board the train for Camp Green, North Carolina.[13]

The Ipswich Corn Palace may not have been competition for the Mitchell Corn Palace, but it still drew attention to the community while fostering a sense of pride, and it enjoyed one of the longest lifespans among the various palaces.

Footnotes for Ipswich Corn Palace, 1909-1920s

1. C.L. Jackson, "Commercial Club to Adv.," South Dakota *Tribune*, October 7, 1909, p. 5.

2. C.L. Jackson, "Where the Name Originated From," South Dakota *Tribune*, November 25, 1909, p. 1.

3. C.L. Jackson, "Partial View of 'Homewood Farm' Ipswich, S. Dak.," South Dakota *Tribune*, October 7, 1909, p. 1.

4. Library Board, "Marcus P. Beebe Memorial Library," Gibson Publishing, 2006, p. 2.

5. Ipswich Commercial Club, Ipswich, 1883-1983: Ipswich, South Dakota Centennial, June 24-25-26 (Aberdeen, S.D.: North Plains Press, 1983).

6. C.L. Jackson, "Great Artesian Basin," South Dakota *Tribune*, November 5, 1909, p. 1.

7. C.L. Jackson, "Today's Ipswich," South Dakota Tribune, March 14, 1910, p. 8.

8. C.L. Jackson, "City News," South Dakota *Tribune*, September 23, 1909, p. 5.

9. Ipswich Commercial Club, Ipswich, 1883-1983: Ipswich, South Dakota Centennial, June 24-25-26 (Aberdeen, S.D.: North Plains Press, 1983)

10. C.L. Jackson, "Commercial Club to Adv.," South Dakota *Tribune*, October 7, 1909, p. 5

11. F.J. Tracy, "Editor's Notes," Edmunds County *Democrat*, October 7, 1909, p. 2.

12. F.J. Tracy, "Notice to Artists," Edmunds County *Democrat*, September 19, 1912, p. 4.

13. Interview with Candy Kub, Parmley Museum volunteer, Ipswich, South Dakota, October 15, 2007.

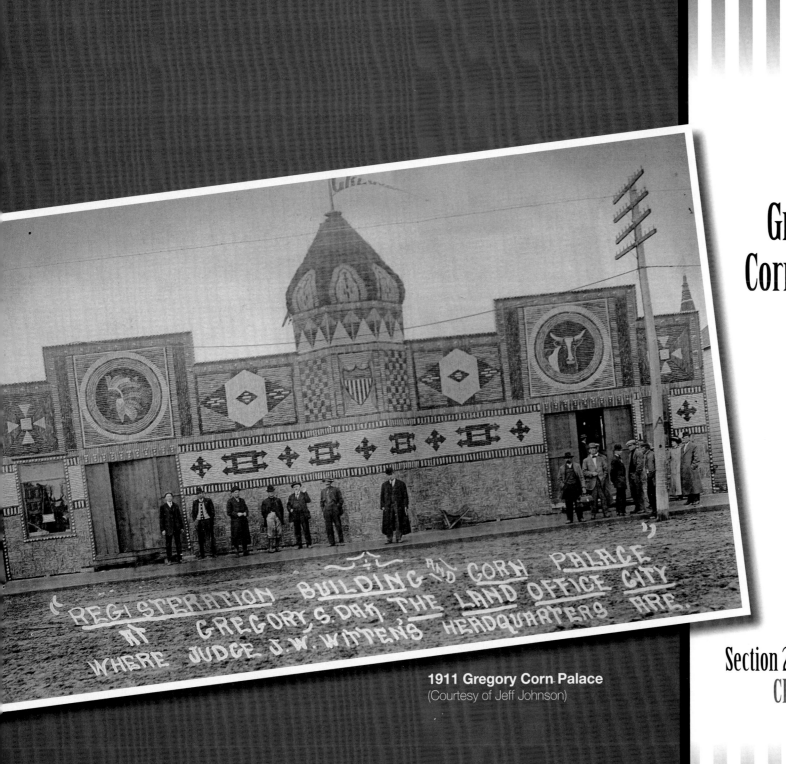

1911 Gregory Corn Palace
(Courtesy of Jeff Johnson)

Gregory Corn Palace 1911

To fully appreciate the significance of the Gregory Corn Palace, one must first explore the turbulent relationship between Gregory and its neighbor, Dallas, along with the rise of the railroad and the decline in the Native American situation as related to the South Dakota reservations.

The town of Dallas was founded in 1896 and named for Dallas, Texas, which was in turn named for George Mifflin Dallas, who was vice president of the United States from 1845 to 1849 under James Polk.[1] Two brothers by the name of Jackson were looking to found a town in western Gregory County and name it Dallas, so their father provided the backing to purchase several town lots where they expected the railroad to pass through in the near future. The Chicago and Northwestern Railway was hoping to extend its line to the northwest out of O'Neill, Nebraska, but it was waiting for more settlers to populate the territory.[2]

By 1902, the C & NW Railroad had surveyed land approximately 32 miles into South Dakota and was ready to expand through Fairfax and as far as Bonesteel, which was five miles over the border. Then in 1904, the U.S. government released nearly 145,000 acres of Rosebud Indian Reservation land for settlement, which had been bought back from the Indians. The 2,412 tracts of land were divided into approximately 160 acres each, and 106,296 people registered for them. A lottery was held to prevent a disaster similar to the Oklahoma Land Rush, and the plan worked for the most part. Only at the "Battle of Bonesteel" was there documented bloodshed, when one gambler was killed and two others wounded by armed guards.[3]

Among the 1904 Gregory County newcomers were several former residents of Butte, Nebraska, some of whom were

The young Gregory, of 1907. The tallest building has a sign on the top part saying: "Samuel Schultz — Gregory Town Hall." (Contributed by Mrs. Mae Whitley.)

The postmark on this picture was November 5, 1908, and was evidenly taken about registration time. (Contributed by Blanch Bailey.)

(Photos courtesy of Gregory Public Library)

(Newspaper courtesy of South Dakota State Archives)

serious settlers, while others were merely speculators. On August 8, 1904, several of them set about to form the town of Gregory three miles north and one and one-half miles west of Dallas, and the speculators got the first jump. Once the town was platted, they purchased all of the lots on Main Street and then quickly offered them for sale at a healthy profit. Those who were there to set up permanent businesses became so angry that they got themselves organized, bought all the lots one block over on Church Street and made that the business district.[4]

Five months later, the new town boasted 150 permanent buildings, and by June 1905, the town had 250 buildings and 500 residents. Many of the new farmers had ties to the Gregory town folk and, therefore, did most of their business with Gregory rather than Dallas, but the biggest problem for Dallas came when Chicago and Northwestern officials announced that it was going to bypass Dallas and extend its line to Gregory. Another Rosebud land lottery was to take place in the near future, meaning that Gregory would have the benefit of being not only *on* the line but at the *end* of the line, which would help the town grow more rapidly. The Jackson brothers did all they could to persuade the railroad officials to change their minds but to no avail; in their minds, it was time for drastic measures.[5]

An Irish building-mover was contacted, and soon businesses were being transported from Dallas to Gregory, giving the appearance that Dallas had given up and had admitted defeat. But when the bank was on its way to Gregory, being pulled by 76 head of horses, the movers suddenly veered around the town and settled on a foundation five miles to the west, which just happened to be the stopping point of the land surveyed by the railroad. Other buildings quickly followed the bank, and it soon was discovered that Dallas residents had been secretly buying up land in that area for some time. The fight was back on and fiercer than ever.[6]

Gregory rose to the challenge and quickly improved its water system, installed electric lights and built a new city hall with an opera house. Dallas city leaders, not to be outdone, pleaded with railroad officials to extend their track beyond Gregory to the farthest point surveyed, which of course was the exact spot where Dallas had set up their new town. Tension mounted as railroad officials assessed the matter, but soon there was celebrating in Gregory when they announced on April 11, 1907, that they would stick to their original plan of ending the line in that town. However, after further considering the situation, officials realized that including Dallas would add one more

(Courtesy of Gregory Public Library)

town to their line and would put the railroad closer to the reservation cattle. In addition, having settlers travel five miles farther down the line would also mean larger fares and more profits. It was soon time for Dallas to take its turn at throwing a party.[7]

Six thousand homesteads were up for grabs on October 5, 1908, and six towns — Chamberlain, Presho, O'Neill, Valentine, Gregory and Dallas — were competing by lottery for the 114,769 registrants. Gregory's citizens came up with several ideas to lure registrants off the trains, and they did manage to coax 7,000 passengers off, but alas, Dallas captured 43,000, second only to O'Neill, Nebraska's 45,000.[8]

Another battle emerged in 1909 when a land office was to be set up in the area for new homesteaders, and the site was narrowed down to Gregory and Dallas. Secretary of Interior James Garfield, son of ex-president Garfield, gave the prize to Dallas, but thanks to past political rivalries, President Theodore Roosevelt stepped in and overrode his decision, awarding the land office to Gregory.[9]

That victory paid off in high fashion in 1911 when

(Newspapers courtesy of South Dakota State Archives)

another lottery was to be held, and the citizens of Gregory were determined to be prepared as they never had before. On August 17, 1911, the Gregory *Times-Advocate* reported the following: "The Commercial Club of this city has decided to build an immense corn palace wherein will be placed exhibits of all farm products for inspection by those who come from the east to register for Mellette and Bennett county homesteads in October. The club is now actively at work on the project and the farmers are enthusiastic over the opportunity to exhibit the fruits of their labors. The corn palace will be located on Main Street and have a frontage of seventy-five feet."[10]

The newspaper article was a little misleading because the city didn't exactly "build" a corn palace, but rather decorated an existing livery barn. It was probably best that they didn't build from scratch because the lottery drawing was to be held on October 5, and the building wasn't finished until October 3. Even then, all of the exhibits weren't in place in time for the drawing because of adverse weather conditions.[11]

The 1911 land lottery was to be much bigger than the one in 1904, with 8,000 names to be drawn, one of whom was an unknown, down-on-his-luck young man by the name of Harry Truman. The 27-year-old couldn't seem to please his father nor the girl of his dreams, so he was out to prove himself worthy of both. He arrived in Gregory on October 18, 1911, in hopes of getting a lucky draw in the homestead lottery. He didn't. No doubt he also hoped to be impressed with the prairie town. He wasn't.[12]

Harry wrote a letter to the young woman he was courting, Bess Wallace, shortly after his arrival, and said,

Krotter Lumber Yard used the Corn Palace building until it was demolished in 1952.

(Courtesy of Jeff Johnson)

In image: REGISTER HERE — MELOY'S HOTEL & SHORT ORDER HOUSE — WHERE WE REGISTERED GREGORY, S.D.

1911 registration building and Corn Palace

(Courtesy of Jeff Johnson)

"Would you like to hear what we did going and coming from notorious Gregory? To begin with, it was just like riding a crowded street car for a day and a night. We took a sleeper to Omaha coming and going. From Omaha up trains are running every hour or so all day. … They had to call special police to handle the crowd at the Union Station. We managed to get seats in the last coach. There were 687 people on the train and nearly all were nice looking Americans. I only saw about a dozen bohunks all the way there and back."[13]

As for the Corn Palace itself, even though it was decorated by an expert who'd decorated the Mitchell

Corn Palace, Harry wasn't very impressed with that, either. He wrote, "After we'd cinched our rooms we went and registered at the Corn Palace, a wooden shack. It takes about one minute to do it. There were about twenty notaries in a hollow square. I bet there was more swearing going on there than ever will be in one place again. I really don't know what a Quaker would have done."[14]

Regardless of what Harry thought, the citizens of Gregory were proud to declare, "The corn palace is one of the greatest objects of interest to those who choose Gregory as the city in which to register for a quarter of Mellette county land."[15]

Even though the Corn Palace wasn't redecorated in later years, it was used by the Krotter Lumber Yard until it was demolished in 1952.[16] And even if the Palace didn't exert a great influence on Gregory's success, no doubt the city's rivalry with Dallas did. The long-standing feud between the two neighbors created a competitive spirit and a strong desire to succeed among Gregory's citizens, and no doubt explains why nearly a century later, the town's population of 1,342 exceeded both the Dallas population of 144 and the combined totals of Gregory's next three closest neighbors as well.[17] What do you think about that, Harry?

Footnotes for Gregory Corn Palace, 1911

1. Doane Robinson, Doane Robinson's Encyclopedia of South Dakota (Pierre: Doane Robinson, 1925), 156.
2. Herbert S. Schell, History of South Dakota (University of Nebraska Press, Lincoln, 1961), 252.
3. Ibid., 254.
4. William McDonald, "The Rosebud Country — Last Great Frontier," Fifty Years in the Rosebud Country of South Dakota (Gregory: Gregory Times-Advocate, 1954), 20.
5. Ibid., 37.
6. Ibid.
7. Ibid., 38
8. Ibid., 44
9. Ibid., 45
10. G. Gill Warner, "Will Build a Corn Palace," Gregory Times-Advocate, August 11, 1911, p. 1.
11. G. Gill Warner, "Corn Palace and Grand Exhibits," Gregory Times-Advocate, October 5, 1911, p. 1.
12. Jeff Johnson and Roger Holtzmann, "When Harry Met Gregory," South Dakota Magazine (November/December 2002): 42.
13. Ibid.
14. Ibid.
15. G. Gill Warner, "Corn Palace and Grand Exhibits," Gregory Times-Advocate, October 5, 1911, p. 1.
16. 4. William McDonald, "The Rosebud Country — Last Great Frontier," Fifty Years in the Rosebud Country of South Dakota (Gregory: Gregory Times-Advocate, 1954), 21.
17. United States Census, 2000.

Timber Lake Grain Palace 1914

TIMBER LAKE

GRAIN 1912 PALACE.

CUNDILL HONYOCKER PHOTO.

The 1914 Timber Lake Grain Palace stood south of the railroad on the west side of Main Street. It is very common to find historic photos marked incorrectly, such as the above photo. Few photographs were dated at the time they were taken, so it was left to later generations to guess at the actual date.

(Courtesy of Timber Lake & Area Historical Society and photographer Frank Cundill)

The first story on the Timber Lake, South Dakota, Grain Palace shared front page space with World War I news, announcing that details were nearly complete with the former and just beginning with the latter. The town had a birthday to celebrate, and no war should dampen a community's enterprising spirit.[1] The dates picked were Thursday, August 27, and Friday, August 28, neither of which fell on the actual day Timber Lake was founded. They were, however, more convenient for farmers at the end of harvest.[2]

The people of Timber Lake went about organizing their event with realistic expectations and honest intentions. They did not empty the pocketbooks of their citizens nor boast that their palace was going to be the most beautiful ever. Instead, they borrowed an existing garage recently vacated by the Darling Brothers and did the decorating themselves without the assistance of outside experts. They admitted that they'd like to invite the entire state to participate, but knew they had room for only their own Dewey County plus portions of adjacent Corson and Zeibach Counties. And when it came to prizes, they were straightforward in saying, "The inducements are not large, that is true, but the honor and glory will be lasting."[3]

A baby show was to be held each day, which people were urged to attend because they might meet a future president of the United States among the contestants, and all couples wishing to get married by Judge Stow during the celebration could do so without paying a fee for the judge or the marriage license. Most other activities were sports related, with the emphasis on baseball. The local team would be playing a tough Isabel team for the

(Courtesy of Timber Lake & Area Historical Society)

The Timber Lake *Topic* newspaper was a consolidation of the Timber Lake *Tribune,* Dewey County *Advocate* and Trail County *Record.*

(Newspapers courtesy of Timber Lake *Topic*)

TIMBER LAKE TOPIC

FRIDAY, JULY 31, 1914

———

For Fourth Anniversary Celebration and Harvest Festival to be held at Timber Lake Aug. 27-28.

———

As to program, little can be said at this time, but Timber Lake has a reputation as an August show town, and you may rest assured that there will be no dull moments in the two days for sane pleasure seekers.

TIMBER LAKE TOPIC

FRIDAY, AUGUST 21, 1914

———

Two Days Program Arranged for Pleasure Seekers Here Thursday and Friday.

———

If you visit Timber Lake next Thursday and Friday and don't have a good time it will certainly be your own fault, for the town and the contents thereof will be at your disposal and the celebration management has labored hard and well in a strenuous effort to make the nineteen fourteen show surpass all others.

"steenth" time, in spite of the fact that Isabel had won most of the games. Prize money would be awarded to the winner of the game between teams representing the Standing Rock and Cheyenne reservations.[4]

Other activities included horse racing, bronco busting, a tug of war, tipi contests and motorcycle races. Activities specifically not included would be anything involving alcohol. Succinctly put, "Bootleggers and grafters might as well save their railroad fare as the town will be a bit crowded and there will be no room for them. In fact, it is the intention to have better policing facilities than heretofore, and no intoxicants of any kind will be tolerated."[5]

$1 prize for best loaf of white bread; 75 cents for best cookies.

$2 prize for best stalk of corn, any variety; $1 for best sheaf of flax.

TIMBER LAKE TOPIC

FRIDAY, AUGUST 28, 1914

CELEBRATION GRAND SUCCESS

Large Crowds Enjoy Two Days of Fun at Timber Lake.

The 1914 celebration and harvest festival held in honor of the fourth anniversary of the foundation of the town of Timber Lake, has come and gone, but the memory will linger in the minds of both the guests and the hosts.

(Newspapers courtesy of Timber Lake *Topic*)

$3 prize for best jar of butter, one pound or more; $1 for best peck of early potatoes.

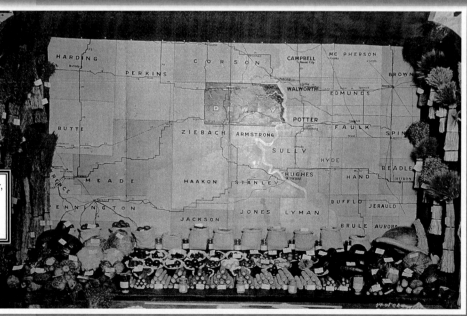

Two Dewey County interior displays
(Courtesy of Timber Lake and Area Historical Society)

Footnotes for the Timber Lake Grain Palace

1. Editor, "Details Nearly Complete," Timber Lake *Topic*, August 14, 1914, p. 1.
2. Ibid.
3. Editor, "Timber Lake to Celebrate," Timber Lake *Topic*, July 24, 1914, p. 1.
4. Editor, "Sports Aplenty Next Week," Timber Lake *Topic*, August 21, 1914, p. 1.
5. Editor, "Timber Lake to Celebrate," Timber Lake *Topic*, July 24, 1914, p. 1.

The 1917 Rapid City Alfalfa Palace was decorated with alfalfa, corn and other grains and was located on the southeast corner of 7th and St. Joe.

(Courtesy of Aberdeen's Dacotah Prairie Museum)

Rapid City Alfalfa Palace 1917

Section 2 ❖ South Dakota
CHAPTER 7

Rapid City could have had the first South Dakota Palace on the Prairie if its citizens had listened to the local newspaper editor in 1890 when he urged a town to build a Tin and Mineral Palace.[1] The idea didn't catch fire, so instead Rapid City was nearly the last South Dakota city to attempt a palace, and it was made mostly of alfalfa instead of metal or mineral.

When Rapid City's Alfalfa Palace opened on September 17, 1917, the attendees were first given a history lesson on Queen Alfalfa, and then when Governor Peter Norbeck took the stage to dedicate the palace, they got a lesson on the history of the state. With the world caught in the middle of World War I, a little talk on patriotism also seemed in order, and South Dakotans were urged to cooperate with the federal government as it increased its military involvement in the war. Performing leopards, vaudeville acts and a variety of music numbers followed, including marches, overtures and a number titled "Custer's Cavalry Charge," which featured Custer's approach and charge of the enemy, the defeat of the enemy and the cavalry pursuit. Obviously, the song was not about Custer's most famous battle.[2]

RAPID CITY DAILY JOURNAL

TUESDAY, SEPTEMBER 18, 1917

———

FIRST ANNUAL ALFALFA PALACE IS DEDICATED BY GOV. PETER NORBECK

———

The first and only Alfalfa Palace in the world was yesterday dedicated at Rapid City by Governor Norbeck of South Dakota, marking a great milestone in the history of Western South Dakota and a greater event in the life of the alfalfa seed capital, Rapid City.

The occasion was most auspicious. The presence of the governor of the state in the metropolis of the western half of the state lent especial significance to the occasion.

The speaker said it was fitting that a man of the absolutely democratic type, such as Governor Norbeck, should be the one to dedicate the Palace. He commended the governor for his great patriotism in the handling of the affairs of the state during the great crisis that has come to the nation.

Governor Norbeck then addressed the gathering. He told of the early days—when as a boy in 1876 he watched the people pass his father's farm in Clay county, bound for the Black Hills.

RAPID CITY DAILY JOURNAL

WEDNESDAY, SEPTEMBER 19, 1917

———

MANY SEE PALACE ON SECOND DAY AND ENJOY CONCERT AND VAUDEVILLE

———

After two days' performances all those who have witnessed the entertainment features the Alfalfa Palace committee have furnished are united in their opinions that the vaudeville acts and band concerts are worth twice the price of admission and could hardly be improved upon from the standpoint of a well balanced program.

MANY SEE PALACE ON SECOND DAY AND ENJOY CONCERT AND VAUDEVILLE

SPELLING CONTEST FEATURE YESTERDAY'S AFTERNOON PROGRAM; FINE EXHIBITS

(Newspapers courtesy of Rapid City Public Library)

FIRST ANNUAL ALFALFA PALACE IS DEDICATED BY GOV. PETER NORBECK

Governor Norbeck who dedicated the Alfalfa Palace yesterday.

With all the visitors in town for the Alfalfa Palace Exposition, the Rapid City *Daily Journal* thought it was a perfect time to inform these individuals why it would be in their best interest to move there permanently. Especially noted were the abundant sources of lumber; the rich mineral deposits of silver, copper, lead and coal, as well as gold mines yet to be discovered no doubt as rich as the nearby Homestake mine in Lead; the absence of empty businesses, the new school, the beef and hog packing plant, and the two cigar factories, one of which had the largest payroll of any cigar factory in the two Dakotas.[3]

The second day's performances were reported to be so popular that audiences were attending sessions a second time. People were especially pleased with the Watertown Fourth Regiment Band, a Hawaiian sextette, Vallecita's five performing leopards and Charging Thunder's Sioux Indian dancers, who were a special added attraction for day two.[4]

Omaha's mayor, Jim Dahlman, headlined the third day;[5] a spelling contest was the featured program on the fourth day;[6] and a Traveling Men's parade was the big event of the fifth and final day.[7] The two unique things about the Alfalfa Palace celebration was that it garnered front page space in the local newspaper each and every day, and its headlines were longer than those of other palace expositions. True, that wasn't much, but it was a start.

TRAVELING MEN PRESENT FINE DEMONSTRATION IN PARADE; TODAY IS LAST

RAPID'S FIRST ANNUAL ALFALFA PALACE ENDS; PARADE IS BIGGEST EVER

RAPID CITY DAILY JOURNAL

SUNDAY, SEPTEMBER 23, 1917

———

RAPID'S FIRST ANNUAL
ALFALFA PALACE ENDS
PARADE IS BIGGEST EVER

———

Rapid City's first annual Alfalfa Palace is now history. It closed last evening and its close marked one of the most successful weeks from the standpoint of a celebration that Rapid City has ever known.

(Newspapers courtesy of Rapid City Public Library)

It is Rapid City Day Today And We Are All Going to Go

Footnotes for the Rapid City Alfalfa Palace

1. Rapid City Republican,"Exhibition Notes," Mitchell *Daily Republican,* August 26, 1892, p. 3.
2. Editor,"First Annual Alfalfa Palace is Dedicated by Gov. Peter Norbeck," Rapid City *Daily Journal,* September 18, 1917, p. 1.
3. Editor,"The Black Hills of South Dakota, Rapid City Especially, An Ideal Place," Rapid City *Daily Journal, S*eptember 18, 1917, p. 2.
4. Editor,"Many See Palace on Second Day and Enjoy Concert and Vaudeville," Place" Rapid City *Daily Journal,* September 19, 1917, p. 1.
5. Editor,"Jim Dahlman Pays Big Tribute to Black Hills Alfalfa at Palace Here," Rapid City *Daily Journal,* September 20, 1917, p. 1.
6. Editor,"Spelling Contest Feature Yesterday's Afternoon Program; Fine Exhibits," Rapid City *Daily Journal,* September 21, 1917, p. 1.
7. Editor,"Traveling Men Present Fine Demonstration in Parade; Today is Last," Rapid City *Daily Journal,* September 21, 1917, p. 1.

(Courtesy South Dakota State Historical Society Archives)

St. Francis
Corn Palace
1932

Section 2 ❖ South Dakota
CHAPTER 8

The St. Francis Corn Palace remains a bit of a mystery for this author. A search through the Todd County *Tribune* revealed nothing of its origins, so the only evidence of the palace's existence so far is a photo found in a 1976 Rosebud Educational Society calendar for the month of July. The date on the Corn Palace door says 1932, but there are indications that the building originally may have been decorated earlier than that. A close look at the larger number "2" offers a clue that maybe it was attached to the door at a different time. The decorations have fallen into disrepair, and there are several corn cobs on the ground, which are additional indications that the photograph was not taken when the building was newly decorated.

The building could have been used previously as a granary, school house or church, though the arched side windows could lead one to pick the church. The center tower could have housed either a school bell or church steeple, but the corner towers probably were added when the building was converted into a corn palace. The fact that the windows are covered leads one to believe that either the building was no longer in use when the photo was taken or that the interior served no function when used as a Corn Palace.

Section 3
Missouri

Flora's Temple, one of several buildings for the 1889 New Era Exposition

(Courtesy of St. Joseph Museums, Inc.)

St. Joseph New Era Exposition 1889

Section 3 ❖ Missouri
CHAPTER 1

St. Joseph, Missouri, may have had a humble beginning as Joseph Robidoux's trading post in the 1840s, but by the 1880s, it was boasting "perhaps no city of its size in the United States has a greater number of elegant mansions. St. Joseph is to her citizens what Athens was to the Athenian of the age of Perricles, what Florence was to the Florentine of the fifteenth century."[1] And while the progressive community previously had been best known for hosting in 1860 the longest horse race with the highest stakes in the U.S. — a $200,000 wager on a 10-day, 1,950-mile Pony Express ride from San Francisco to St. Joseph — the city decided in 1889 to seek new fame with a project called the New Era National Exposition.[2]

While considerably different in concept, the St. Joseph Exposition was chiefly inspired by the Sioux City Corn Palace and the Ft. Worth Spring Palace. Not long after Mr. Perky was named manager of the New Era Expo, its secretary, Mr. Hutchinson, made a trip to Ft. Worth in June to pick up pointers from the Spring Palace personnel and intended to return with ideas that would allow the lady decorators of St. Joseph to outshine those in Ft. Worth. For even though the citizens of St. Joseph had nothing but respect for the "refinement, intelligence, and artistic taste"[3] of Ft. Worth women, the "wide-awake and progressive" ladies of St. Joseph certainly could do better.[4]

Instead of building one large palace, the New Era board of directors decided to construct several buildings,

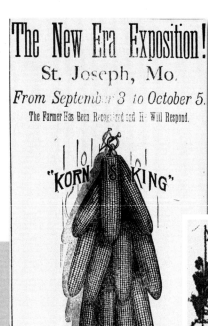

Ladies' Palace of Delights, or Ladies' Bowar

(Illustration from the September 18, 1889, issue of the St. Joseph *Herald,* courtesy of State Historical Society of Missouri; photograph courtesy St. Joseph Museums Inc.)

The New Era Exposition!

St. Joseph, Mo.

From September 3 to October 5.

The Farmer Has Been Recognized and He Will Respond.

"KORN IS KING"

(Illustrations from the September 18, 1889, issue of the St. Joseph *Herald,* courtesy of State Historical Society of Missouri)

each to be decorated in grains and grasses, "to prove to the people that northwest Missouri is richer than all in its agriculture."[5] One of the first to be built was a pavilion called the W.C.T.U. headquarters. It was to be used as a resting place for all, which apparently included even those who were not inclined to practice temperance.[6] The building also was referred to as the Ladies' Palace of Delights or the Ladies' Bowar, and was called "peculiar, odd and striking, being of a composite style of architecture, and might be classed as a Moorish dome-shaped structure."[7]

Other Exposition buildings within the 65-acre grounds included the Reporters Lodge, which also was referred to as the Press Lodge and which was built to attract newspapers from around the country and abroad; the Builders' and Traders' Exchange; Pomona's Pavilion, a square structure decorated with baskets of flowers, wreaths and a border of grape vines; Ceres Palace, also called the Ceres Arbor, which had large ears of corn on the corners to simulate turrets; Cupid's Bowar, with a mosque dome made of oats surmounted by a cross of corn; Sunnyside, an unusual structure shaped like a huge sack of wheat; Flora's Temple, a two-story pagoda; Horticultural Hall; a grand amphitheater; and a 1,040-foot Machinery Hall, which housed numerous exhibits and restaurants.[8]

(Illustrations from the September 18, 1889, issue of the St. Joseph *Herald,* courtesy of State Historical Society of Missouri)

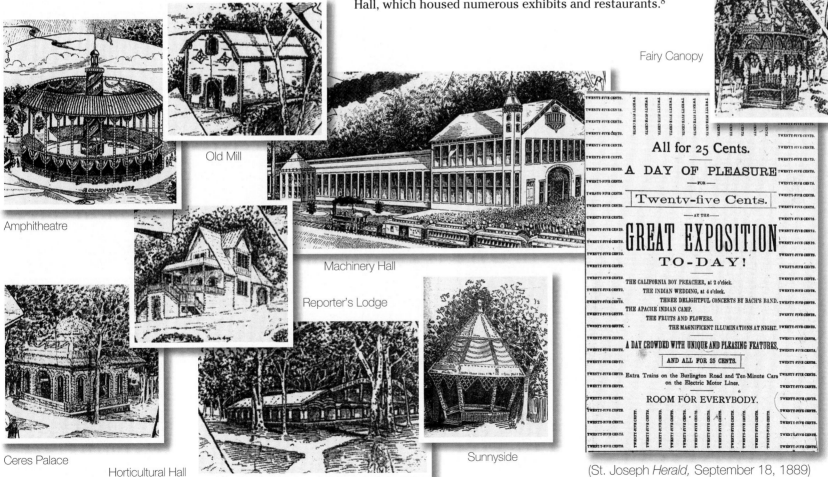

Fairy Canopy

Old Mill

Amphitheatre

Machinery Hall

Reporter's Lodge

Ceres Palace

Horticultural Hall

Sunnyside

All for 25 Cents.

A DAY OF PLEASURE

—FOR—

Twenty-five Cents.

—AT THE—

GREAT EXPOSITION
TO-DAY!

THE CALIFORNIA BOY PREACHER, at 2 o'clock.
THE INDIAN WEDDING, at 4 o'clock.
THREE DELIGHTFUL CONCERTS BY BACH'S BAND.
THE APACHE INDIAN CAMP.
THE FRUITS AND FLOWERS.
THE MAGNIFICENT ILLUMINATIONS AT NIGHT.

A DAY CROWDED WITH UNIQUE AND PLEASING FEATURES,

AND ALL FOR 25 CENTS.

Extra Trains on the Burlington Road and Ten-Minute Cars on the Electric Motor Lines.

ROOM FOR EVERYBODY.

(St. Joseph *Herald,* September 18, 1889)

Corn Palace

(Illustration from the September 18, 1889, issue of the St. Joseph *Herald,* courtesy State Historical Society of Missouri; photograph courtesy of St. Joseph Museums Inc.)

Cupid's Bowar

(Illustration from the September 18, 1889, issue of the St. Joseph *Herald,* courtesy State Historical Society of Missouri; photograph courtesy of St. Joseph Museums Inc.)

ATTRACTIONS.

Daily Attractions of More than Ordinary Merit will be Offered to the Amusement Loving Public.

Bach's Celebrated Band and Orchestra!

Will Give Concerts Every afternoon and Evening in the Amphitheater.
Thousands of Prismatic Lights will Illuminate the Grounds. Numerous Buildings, Covered with Cereal Decorations will Delight the Eye of the Visitor.

A REALISTIC INDIAN FIGHT

And a Mimic Representation of the

Custer Massacre!

100 Apache Indians, 100 Indian Fighters Under the Celebrated Scout,

Capt. Jack Crawford

And 500 Soldiers will Participate.

Sermons will be Delivered in the Amphitheater on Sunday by the Most Celebrated Divines in the Country. Music by a Chorus of 1,000 Voices. A Congress of the Most Celebrated Agriculturists in the Country. A Carnival of Song Birds. A Magnificent Art Exhibition. A Wonderful Display of Historical Relics, Sham Battles between Companies of Soldiers Numbering over 1,000. Balloon Ascensions and Parachute Jumping. A Day of Field Sports.

The Celebrated Woody Quartette

Of Male Voices will sing during the Exposition.

ELSA VON BLUMEN and JOSIE HAWKS

Champion Lady Bicyclists of the World, will give daily Exhibitions of Fancy Riding, and will Engage in Trials of Speed with Running Horses.

The Celebrated Kemp Brothers

Great Bareback Hippodrome Riders, will give a Series of Roman Hippodrome Races.

CAPT. A. H. BOGARDUS

And Three Sons will give Exhibitions of Fancy Rifle Shooting.

A Hall Filled With Machinery

And 500 Men Engaged in Manufacturing.

For Complete Premium List, Rules and Regulations, Railroad Rates, and General Information about the Exposition, address

NEW ERA EXPOSITION, St Joseph, Mo.

(Illustrations and newspapers courtesy of State Historical Society of Missouri)

Fifty-eight men were hired for the Exposition police force, and other than a few unfinished exhibits, the grounds were declared ready for the opening on September 3. A 50-cent admission charge got the ticket holder into all events, and the biggest draw was expected to be Captain Jack Crawford's Wild West Show (he was once part of Buffalo Bill's Wild West Show). Captain Jack featured Bronco John and his Band of Cowboys, fancy shooting by Captain Bogardus and an Indian warfare exhibition featuring numerous Apaches from Arizona who were hired specifically for the St. Joseph event. Only three members of the tribe had even seen a train before taking their first ride to the city.[9]

A GREAT DAY.

The Large Crowd at the Exposition Witness a Fine Arena Exhibition.

Hurdle Races by Gentlemen and Cowboys an Interesting Feature.

Scenes on the Grounds Illustrated by "The Herald" Artist--Making a Mash---The Wild West and Bucking Broncos.

To-Day's Programme the Most Interesting One Yet Arranged for Sunday.

A Successful Balloon Ascension--Monday Iowa Day--Governors Larrabee and Francis to Be Present--An Entire Change of Programme--The New Building--Exhibitions of Corn.

TO-DAY!

A LEAP FROM THE CLOUDS.

A Thrilling Spectacle!

Prof. Chas. Walcott

Ascends in a Balloon to the height of ONE MILE, then drops
to the earth by means of a PARACHUTE.

TO-DAY AT 4:30 P. M.
AT THE
NEW ERA EXPOSITION.

ST. JOSEPH, MISSOURI.

(Illustrations and newspapers from
the St. Joseph *Herald,* courtesy of
State Historical Society of Missouri)

The second day was plagued by dreary weather, and some people felt the third day was marred because some of the Apaches "were not properly clad and modesty demands a more careful adjustment of apparel."[10] It wasn't until the fourth day that everyone knew their parts well enough for the show to run smoothly,[11] and it wasn't until the fifth day that the grounds and all of the exhibits were completed to satisfaction.[12] The biggest excitement on the sixth day was a balloon ascension that nearly ended in tragedy when the wind took the balloon more sideways than upward.[13]

An unusual and uninvited musician caused a stir on the eighth day when the management was neither entertained nor humored by the presence of Count Von Pieodiabaskrumeymbois and his one-man band. He was quickly escorted from the grounds without a 50-cent refund in spite of the fact that he could play the accordion, pipe, snare, bass drum, triangle, cymbals and bells all at the same time.[14]

Refunds were handed out on the 10th day to several angry mothers who brought their young children to a baby contest that had, unknown to them, been canceled because of inclement weather. Those who had arrived by train also were reimbursed for their fare and given a free rail pass for a return trip.[15]

The big event for Sunday, September 15, was to be an official Apache wedding. The groom, Fight A Bear, was the great-great-grandson of Old Gabriel, who was believed to be 150 years old and the world's oldest living human. Old Gabriel was reportedly already a grandfather six years before the signing of the Declaration of Independence, and married his sixth wife in 1845 at the age of 110.[16] The wedding, as spectacular as it may have been, most certainly was upstaged by a fire that broke out later that night in Machinery Hall. The flames destroyed the structure and most of the contents, and took the life of one man.[17]

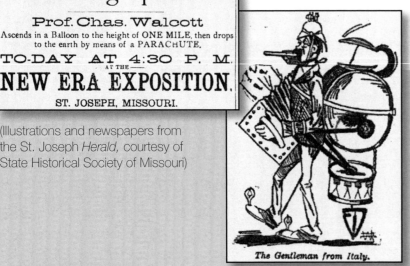

The Gentleman from Italy.

THE WEDDING.

Machinery Hall on Fire.

(Illustrations and newspapers from the St. Joseph *Herald,*
courtesy of State Historical Society of Missouri)

A TERRIBLE FIRE.

The Art and Main Hall at the Exposition Grounds Destroyed by Fire.

It Is Supposed to Have Caught From a Spark Off of the Electric Wire.

The Flames Spread in an Alarming Manner and It Was An Impossibility to Attempt to Control Them.

Capt. Johnson Foster, an Employe, Perishes in the Flames.

$300,000 the Estimated Loss—Little Insurance on the Building or Contents—The Steel Car Destroyed—Incidents and Stories of the Fire—The Exposition Will Go On.

BARELY SCORCHED

THE -:- FIRE

HAS NOT HURT THE EXPOSITION.

Only One Building Burned!

ALL OTHERS INTACT.

TEN THOUSAND DOLLARS WILL BE RAISED

500 MEN

WILL BE PUT AT WORK, AND

A New Building will Rise in a Day!

EVERY ATTRACTION

ON THE GROUNDS,

AND SCORES OF NEW ONES WILL BE ADDED.

Not an Hour will be Lost.

THE PROGRAMME

Will Not Be Changed in Any Detail.

Open Every Day and Evenings.

The only item salvaged was a carriage that had belonged to General Lafayette, and it was saved by the Apaches. They perhaps could have saved more valuable artifacts, but some of the police officers mistakenly thought the Indians were stealing items and held them at gunpoint for several minutes.[18]

Devastating as the fire may have been, it actually spurred the Exposition forward. Newspaper articles promoting the event suddenly appeared on page one instead of being stuck somewhere in the middle of the papers, large advertisements suddenly appeared, attractive sketches of the various pavilions adorned the pages and the admission price was reduced to 25 cents per day. The efforts resulted in the biggest crowds ever, though some of the increased attendance was no doubt due to human curiosity for witnessing carnage first hand.[19] Attendance probably could have been increased even further had gambling and alcohol not been strictly forbidden on the grounds, but the *Herald* editor exclaimed, "All hail to this body of gentlemen who are brave enough

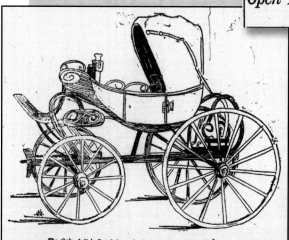

The Only Article Saved from the Flames—Gen. Lafayette's Carriage.

in the city of St. Joseph to say 'thus far and no farther; and who, even though they knew their attendance would be largely increased, could not be bought."[20]

Plans were drawn up for a new Main Hall, and even though construction funds were a bit short, the city's newspapers guaranteed the difference so building could begin on Friday morning, September 20.[21] A call for volunteers went out in an attempt to complete the structure within 48 hours. That lofty goal came up a little short, but by the following Tuesday, the *Herald* was proud to report that construction was completed "excepting the finishing touches on interior and exterior."[22]

The Exposition officially ended on October 5, but the grounds were kept open the following week and limited attractions were still available for the employees. It was noted that some employees had not been paid for their services, but the adult Apaches were each paid $22.50, as stated in their contract. They also received many gifts from awestruck white visitors, and seemed well-pleased with the "white man's big pow-wow."[23]

(Illustrations and newspapers from the St. Joseph *Herald*, courtesy of State Historical Society of Missouri)

To-day at the Exposition.

Vote for Your Friends!

K. H. CLARKE will give a handsome silver manicure set to the most popular lady in St. Joseph.
AUG. WETTEROTH will give a gold-headed cane to the most popular gentleman in St. Joseph.
Tickets will be given at the gate. Voting will take place in the main building.

READ THE SUNDAY PAPERS FOR TO-MORROW'S ATTRACTIONS!

They are Great!

Delightful Afternoon and Evening Concerts
— BY —
BACH'S CELEBRATED MILITARY BAND AND ORCHESTRA.

The Grounds at Night are Lighted by 5,000 Prismatic Lamps, and Present
A Beautiful and Fairy-Like Scene!

25c   SUNDAYS AND EVENINGS   25c

The Burlington Route and the Electric Cable Car Lines will run plenty of cars at short intervals, and there will be plenty of room for everybody.

TO-DAY :-: LEADS

ALL FORMER DAYS

IN ATTRACTIONS

At the Exposition.

SECRETARY RUSK

WILL ARRIVE THIS MORNING, AND

Speak on the Grounds at 2 O'clock this Afternoon.

He will be followed by Prominent Speakers of Washington.

TRAVELING MEN'S DAY.

There will be a parade at 10 o'clock this morning, at which 1,000 Traveling Men are expected to take part.

The Great Hippodrome Chariot Races!

This Evening Bach's Military Band and Orchestra
Will give the Greatest Musical Programme of the Exposition.

ADMISSION, EVENING, ONLY 25 CENTS.

EXPOSITION

—UNDER—

-:New Management:-

—TO BE—

CONTINUED ONE WEEK

—FOR THE—

Benefit of the Employes

—OF THE—

OLD-:-ASSOCIATION.

Concerts Every Afternoon and Evening

—BY—

PRYOR'S BAND OF 20 PIECES.

Tuesday, Oct. 8th.

Capt. A. H. Bogardus and his three sons in fancy shooting.
Ring tournament. Prizes $10.00 and $5.00.
Fast mule race. $5.00.
Pony race, ridden by boys under 15. $5.00.
Best boy rider, under 12. $5.00.
Best saddle pony, thirteen hands high and under, style and speed combined. $5.00.
Amateur wrestling match, catch-as-catch-can. Pair of Indian Clubs.
Burlesque on the "Lone Trapper."
Exciting race for a bride.

ADMISSION, 15 Cents; CHILDREN, 15 Cents.

Carriages Free.

GRANNIS -:- SPECIALTY -:- COMPANY.

1. Overture...Pryor's Band
2. Ballad, "Mother's Last Request".......................J. C. Thompson
3. Comic, "Silver King"..................................H. Goodliffe
4. Give Me Back My Heart Again..........................H. Grannis
5. Comic, "Gal from the South"............................H. Jordan
6. "Sweet Genevieve".....................................C. J. Sullivan
7. Grand Finale Medley..................Grannis, Thompson and Company

SECOND PART.

1. Overture..Pryor's Orchestra
2. Comic Songs..H. Jordan
3. Motto Sings...H. Grannis
4. Burlesque Boxing Match, David and Goliah...........P. Sneed and J. Cline
5. Comic Song...H. Goodliffe
6. Sketch..Grannis and Thompson
7. "Nornen Murricno".....................................C. J. Sullivan
8. Concluding with a Laughable Farce, entitled "Razor Mania," by the full company.

Don't forget the Great Boxing Match between J. Cline, the pop corn man, and P. Sneed, the giant of the Police Force,

FOR ONE HUNDRED DOLLARS A SIDE!

All the above at the EXPOSITION GROUNDS for

ONLY 25 CENTS.

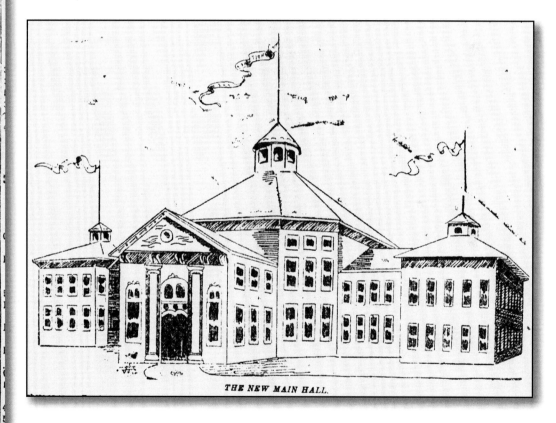

THE NEW MAIN HALL.

Footnotes for St. Joseph New Era National Exposition, 1889

1. Raymond J. Hekel, History of Buchanan County, Missouri (Cape Cirardeau: Birdsall, Williams & Co., 1881) 644.

2. Ibid. 643.

3. Gazette Publishing, "The Ladies' Movement," St. Joseph *Daily Gazette,* June 16, 1889, p. 4.

4. Ibid.

5. The Herald Publishing Co., "Exposition Notes," St. Joseph *Herald,* July 23, 1889, p. 3.

6. Ibid.

7. The Herald Publishing Co., "The Fifth Day," St. Joseph *Herald,* September 8, 1889, p. 6.

8. Ibid.

9. The Herald Publishing Co., "The Opening Day," St. Joseph *Herald,* September 3, 1889, p. 5.

10. The Herald Publishing Co., "The Third Day," St. Joseph *Herald,* September 6, 1889, p. 3.

11. The Herald Publishing Co., "The Fourth Day," St. Joseph *Herald,* September 7, 1889, p. 8.

12. The Herald Publishing Co., "The Fifth Day," St. Joseph *Herald,* September 8, 1889, p. 6.

13. The Herald Publishing Co., "The Sixth Day," St. Joseph *Herald,* September 9, 1889, p. 3.

14. The Herald Publishing Co., "Opposition to Bach's Band," St. Joseph *Herald,* September 11, 1889, p. 3.

15. The Herald Publishing Co., "An Explanation," St. Joseph *Herald,* September 13, 1889, p. 3.

16. The Herald Publishing Co., "Fight-A-Bear Will Marry," St. Joseph *Herald,* September 14, 1889, p. 3.

17. The Herald Publishing Co., "A Terrible Fire," St. Joseph *Herald,* September 16, 1889, p. 1.

18. The Herald Publishing Co., "A Blue Monday," St. Joseph *Herald,* September 17, 1889, p. 1.

19. Ibid.

20. The Herald Publishing Co., "Something New," St. Joseph *Herald,* September 18, 1889, p. 10.

21. The Herald Publishing Co., "A New Main Hall," St. Joseph *Herald,* September 19, 1889, p. 6.

22. The Herald Publishing Co., "Governors' Day," St. Joseph *Herald,* September 24, 1889, p. 2.

23. The Herald Publishing Co., "Exposition's Finis," St. Joseph *Herald,* October 6, 1889, p. 2.

Missouri Corn Palace Exhibit

(Courtesy of Irwin Lyndon, Professor of Agriculture, Missouri State University)

St. Louis World's Fair 1904

Section 3 ❖ Missouri
CHAPTER 2

The St. Louis Louisiana Purchase Exposition was held in 1904, a year later than originally was planned to celebrate the centennial of the United States' largest-ever real estate deal in 1803. The 1904 exhibition covered nearly twice as many acres as any previous world's fair — 1,272 acres vs. 686 acres for Chicago's Columbian Exposition in 1893 — and the St. Louis Palace of Agriculture, covering nearly 20 acres, could boast of being the largest building ever constructed for a world's fair. The emphasis on size could have occurred because St. Louis was still behind its rival, Chicago, in population, or maybe because St. Louis had no structure to best the Eiffel Tower, which attracted significant attention for Paris at the *Exposition Universelle* in 1889, or the colossal Ferris Wheel that made its debut at the Chicago World's Fair. It's true that St. Louis also had a large Ferris Wheel, but that was because the city borrowed it from Chicago.[1]

The massive Palace of Agriculture contained some of the most interesting and beautifully decorated exhibits ever seen along its nine miles of aisles, and among them were the Missouri Corn Palace, along with other exhibits shown here from Kansas, Oklahoma, Nebraska and North Dakota.

Kansas Exhibit

(Courtesy of Irwin Lyndon, Professor of Agriculture, Missouri State University)

Kansas Exhibit
(Courtesy of
Irwin Lyndon,
Professor of
Agriculture,
Missouri State
University)

Oklahoma Exhibit

(Courtesy of Irwin Lyndon, Professor of Agriculture, Missouri State University)

Nebraska Exhibit

(Courtesy of Irwin Lyndon, Professor of Agriculture, Missouri State University)

North Dakota Exhibit. The sign over the door reads, "The Roosevelt Cabin. This is the original cabin occupied by Theodore Roosevelt for three years when he was a cattle owner in western North Dakota 1883 to 1886."

(Courtesy North Dakota State Archives)

Pres. Roosevelt's Log Cabin. N. Dakota Exhibit. Agricultural Building. Louisiana Purchase Exposition. Copyright 1904 by C. H. Graves.

St. Louis World's Fair Footnotes

1. Erik Matte, World's Fairs (Princeton Architectural Press, New York City, N.Y., 1998), 117-121.

1889 Texas Spring Palace
(Courtesy of Ft. Worth Public Library)

Texas
Spring Palace
1889

Section 4 ❖ Texas
CHAPTER 1

The promoters of the Texas Spring Palace karporama traced the inspiration for their event all the way back to the Egyptians, Greeks and Romans, whose ancient gatherings celebrated a variety of events. They also admitted to being inspired by the numerous world's fairs from London's in 1851 to Paris' in 1889. Notice was taken of the millions of people who visited the World's Fair cities during their international exhibitions, and Fort Worth wanted to reap similar benefits on a smaller scale.[1]

Fort Worth citizens were somewhat envious of St. Paul's ice palaces and Sioux City's Corn Palaces, and therefore pledged to be better than either. Rather than celebrate one crop, as they claimed Sioux City did, Fort Worth would "present to the visitor a sample of all the products of Texas,"[2] and rather than copy St. Paul, the city would construct something of permanence instead of a structure that, although beautiful and grand, "melteth away before the god of day."[3]

In mid-January of 1889, General R.A. Cameron, commissioner of immigration for Fort Worth and Denver, was invited to express his thoughts on what would best promote the area. He proposed a Texas Spring Palace or Texas June Palace because "in the month of June Texas was at her best — golden grain would be waving on thousands of acres, all the grasses would be growing luxuriantly, peaches and other fruit would be ripe. Potatoes and all sorts of vegetables would be at their best, and flowers of the state would all be in bloom. In short, Texas could show to the visitor from the north what could be found here."[4] An exposition was to run for three weeks in June and encompass all of the products produced by the state. In other words, "it would be a wheat palace, a corn palace, a cotton palace, an art palace, a sorghum, millet, rye, barley and jute palace."[5]

Not only would crops be featured, but minerals as well, including coal, iron, copper, platinum, granite, marble, limestone (red, white and blue) and sandstone. Then add to that flowers, fruit and wildlife. The exterior

TEXAS SPRING PALACE.

Chairman Sommerville and the Committee Buckle Down to Work.

People from All Over the State Delighted with the Plan—The Public Meeting To-Night.

(Illustrations, ads and articles courtesy of Ft. Worth Public Library)

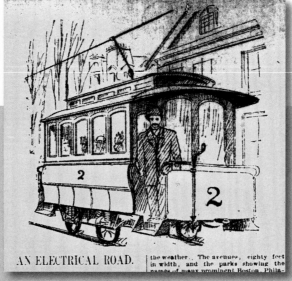

AN ELECTRICAL ROAD.   the weather. The avenues, eighty feet in width, and the parks showing the names of many prominent Boston, Phila-

FAT AND LEAN MEN'S SUITS
—IN—
ENDLESS VARIETY.

L. AUGUST & CO.,
LEADING FASHIONABLE CLOTHIERS,
311 and 313   Houston Street.   311 and 313

would boast eight towers and a magnificent dome, all covered in grains and grasses, and the interior would be lined with attractive displays.[6] The general later added gold and silver to his list of minerals.

A committee headed by W.F. Sommerville was appointed to canvas businessmen and passers-by on the streets of Fort Worth for two days and poll their thoughts on the palace. Many locals and out-of-towners couldn't wait for the canvas and quickly contacted the *Gazette* to voice their support. The paper received positive responses from individuals in Beaumont, Denver, Galveston and New Mexico, and one local businessman stated the magic words, "A fine thing and I will invest in it."[7]

At 8 p.m. on the evening of January 16, 1889, 200 men and women packed Huffman's Hall to hear the committee's report, which followed another pep talk by General Cameron. The committee reported a favorable response from Fort Worth's citizens but noted that time was short, so it suggested another

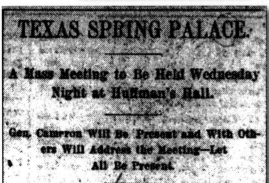

(Articles courtesy of Ft. Worth Public Library)

(1889 Texas Spring Palace ribbon, employee pass and invitation courtesy of Ft. Worth Public Library)

committee be formed of not less than 50 members who would move energetically to form a stock company and provide "the necessary inquiry as to cost, location, etc., the design and erection of a building; as well as arrangements with railroads for excursions and advertising of same."[8] The citizens present were asked to stand if they were in support of the project, and every chair was quickly vacated.[9]

On the following day, which was a Thursday, 36 of the 50 appointed committee members returned to Huffman's Hall and unanimously passed a resolution to "take immediate steps to organize a Texas Spring palace company. Its object shall be to secure grounds and erect a palace thereon for the exhibition of all the agricultural, horticultural, mineral and other products of the state of Texas. Its authorized capital stock shall be $100,000, divided into 10,000 shares of $10 each, which, when issued, shall be full paid, and not subject to any assessment."[10]

The company would organize as soon as it had raised $25,000 in stock, and each committee member signing the resolution pledged to invest in the company. (It was later decided that a third of the authorized stock should be raised before officially organizing.) The chairman was given the authority to appoint another 50 members to the general committee, and a body of 10 also was appointed to solicit stock. The next meeting was set for following Tuesday, and the intent was to have $50,000 in pledges by 4:00 that afternoon.[11]

In spite of the fact that the editor of the El Paso *Herald* thought the name "Spring Palace" was a little peculiar, he pledged his support along with the editors of the Gainesville *Hesperian* and the Waco *Trade Review*. All claimed to understand why the worthy project came together so quickly.[12]

The *Gazette* editor speculated that perhaps the popularity of the Spring Palace idea was a fashion statement. He noted that previously the fashion had been croquet, now it was lawn tennis; before it had been roller skating, today it was the palace. He went on to say, "This latest novelty craze seems to have taken its rise in the success of the 'Ice Palace' at Montreal, an erection which attracted very wide attention and proved a most successful novelty. It was followed by others of a similar kind — all more or less successful; but the most original and perhaps the most successful of all is the Corn Palace at Sioux City, Iowa. It was the marvelous success of this — both artistically and financially — that suggested to Gen. Cameron the idea of the Texas Spring Palace."[13]

McLennan County tower, 1889 Texas Spring Palace
(Courtesy of Ft. Worth Public Library)

Hardeman County tower, 1889 Texas Spring Palace
(Courtesy of Ft. Worth Public Library)

Tom Green County tower, 1889 Texas Spring Palace
(Courtesy of Ft. Worth Public Library)

Webb County tower, 1889 Texas Spring Palace
(Courtesy of Ft. Worth Public Library)

The editor went on to offer a suggestion for decorating the dome. He thought it would be a good idea to accept Wichita Falls' offer to donate the wheat and find an artistic way to give the appearance of a vast field in the various stages of harvest — with one area partially cut, another in shocks, and another being hauled off and stacked. He thought "the effect as seen from a little distance would be very realistic."[14]

The general committee's fundraising goal for the end of January was short $18,500, so it was time for another pep meeting in Huffman's Hall. A special invitation went out to the ladies in the community, and the local newspaper paraphrased the opening speaker's remarks by stating, "The men of Texas had been at work for years past but this was the first opportunity given the ladies of Texas a chance to help the state."[15] It's hard to image many women being rallied by that remark, but maybe the next speaker had better results when talking dollars and cents. He stated that the 1887 Sioux City Corn Palace had been a financial success even though it cost $30,000 to build, and the 1888 Corn Palace had been even more successful at a cost of $55,000. Hurley & Co., who had built the exposition building at the New Orleans World's Fair, claimed they could finish the Spring Palace in 55 days at a cost of only $26,000, which was $4,000 under the original estimate, and still could produce a building far overshadowing the Sioux City palaces. A call then went out worthy of the most assertive revivalist for on-the-spot subscriptions in the amount of $100, $300 and $500. The result was an additional $6,500 in pledges, but that still left the committee short at least $13,000.[16]

A few more pledges trickled in during the next few days, but when adequate funds still were not secured by the following week, women supporting the Spring Palace called for another meeting to be held in Huffman's Hall on the evening of February 8. The call was heeded and the hall was filled to standing room only. After warming up the crowd with a European slide show and a musical number, a picture of the proposed Spring Palace was projected onto a screen, a speech was made by an orator especially chosen by the ladies, and then committee members strode through the aisles seeking new stockholders. The plan

worked well enough to raise another $6,100, which finally provided enough capital to organize the stockholding company.[17]

The following evening, 150 men capitalized on the success of the women by unanimously passing a resolution to form the Texas Spring Palace Company. Also passing by a unanimous vote was "a motion offered by W.L. Malone that the thanks of the stockholders be given the ladies of Fort Worth for their successful efforts in behalf of the Spring Palace and that all the ladies of Fort Worth are requested to organize permanently for the work to be done and only to be accomplished by them."[18]

A local law firm offered to draw up the charter free of charge, and two architectural firms were willing to design the Spring Palace at no cost to the newly formed company. The *Gazette* declared, "This Palace will bring men and money to Texas, and, better than all, it will send back to all the states of the Union those who can testify of the truth as it was made manifest to their own eyes, and thus turn to Texas the great tide of home-seekers and investors."[19]

General Cameron was in Sioux City the following week to learn from city officials how to best organize the Spring Palace Exposition, which was then scheduled to run from June 1 to July 1. The Sioux Citians found the general to be most pleasant, and encouraged all Americans to lend their support to the success of the Fort Worth enterprise.[20]

At a director's meeting held on February 20, a palace design was selected from those offered by seven architects, and a contract was awarded to Messrs. Armstrong & Messer. It was reported that, "The building according to the plans adopted will be 250 feet long, 60 feet wide, with a transcript 150 feet long and 50 feet wide. The center of the building is circulated with a diameter of 80 feet, with a clear space to the top of the dome, 110 feet from the ground and 55 feet in diameter. In the center of the building will be a pool 40 feet in diameter, in the center of which will be a pyramid of native rock with arched grottos, in which will be a fountain, of changeable colors, and outside at the top will be another fountain flowing over the whole pyramid. In the pool at the base will be fish from the Texas streams, and around the edge will be flowers, plants and shrubs, from the rosebush to the century plant, including all the flora of the state. Near this fountain will be the grand music stand, rising from front to rear, the entrance being from the gallery. Around the building project twelve towers, from one to three stories, with numerous balconies, all of which are capable of fine decorations. Four of the towers have stairs of ample width leading to the galleries under which will be the retiring room for ladies and gentlemen. The galleries, which are spacious, have numerous niches and alcoves for displaying specimens of our many resources. The exterior is especially designed for rich decorations. Each of the towers has a flag staff on which will be displayed many-colored flags. Over the lantern of the dome will be a flag staff thirty feet high, making a total of 130 feet from the ground to the top of the flag staff from which will float the stars and stripes. From east of the towers to the lantern wires will be run and decorated with wheat and other products in fantastic shapes. Strung in between these will be about one thousand incandescent electric lamps of various colors to be lighted at night to give a rich and beautiful effect to the Palace. Arc lights will be around the four entrances and within the building."[21]

Several areas within Fort Worth competed for the palace's location with promises of land, stock, cash, bridges and electric railway service. A decision was made to set the matter aside for further discussion and additional proposals. It also was decided to change the opening date from June 1 to May 29 and to run the Exposition for three weeks instead of four.[22]

The next meeting dealt mainly with discussing the best location for the future palace, and the directors' main objective was to pick one without provoking a big fight among partisan stockholders. Their goal was to pick a site that would benefit the city as a whole, both immediately and in the future; offer the most convenience for visitors; and result in the largest financial return to investors. While the men were dealing with the location pros and cons, the ladies were planning a fundraiser by sponsoring a supper and dance. Admission would be 50 cents, India tea would be served and the young ladies doing the serving would be dressed in "India costumes."[23]

In spite of the continuous fundraising efforts to fulfill the palace's grand design, the 1889 Spring Palace Exposition still failed to attract the number of visitors needed to turn a profit. However, the event was not necessarily considered unsuccessful because the city refused to admit defeat. Even the city of Jefferson said that Fort Worth had never failed at anything except religion. If blame were to be placed anywhere, it was ascribed to the railroads, which were taken to task by the *Gazette* when it declared, "Some railroads in the North furnish their passengers with stenographers. Some railroads in Texas do not furnish their passengers with seats."[24]

1890 Texas Spring Palace
(Courtesyof Ft. Worth Public Library)

Texas
Spring Palace
1890

Section 4 ❖ Texas
CHAPTER 1

Even though it was tantamount to showing a profit in 1890, the *Gazette* was adamant that there would be no gouging of visitors. "Dallas, Galveston and Austin should be permitted to maintain unquestioned their monopoly in the gouging business when strangers enter their gates."[25] To give credence to Fort Worth's stand against gougers, all fakirs and "catch-penny" artists were discouraged from preying on Fort Worth's guests, and exposition committees were advised to put their inquiries for showing their wares directly in the waste basket.[26]

Promoters raised $50,000 to double the size of the 1890 palace and the construction contract was awarded to the Fort Worth Loan and Construction Company. Everyone raising colored corn was asked to save it for the palace so chief decorator E.D. Allen could make good on his pronouncement of the new palace being "the most beautiful structure of the kind ever constructed."[27] When the remodeling was commenced on February 18, a goal was set to triple the number of visitors to the city and thereby turn previous losses into huge profits.[28]

Other than a few opening-day glitches, events were proceeding according to schedule until suddenly catastrophe struck.

TEXAS SPRING PALACE

Opens May 10, 1890.

The second season of the grandest and most unique exhibit of the products of the soil ever presented to the public will be opened at

FORT WORTH, TEXAS,

May 10, 1890,

And continue twenty-one days. The buildings are being greatly enlarged and improved, and the decorations and arrangements of exhibits more elegant and superb than last year's Exposition.

(All items courtesy of Ft. Worth Public Library)

(1890 ticket courtesy of Ft. Worth Public Library)

At 10:25 p.m. on May 30, 1890, a dropped match sent flames shooting up a grass-covered pillar on the second story. With fire spreading quickly around the 7,000 guests, the large structure would have been a certain death trap for most had not festival organizers guarded against such potential tragedy by providing extra exits throughout the building. Their planning would have proved adequate in all areas had not a man stumbled while carrying a child to safety at the south exit, thereby causing a jam that resulted in injury to several people who were crushed or trampled.[29]

There were many reports of bravery as numerous men, women and older children rushed about rescuing those in need, while others stood below windows to catch children who were dropped from the second story to escape the flames. Fittingly, the last person to exit the burning building was the exposition's president, B.B. Paddock, who had remained inside to instill a sense of calm and order to his frightened guests.[30]

Rumors were running rampant of scores of deaths, but when the smoke cleared there was only one fatality — Mr. Al Hayne, a British national who had safely exited the building, but then went back inside to rescue others. His clothing caught fire, and even though he was removed from the building, he was unable to survive the terrible burns received in his heroic attempt to put the welfare of others before his own. There were, however, at least 50 lesser casualties ranging from cuts and bruises to burns and fractures.[31]

Several attempts were made to rebuild, but there was never enough support or money to restore the grandest structure in Fort Worth's history.

A Great Calamity.

THE FIERY END OF THE PRIDE AND GLORY OF TEXAS.

The Terrible, yet Grand Scene, Amid which the Spring Palace Went Down.

Noble Acts of Heroism, and Rare Bravery of Women in a Terrible Ordeal in the Burning Building.

One of the Most Remarkable Conflagrations in History, from which Thousands Escaped and Only One Died.

A Palace Grander and More Beautiful Than Ever to be Erected in 1891—Scenes at the Fire and a List of the Injured.

(Items courtesy of Ft. Worth Public Library)

**1890 Texas Spring
Palace interior**

(Courtesy of Ft. Worth Public Library)

1890 Texas Spring Palace interior
(Courtesy of Ft. Worth Public Library)

Footnotes for the Texas Spring Palace in Fort Worth, 1889-1890

1. Democrat Publishing Company, "The Spring Palace," Fort Worth *Daily Gazette,* May 1, 1890, p. 2.
2. Ibid.
3. Ibid.
4. Democrat Publishing Company, "Texas Spring Palace," Fort Worth *Daily Gazette,* January 15, 1889, p. 2.
5. Ibid.
6. Ibid.
7. Democrat Publishing Company, "Texas Spring Palace," Fort Worth *Daily Gazette,* January 16, 1889, p. 8.
8. Democrat Publishing Company, "Texas Spring Palace," Fort Worth *Daily Gazette,* January 17, 1889, p. 5.
9. Ibid.
10. Democrat Publishing Company, "Texas Spring Palace," Fort Worth *Daily Gazette,* January 18, 1889, p. 8.
11. Ibid.
12. Democrat Publishing Company, "Spring Palace," Fort Worth *Daily Gazette,* January 25, 1889, p. 8.
13. Democrat Publishing Company, "Texas Spring Palace," Fort Worth *Daily Gazette,* January 27, 1889, p. 8.
14. Ibid.
15. Democrat Publishing Company, "Texas Spring Palace," Fort Worth *Daily Gazette,* January 31, 1889, p. 5.
16. Ibid.
17. Democrat Publishing Company, "Texas Spring Palace," Fort Worth *Daily Gazette,* February 9, 1889, p. 8.
18. Democrat Publishing Company, "Texas Spring Palace," Fort Worth *Daily Gazette,* February 10, 1889, p. 5.
19. Ibid.
20. Democrat Publishing Company, "Texas Spring Palace," Fort Worth *Daily Gazette,* February 17, 1889, p. 3.
21. Democrat Publishing Company, "Texas Spring Palace," Fort Worth *Daily Gazette,* February 21, 1889, p. 5.
22. Ibid.
23. Democrat Publishing Company, "Spring Palace," Fort Worth *Daily Gazette,* February 25, 1889, p. 8.
24. Democrat Publishing Company, "Local Notes," Fort Worth *Daily Gazette,* February 11, 1890, p. 4.
25. Democrat Publishing Company, "Local Notes," Fort Worth *Daily Gazette,* February 14, 1890, p. 4.
26. Democrat Publishing Company, "Spring Palace Notes," Fort Worth *Daily Gazette,* February 14, 1890, p. 4.
27. Ibid.
28. Democrat Publishing Company, "Spring Palace Notes," Fort Worth *Daily Gazette,* February 19, 1890, p. 4.
29. Democrat Publishing Company, "A Great Calamity," Fort Worth *Daily Gazette,* June 5, 1890, p. 3.
30. Ibid.
31. Ibid.

1894 Waco Cotton Palace
(Courtesy of Baylor University)

Waco
Cotton Palace
1894

Section 4 ❖ Texas
CHAPTER 2

In the late 1800s, every city that built a grain or mineral palace had a big celebration for its opening day festivities, but Waco, Texas, held a party to equal all others on June 22, 1894, when it merely laid the cornerstone for its future Cotton Palace. The celebratory noise had to have been deafening when starting at 1 p.m., and continuing for the next hour, churches rang their bells, factories blew their whistles and locomotives blasted their horns to announce the 200-float parade that would fill the city streets at 2 p.m. that afternoon.[1]

In describing the procession, the newspaper that evening reported, "Some of the cars had steeples built of corn stalks and decorated with cotton; others were towers and everything was covered with cotton spangled with frost work of glass that sparkled in the sun. It was like the white city on wheels."[2]

Judge Herring, one of the day's main speakers, praised the city and the parade itself by comparing the event to what he thought it would have been like five decades earlier. "A trades' procession of Waco half a century ago might have consisted of a bale of cotton, a long horn steer, a jack rabbit, and a horned frog. The procession today embraced all arts, all commerce, all civilization, all manufacturing, and even at that it was not a complete index of the prosperity of Waco."[3]

More than 10,000 people were on hand to witness the Masonic fraternity's Grand Master as he laid the Cotton Palace cornerstone and conducted rites suited to the occasion. No doubt all looked forward to the near future when "the Cotton Palace with its permanent exposition of the fruits of the land would draw settlers not only to Waco and McLennan County, but to all Texas and by legitimate demand would enhance values so that people becoming more comfortable would grow happier and better."[4]

Planning for the palace had been in full swing since March of that year when stockholders met to organize and elect a slate of officers. By the end of that month, a block of land had been purchased for the construction site, and the grand opening was expected to be held on October 1.[5]

Confusion reigned briefly in May when a rumor spread through the Waco Ladies' Auxiliary "that the cotton palace enterprise would likely be abandoned."[6] The rumor was quickly squelched by James Moore, vice president of the Cotton Palace Association, when he assured the ladies that building blueprints would be ready by May 21 and construction would begin by June 1.[7]

An impressive 400- by 800-foot structure soon arose at a cost of $250,000, and although the opening didn't quite meet the October 1 deadline, the exposition did enjoy a profitable run from November 8 to December 6, 1894.[8] Unfortunately, the Cotton Palace burned to the ground five months later, and an exposition wasn't attempted again until 1910, whereafter it operated successfully for more than 20 years.[9]

THE COTTON PALACE.

Ten Thousand People Gathered to Witness the Laying of the Corner Stone.

An Invitation Wired President Cleveland—The Decorated Floats—The Speakers and Their Addresses.

Dallas *Morning News*, June 23, 1894
(Courtesy of Baylor University)

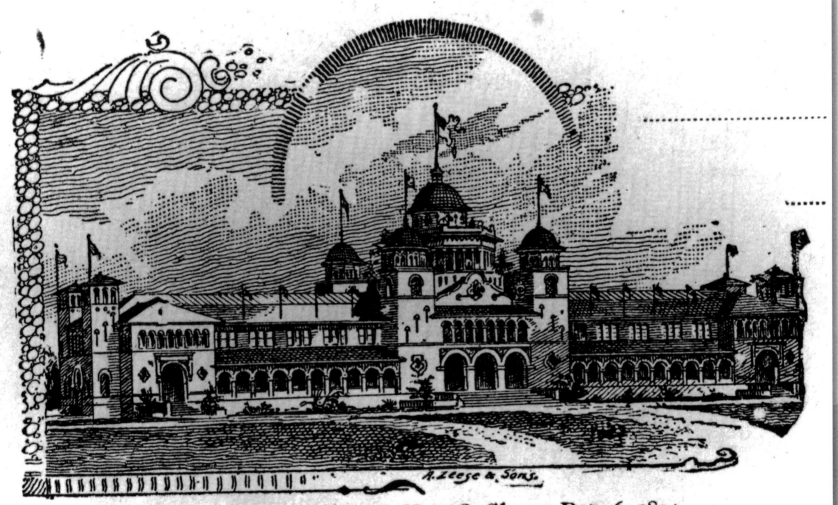

Open at Waco, Texas, Nov. 8, Closes Dec. 6, 1894.

Footnotes for the Waco Cotton Palace, 1894

1. Alfred O. Anderson, "The Cotton Palace," Dallas *Morning News*, June 23, 1894, p. 4.
2. Ibid.
3. Ibid.
4. Ibid.
5. Alfred O. Anderson, "Waco News," Dallas *Morning News*, March 3, 1894, p. 6.
6. Alfred O. Anderson, "Waco Cotton Palace," Dallas *Morning News*, May 17, 1894, p. 5.
7. Ibid.
8. Editor, "Where Cotton Reigns," Columbus *Daily Enquirer*, November 30, 1894, p. 3.
9. Dayton Kelley, Ed., The Handbook of Waco and McLennan County, Texas (Waco: Texian, 1972), 1.

Section 5
Illinois

Springfield Coal Palace, from the Illinois
State *Journal,* September 3, 1889

(Courtesy of State Historical Society of Illinois)

Springfield Coal Palace 1889

Section 5 ❖ Illinois
CHAPTER 1

The Springfield Coal Palace had perhaps the most inauspicious beginning of all the Midwestern palaces when on Saturday, August 24, 1889, a staff member of the Illinois State *Journal* made an off-the-cuff suggestion to Colonel Mills that perhaps there should be a Coal Palace at the upcoming Sangamon County Fair. The staff member didn't expect his remark to be taken seriously, but Colonel Mills, who was secretary of the fair board, took an immediate interest in the Coal Palace concept and called for an executive board meeting to be held on the following Monday morning. The board unanimously approved the idea and passed a resolution inviting the area's 23 coal operators to an 8 p.m. meeting that very night. The coal officials quickly agreed to supply the coal required for construction, and within one day's time, the Coal Palace was on its way to becoming reality.[1]

There was an informal discussion as to the dimensions of the Coal Palace, with suggestions that it should be 40 feet long, 20 feet wide and 16 feet high, but it was realized that the actual size would have to be determined later depending on the availability of coal and financing. The architect would no doubt also want a say in the matter, so it was all left for a committee to decide at a later date. The date couldn't be much later, however, because the fair was set to open in two weeks. It spoke well of the organizers that the only real challenge they foresaw was "shortness of time for work."[2]

If one wonders at the magnitude of optimism and speed with which plans moved forward, perhaps the answer lies with the local economy at that time. 1889 was a prosperous year for Springfield and the surrounding area, and business was booming. Crops

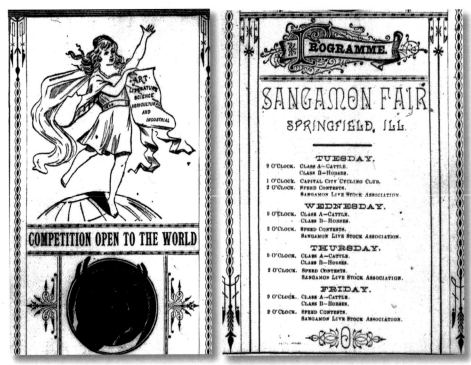

Illinois State *Journal*, September 8, 1889
(Courtesy of State Historical Society of Ilinois)

On the other side of the coin, the article to the left indicates that conditions were quite dire in the mining industry. Illinois State *Journal*, September 3, 1889.

(Courtesy of State Historical Society of Ilinois)

Illinois State *Journal,* September 9, 1889
(Courtesy of State Historical Society of Ilinois)

Illinois State *Journal,* September 3, 1889

(Courtesy of State Historical Society of Ilinois)

were good, with 20,000 bushels of wheat coming to the Springfield wheat mills each week, which meant that 24-hour shifts were required at the mills to meet British import demands. The influx of money allowed the city to pave its major streets with cedar blocks and brick and to replace wooden sidewalks with stone and brick. Seven new churches were built within the last year; several new businesses were springing up, including an ice factory; and residents were spending upwards of $4,000 for handsome Queen Ann-style homes.[3]

Perhaps the most unusual aspect of Springfield's Coal Palace was the original intention to use the building to promote the area's corn production, as noted in the first Illinois State *Journal* headlines on the subject proclaiming "King Corn's Coal Palace." The promotion

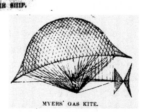

In 1889, there was a fascinating interest in flying machines, as evident in newspaper articles that contained stories with various illustrations of the unusual objects, as well as advertisements that took the shape of hot air balloons. Illustrations: Illinois State *Journal,* August 7, 1889; Ads: Illinois State *Journal,* September 9, 1889.

(Courtesy of State Historical Society of Ilinois)

The Sangamon County Fair was followed by the Illinois State Fair.

GO TO THE SPRINGFIELD FAIR.

Some Very Good Reasons for Attending the Great Exhibition.

The principal theme of conversation among the farmers, stockmen and the residents of all the towns in Central Illinois is the great Fair and Exposition to be held at Springfield Sept 10-18. The papers published in all portions of the State have called frequent attention to the extensive and attractive exhibits already secured for all the departments of the Fair, and all the railroads have granted the lowest rate ever given for an exhibition of this character. It is safe to say that the largest crowd of people ever collected in the State will be seen at the Springfield Fair. The writer desires to say a word to farmers, mechanics and fruit growers.

GO TO THE SPRINGFIELD FAIR, and see the magnificent specimens of the products and resources of Illinois the Premier Agricultural State of the Union.

GO TO THE SPRINGFIELD FAIR and see the best products of the Northern, Southern, Eastern and Western States. The large premiums offered attract the best productions of the farm to the Springfield Fair from all parts of the country.

GO TO THE SPRINGFIELD FAIR and see the most attractive and extensive exhibit of horses, cattle, swine, sheep and poultry ever collected together in this county.

GO TO THE SPRINGFIELD FAIR and see the unmistakable evidence that the farmers of this State are justly entitled to a foremost position as intelligent and progressive breeders of live stock and successful growers of the best specimens of of farm products.

GO TO THE SPRINGFIELD FAIR with your flocks, herds, products, etc., and demonstrate your skill as a breeder.

THE GREAT
ILLINOIS STATE FAIR.

JEFFERSON PARK,
PEORIA.

SEPT'R 23-27, 1889.

$75,000 EXPENDED IN MAGNIFICENT IMPROVEMENTS.

Nearly $25,000 in Cash Premiums,

DIVIDED AS FOLLOWS:

Cattle	$5,500
Horses	7,942
Swine	1,760
Sheep	1,620
Poultry	711
Dairy	1,347
Farm Produce, etc	1,638
Miscellaneous	2,060
Special Attractions	2,000
Total	$24,578

The Special Attractions will consist of the following features.

NO EXTRA CHARGE.

The Blind Cadets from the Illinois Institution for the Education of the Blind.—The Great Marantette Equestrian Combination —The Flock of African Ostriches.—Four Great Balloon Ascensions.—Four Parachute Leaps.—The Fish Hatchery.

was to be accomplished by trimming the outside of the building in corn and featuring corn displays throughout the interior.[4] Perhaps the coal operators objected to donating coal to promote corn because four days later an article in the newspaper declared that the object of the Coal Palace was "simply to furnish a novel attraction for the Fair and to call attention to the superior character of the coal which is mined in this vicinity."[5]

Coal was indeed extremely important to the area, providing employment to roughly 1,500 men in the county while reaping 95 cents per ton for the 1 million tons mined each year and shipped by rail to Wisconsin, Iowa, Minnesota, Dakota Territory and the Northwest. Therefore, it was only appropriate that the Coal Palace should be positioned just inside the main entrance to the fairgrounds where everyone would see it "in line with the west entrance to the Fine Arts Hall."[6]

Detailed plans for the construction of the Coal Palace were made public only two days following the decision to build. According to the August 29 issue of the Illinois State *Journal,* "The structure will be imposing in size, with walls sixteen feet to the plate, built in rough, broken range masonry of blocks of coal from Springfield mines laid in black mortar. At each corner of the palace will be a circular buttress carried up into a turret twenty-six feet high and containing a flag staff nine feet higher at the point. In the center of each side and end of the palace there will be a massive and imposing arched doorway six feet wide and nine feet high. The door jambs will be adorned with semicircular buttresses, which will continue up with finials at the top of the wall.

"The building will be covered with a hip roof with a coating of tar and nut coal. A fancy dormer window will be built in each side of the roof directly over each entrance. The point of the roof will be finished with two flag staffs, and the hips and combs of the roof and dormers are to be trimmed with ears of bright yellow corn. The interior of this large palace will be lined with woodwork and will be fitted up with booths by the several coal companies. The large windows in the masonry will provide sufficient light for the interior of the black diamond palace. The design for the beautiful palace was made by Messrs. Bullard & Bullard, architects, and it will be a model of artistic and novel architecture. Hundreds of tons of black diamonds will be used in the construction of this novel palace — a trifling amount when compared with upwards of six thousands tons of coal raised from the Springfield mines each day in the year."[7]

The Sangamon County Fair opened on Tuesday, September 10, and the Illinois State *Journal's* lead sentence the following day summed up the opening very cleverly when it said, "There was no dust yesterday at the Sangamon Fair."[8] In other words, the day was a washout, thanks to a two-hour downpour. Yet attendance was still more than 10,000, mostly thanks to the opening being declared Kids' Day, but the Coal Palace dedication was postponed until the morning of September 12.[9]

The palace did its part in helping the fair reach an attendance of 20,000 on the third day. It was reported that one family drove its horse-drawn carriage 57 miles, leaving home at midnight to arrive before the heat of the day.[10]

The Sangamon County Fair was declared a huge success, realizing a $6,500 profit to carry the event through to the next year.[11] The Coal Palace itself, however, would not be a part of the fair's future. Because of the rapidly deteriorating quality of coal, the fair organizers knew from the outset that the palace's lifespan would be limited to one year and took solace in the fact that the coal blocks from the demolished palace would be donated to some of the city's charitable institutions.[12]

Footnotes for the Springfield Coal Palace, 1889

1. C.R. Paul, "King Corn's Coal Palace," Illinois State *Journal*, August 27, 1889, p. 4.
2. Ibid.
3. C.R. Paul, "Recent Improvements," Illinois State *Journal*, August 29, 1889, p. 1.
4. C.R. Paul, "King Corn's Coal Palace," Illinois State *Journal*, August 27, 1889, p. 4.
5. C.R. Paul, "It Will Be A Coal Day," Illinois State *Journal*, August 31, 1889, p. 4.
6. Ibid.
7. C.R. Paul, "That Curiosity In Coal," Illinois State *Journal*, August 29, 1889, p. 4.
8. C.R. Paul, "It Was Children's Day," Illinois State *Journal*, September 11, 1889, p. 4.
9. Ibid.
10. C.R. Paul, "Many Thousands There," Illinois State *Journal*, September 13, 1889, p. 1.
11. C.R. Paul, "A Financial Success," Illinois State *Journal*, September 14, 1889, p. 1.
12. C.R. Paul, "It Will Be A Coal Day," Illinois State *Journal*, August 31, 1889, p. 4.

Arcola Broom Palace
(Courtesy of Dale Yoder)

Arcola
Broom Palace
1898

Throughout history, few people have given much thought to their brooms until they've seen a floor that has needed sweeping, and even fewer have realized that the cleaning tool actually was named for the plant used to make it. However, in 1898, Arcola, Illinois, the self-proclaimed Broom Capital of the World, set in motion plans to not only give broom owners a new appreciation of their sweeping instrument, but to celebrate the usefulness of that handy device. The usefulness the city fathers had in mind, however, involved more of a financial boost for the town itself, and what better way to promote both the crop and the city than with a street carnival?[1]

It took hundreds of years for broomcorn to make its way to America from Africa and Europe, and it might have taken even longer had not Ben Franklin's bifocals zoomed in on the tall sorghum plant during his European travels in

Arcola Broom Palace and Street Fair (Courtesy of Dale Yoder)

the early 1700s. Within 150 years of Franklin's introduction of broomcorn to North America, Illinois was the crop's leading producer.[2] Arcola wanted to show its appreciation of the crop that had made its community "wealthy and happy," so a celebration was held in its honor from September 28 to October 1, 1898.[3]

Twelve thousand attendees crowded Arcola's streets to play games, listen to music, browse through the displays and marvel at its main attraction — the 45-foot-square Broomcorn Palace that was decorated inside and out with intricately designed plumes of broomcorn. It boasted a center tower with a bandstand, minarets on each corner, arched doorways on each side and "exhibits in all lines beyond anything the management had expected."[4]

Arcola Broom Palace under construction

(Courtesy of Dale Yoder)

(Courtesy of Dale Yoder)

Arcola Broom Palace interior

(Courtesy of Dale Yoder)

Footnotes for the Arcola Broomcorn Palace, 1898

1. Editor, "Arcola Broom Corn Palace Nearing Completion," Chicago *Tribune*, September 24, 1898.

2. D.R. Hicks, Alternative Field Crops Manual (University of Minnesota, St. Paul, Minnesota, 1990), 1.

3. Editor, "Arcola Broom Corn Palace Nearing Completion," Chicago *Tribune*, September 24, 1898.

4. Editor, "Arcola's Broomcorn Fair," Chicago *Tribune*, September 18, 1898.

Peoria Corn Palace, 1898
(Courtesy of Peoria Public Library)

Peoria Corn Palace 1898-1900

Section 5 ❖ Illinois
CHAPTER 3

P eoria, Illinois, may not have had the world's only corn palace nor the first, but it was the first and only city to turn a tabernacle into a corn palace, which it did in 1898 to advertise the Peoria Corn Exposition and help spread the word that Peoria was the corn capital of the world. The city was also not the first nor last to make the bold "Corn Capital of the World" claim, but that didn't seem to bother its citizens as long as the hype had the desired effect — to get President McKinley and thousands of ordinary countrymen to visit Peoria and see what all the fuss was about.[1]

What a fuss it was each fall as nearby states brought their products for display in order to help boost Peoria's effort while at the same time engage in a little friendly competition. What could be sweeter for Iowa, Ohio, Kansas, Nebraska or Missouri than to prove Illinois wrong — that one of their states was the true Mecca for corn production.[2]

The railroad encouraged a select group of Illinois farmers by offering prizes to the best corn grown within six miles of its tracks, and one can only assume the boundaries did not extend beyond the state. First prize was a 1,000-mile ticket to the winning husband and wife, which would of course only cost the railroad actual cash if a train should happen to be filled to capacity.[3]

The Peoria exposition contained the usual number of parades, musical entertainments and speeches, and also offered spectators a rare opportunity to see a woman jump from a hot air balloon. Madame Frazer was a dancer turned parachutist who feared not the jump itself, but the landing if it happened to be upon the spires of a local church.[4] There was no mention in the newspaper whether she touched down safely or was stranded on the church roof.

Peoria Corn Palace Footnotes

1. Editor, "A World Famous Corn Show," Peoria Transcript, 1927, p. 8.
2. Leo A. Gruba, "The Whole Town Went in for Corn," Peoria *Journal Star.*
3. Ibid.
4. Alice Oakley, "The Way it Was," Peoria *Penny Press*, 1976, p. 5.

Peoria Corn Palace, 1899 (Courtesy of Peoria Public Library)

Peoria Corn Palace, 1900 (Courtesy of Peoria Public Library)

Bloomington Corn Palace, 1915.

Bloomington Corn Palace, 1915
(Courtesy of Abraham Lincoln Presidential Library,
Springfield, Illinois)

Bloomington Corn Palace 1915-1916

Section 5 ❖ Illinois
CHAPTER 4

The Bloomington Corn Palace, built in 1898 on Front Street and Roosevelt Avenue, was actually a full-time coliseum except from 1915 to 1916, when a façade disguising it as a corn palace declared "Corn is King." The decorations were designed by A.L. Pillsbury and applied by local citizens, but their efforts were not able to generate enough enthusiasm to sustain a permanent harvest celebration. The building was demolished in 1961.

Footnotes for the Bloomington, Illinois, Corn Palace

1. William D. Walters Jr., The Heart of the Cornbelt: An Illustrated History of Corn Farming in McLean County (McLean County Historical Society, Bloomington, Illinois, 1997), 79.

Bloomington Corn Palace, 1915
(Courtesy of McLean County Historical Society)

Bloomington Corn Palace, 1916
(Courtesy of McLean County Historical Society)

CORN PALACE
SIDNEY, NEBR.

Section 6
Nebraska

1890 Grand Island Beet Sugar Palace,
200 Block Northeast Front Street
(Courtesy of Fred Roeser, Hall County Historical Society)

Grand Island
Beet Sugar
Palace
1890

Section 6 ❖ Nebraska
CHAPTER 1

When most cities attempted to build a grain or mineral palace of one kind or another, a local newspaper editor was generally a powerful force, if not the driving force, in getting the project off the ground. In the case of Grand Island, however, the editor of the *Daily Independent* freely admitted in July of 1890 that he'd given only spotty coverage to the planning of a sugar beet palace that had been taking place during the past four months.[1] He gave no excuse for his lack of coverage, nor did he give any reasons why he instead concentrated his reporting on fires, cyclones, train wrecks and Prohibition.

While there was certainly no shortage of natural or man-made disasters to write about, the issue of Prohibition had been around since Nebraska had become a territory in 1854. However, the editor apparently considered the world's first Sugar Palace less significant than the world's first Bootleggers Convention! That event was held in Decorah, Iowa, during the summer of 1890, and the first order of business for the 100 delegates was to recognize the prohibitionists as true friends, for without them, bootleggers would be unemployed. The delegates also were resolved to improve the quality of their liquor and to set a uniform price of $1.10 a gallon. The final resolution was to offer a liberal premium "to the tailor who can get up a suit of clothes that will hold the most bottles and attract the least attention."[2]

When the *Daily Independent's* editor finally turned his attention to the palace project, he did so with bold headlines reading "Grand Island Beet Sugar Palace!"[3] He explained that the construction contract had been let the previous day on July 16, that sufficient funds already had been raised, that 30 men already had begun working on the building and that completion was expected by September 1. The palace was to measure 184 feet by 194 feet, with a center tower 160 feet high, and was to be located "directly west of the Union Pacific passenger depot, and south of the Estes hotel, in plain view of all the railroads, and in the business center of the city."[4]

A miniature sugar beet factory was to be assembled in the interior, and the palace was expected to be the chief attraction in the city next to the sugar factory itself.[5]

The Grand Island area was investing heavily in the sugar beet industry, and articles encouraging good husbandry of the land were printed in the newspaper quite frequently. Tips were offered on how to keep the fields clean because beet fields required more care than corn fields but offered seven times the profit of corn. The sugar beet industry was still in its infancy, so farmers were encouraged to experiment with different types of moisture and pest control. When harmful insects were found on a plant, farmers were requested to capture the insects alive and send them to the experiment station for study at the nearest agricultural university.[6]

Grand Island had been incorporated as a town in 1872, and due to its steady growth to 15,000 citizens, drew up a new charter in 1890 to incorporate as a first-class city, a designation for cities with a population between 8,000 and 25,000. The city government, which was considered quite progressive, was made up of nine men with varied backgrounds. The mayor, W.H. Platt, was a 55-year-old lawyer who was born in New York, while the council members consisted of a newspaperman of Scotch ancestry, a former legislator born in Germany, a cigar

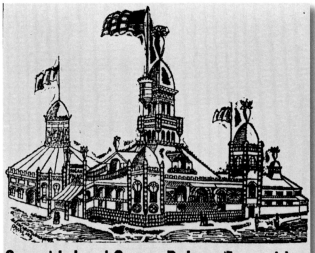

Grand Island Sugar Palace Exposition

Open September 1 to 19, 1890.

Grand Island Sugar Factory

Will open September 1, 1890.

G. A. R. Reunion Dept. of Nebraska

Will open September 1, 1890, and continue one week.

(Advertisement courtesy of Nebraska State Historical Society)

MAIN BUILDING BEET SUGAR FACTORY.

NEW CITY HALL BUILDING.

Illustrations from The Grand Island
Daily Independent

(C)ourtesy of Nebraska State Historical Society

manufacturer from Illinois, a real estate and insurance agent from Illinois, a blacksmith from New Jersey, a factory superintendent from Ohio, an opera house proprietor from Germany and a painter of Irish ancestry.[7]

Recent improvements included a $60,000 sewer system, a $50,000 water system and a new $25,500 three-story, brick and stone city hall measuring 66 by 66 feet. The building, which provided separate areas with modern conveniences for male and female prisoners, was "heated throughout by steam and illuminated by gas and electric lights."[8]

What pride residents felt to have all that plus a new $25,000 beet sugar palace and a $500,000 beet sugar factory (backed mostly by New York capitalists), which would be the largest operation of its kind in the United States and the fourth largest in the world![9]

The function of the palace was more to promote the industry than the city, an approach quite different from most municipalities that built or were to build grain or mineral palaces. The area had a lot invested in the sugar beet industry, and it was imperative that it be successful. One hundred and sixteen railroad car loads of machinery costing $160,000 were imported from France, and requirements to make the plant operable included 12 large steam boilers, three engines of 400 horsepower each and 80 wells to supply the necessary 800 gallons of water per minute to wash the beets. The plant would operate 24 hours a day for four months, including Sundays, which some laborers thought excessive, but which management considered absolutely necessary.[10]

The goal was to refine 100 tons of sugar — equal to about 450 barrels — from every 700 tons of beets. It cost the

Advertisement from The Grand Island *Daily Independent*

(Courtesy of Nebraska State Historical Society)

farmers about $25 per acre to raise the beets, but they were guaranteed a market if they contracted with the factory and could expect to sell their crop for $60 to $80 per acre, realizing a sizable profit.[11] In contrast, wheat farmers in North Dakota were experiencing near ruin due to unfair practices by elevator operators. It had long been the practice for farmers to receive 15 days of free storage in elevators at harvest time, after which they could choose to sell the grain or pay a reasonable storage fee. But when the North Dakota Legislature placed a tax on public grain enterprises, the elevators declared themselves private rather than public and refused to pay the license fee or allow any grain to be stored in their facilities. Farmers had not yet found a need to build storage bins on their farms, and there were not enough railroad cars to haul even one-tenth of the harvest to Duluth or Minneapolis mills. And to add insult to injury, many of the farmers had received their seed wheat from those very elevators on a loan basis, thereby giving the elevators a lien on each farmer's crop. That meant the farmers were forced to sell their wheat at the time of harvest no matter how low the price.[12]

Even with profits nearly guaranteed for the Nebraska sugar beet growers and processors, there were calls for a federal tariff to protect the domestic industry, which is interesting when considering the local opposition to the high tariffs proposed by Senator William McKinley for other products.[13]

With all the preparations going on for the factory and the palace, someone still found time to make detailed scale miniatures of the buildings for exhibit at the Sugar Palace and later at the Nebraska State Fair, which was held 90 miles to the east in Lincoln. All available hands were required to complete the palace interior, which was to include a maple sugar camp scene with artificial snow, a cereal room displaying every cereal known and a grass room, plus a blue and white room. On August 21, it was stated that "fifty men, women, and children have been employed for two weeks, and yet the work is not half completed."[14]

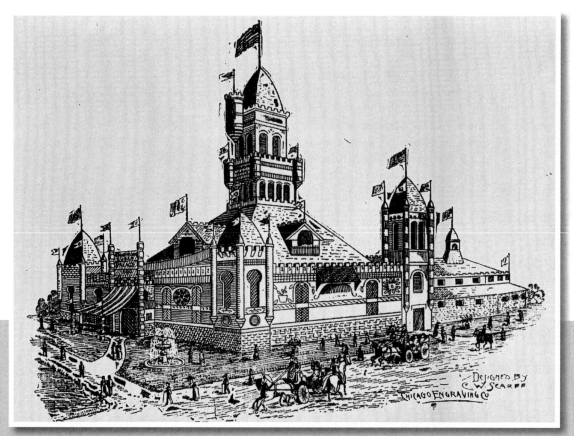

Illustration from The Grand Island
Daily Independent
(Courtesy of Nebraska State Historical Society)

Interior of the Grand Island Beet Sugar Palace

(Courtesy of Stuhr Museum of the Prairie Pioneer)

It was doubly important to draw attention toward Nebraska sugar beets because the world markets were experiencing radical changes. Germany had been importing sugar beets only a few years earlier but, by 1890, they were exporting several million dollars worth, thereby supplanting cane sugar from Puerto Rico, Cuba, Central America and South America.[15] Locally, there was considerable competition from neighboring Colorado, but less so from the states to the east because they did not have the dry, sandy soil necessary to produce a high sugar content in the beets. Nebraska took advantage of Germany's expertise by hiring a German to plant and test local beets.[16]

According to an August 22 report, the dimensions of the Sugar Palace had grown to 200 feet square, though the height had shrunk from 160 feet to 150 feet. The increase in square footage was due to an addition built for the purpose of displaying a panorama of the Battle of Gettysburg, but there was no explanation for the height

shrinkage. The lower 8 feet of the three pavilions appeared to be made of sugar barrels cut into three parts, and each tower all the way to the top seemed to be made of barrels as well. The idea was to give the exterior a soft, rounded look without the use of grain decorations, making it the only palace promoting a cereal that was expressly designed without external ornamentation using any type of grain.[17]

Be Sure

If you have made up your mind to buy Hood's Sarsaparilla do not be induced to take any other. Hood's Sarsaparilla is a peculiar medicine, possessing, by virtue of its peculiar combination, proportion, and preparation, curative power superior to any other article. A Boston lady who knew what she wanted, and whose example is worthy imitation, tells her experience below:

To Get

"In one store where I went to buy Hood's Sarsaparilla the clerk tried to induce me buy their own instead of Hood's; he told me their's would last longer; that I might take it on ten days' trial; that if I did not like it I need not pay anything, etc. But he could not prevail on me to change. I told him I knew what Hood's Sarsaparilla was. I had taken it, was satisfied with it, and did not want any other.

Hood's

When I began taking Hood's Sarsaparilla I was feeling real miserable, suffering a great deal with dyspepsia, and so weak that at times I could hardly stand. I looked, and had for some time, like a person in consumption. Hood's Sarsaparilla did me so much good that I wonder at myself sometimes, and my friends frequently speak of it." MRS. ELLA A. GOFF, 61 Terrace Street, Boston.

Sarsaparilla

Sold by all druggists. $1; six for $5. Prepared only by C. I. HOOD & CO., Apothecaries, Lowell, Mass.

100 Doses One Dollar

Advertisement from The Grand Island Daily Independent

(Courtesy of Nebraska State Historical Society)

All interior decorative materials were dipped in a solution of alum (probably aluminum sulfate) and ground glass to give them a sparkly appearance similar to sugar. The building designer, Charles W. Scarff, claimed that the effect would be so brilliant people would have to look at it through smoked glass. It would have to be dazzling to keep visitors awake during a two-day senatorial debate concerning the pros and cons of the sugar tariff.[18] Such programming might explain why the Sugar Palace concept was abandoned after the first year.

A report four days later cut the building's size down to 189 feet square and only 100 feet tall, but Mr. Scarff still was being praised for doing more to promote Grand Island than any other man. His attributes included courage, confidence, creativity and executive ability — all necessary qualities to pull off an enterprise of such magnitude.[19]

Another article in the same issue listed the population of Grand Island as 9,000 as opposed to the 15,000 figure given at an earlier date in the same newspaper. It also went on to say that the citizens of Grand Island "have always discouraged all foolish efforts to deceive the great public by 'bragging efforts,' which have hurt the growth of other cities."[20]

By August 28, the Sugar Palace had again reportedly reached a height of 150 feet, just in time for the September 1 opening. It was admitted that the palace was "drafted after the Sioux City Corn Palace in design and decoration, only that beets are used more extensively in the trimmings and decorations."[21] However, large maps of Nebraska and the U.S. were made not of beets, but of corn, wheat and oats. And while the Sioux City Corn Palace was admittedly interesting and successful, "it had none of the element of novelty which attracts the wideawake people of the west to Grand Island."[22]

The Union Pacific Railroad gave the Beet Sugar Palace Company a welcome boost on September 2 when it offered a free 24-hour Grand Island layover pass for all passengers returning from the State Fair in Lincoln. The local editor acknowledged that it would benefit the "sugar palace, the sugar factory, and the Sugar City."[23]

The following week a visiting newspaper editor gave the most detailed description of the palace's interior, and he freely noted the parts he liked best. "One of the most attractive features of the palace is the miniature beet sugar machinery, showing the process of manufacture from the pile of beets on the ground to the finished sugar as it falls in the barrels ready for market. The ladies pronounce this exhibit 'just too sweet for anything.' One space that receives its share of attention is a Nebraska farm scene, with the house and fences built of corn and ground … devoted to beet raising. A beautiful motto on the wall, made from sectional pieces of corn cobs, reads: 'For sugar, sheep, hogs, cattle, potatoes, wheat, oats, corn, babies. Nebraska Beets the World.' The adjoining scene represents a quiet Nebraska fireside, the decorations of corn and other grains and the carpet in squares of red and white corn. The lace curtains are made of popcorn and short pieces of straw threaded on string. The balcony is graced with a large motto worked in corn, 'Sugar is King and Nebraska His Kingdom,' and in the center of the palace is a stairway leading to the roof, where a fine view of the town can be obtained."[24]

Very little else was reported on the Sugar Palace, even though the doors were kept open until September 26, one week longer than originally scheduled. The one program held in the palace that did receive considerable coverage was a debate about Prohibition on September 19, which was undoubtedly more interesting and spirited (pardon the pun) than the tariff debate. For that three-hour event, "A fair audience of about 400 or 500 of our most intelligent citizens was present, and showed great interest in the subject."[25] The editor noted that "Mr. Rankin, the professional prohibition speaker, opened the debate with the promise to annihilate the anti-prohibitionists' common arguments. Mr. Rankin's power consists mostly in a powerful voice and rather wild gestures. Logic and veracity are not his main force."[26] The second speaker for Prohibition was Kansas Attorney General Mr. Bradford, of whom it was said "such a falsifier might have been excusable to a certain degree, if he was under the influence of liquor. But we believe he was not, though he spoke like a man who did not know what he said."[27]

Surprisingly enough, the sugar beet factory's opening was somewhat tied to the Prohibition issue; the factory was expected to spawn a distillery as well as a local chewing gum industry if statewide prohibition were to be repealed.[28]

Epilogue

The growing of beets has been recorded as far back as the Greeks and Romans, but it was not until 1747 that a German scientist was able to extract sugar from beets. A French refugee in Prussia, Karl Achard, first attempted the process on a commercial scale in 1797. In 1798, a London society of cane sugar investors tried to head off the beet sugar competition by offering Achard $120,000 to abandon his work, but he refused. Frederick William III of Prussia helped build the first beet sugar factory in 1799, and during the 1800s, France and Germany became the leading producers of sugar beets.[29] Sugar beets were first grown in the U.S. in 1830 near Philadelphia, and the first factory was erected in Massachusetts in 1838. However, the beets planted were low in sugar and the factory shut down in 1840. The first successful American beet sugar factory was built in 1879 in California, and before long, Henry Oxnard and his brother Robert became interested in sugar beets. After studying the beet sugar industry in Europe, the brothers built beet sugar factories in Grand Island and Norfolk, Nebraska, as well as in Chino and Oxnard, California (the town built up around the factory and was named for Henry). The four factories combined in 1899 to become the American Beet Sugar Company, which later became the Crystal Sugar Company in 1934. The Grand Island factory remained in operation until 1964.[30]

Perhaps it also should be noted that the sugar industry got the tariff it asked for in the form of the Sugar Bounty Act of 1890.[31]

Advertisements from The Grand Island *Daily Independent*
(Courtesy of Nebraska State Historical Society)

Footnotes for the Grand Island Sugar Palace, 1890

1. Fred Hedde, "Grand Island Beet Sugar Palace," The Grand Island *Daily Independent*, July 17, 1890, p. 4.

2. Fred Hedde, "A Boot-Leggers Convention," The Grand Island *Daily Independent*, June 9, 1890, p. 2.

3. Fred Hedde, "Grand Island Beet Sugar Palace," The Grand Island *Daily Independent*, July 17, 1890, p. 4.

4. Ibid.

5. Ibid.

6. Fred Hedde, "The Hall," The Grand Island *Daily Independent*, July 16, 1890, p. 2.

7. Fred Hedde, "Our City Government," The Grand Island *Daily Independent*, July 19, 1890, p. 3.

8. Ibid.

9. Fred Hedde, "The Hall," The Grand Island *Daily Independent*, August 6, 1890, p. 2.

10. Fred Hedde, "The Hall," The Grand Island *Daily Independent*, July 23, 1890, p. 2.

11. Fred Hedde, "The Hall," The Grand Island *Daily Independent*, August 22, 1890, p. 2.

12. Fred Hedde, "Face to Face with Ruin," The Grand Island *Daily Independent*, July 31, 1890, p. 4.

13. Fred Hedde, "The Hall," The Grand Island *Daily Independent*, August 1, 1890, p. 2.

14. Fred Hedde, "The Hall," The Grand Island *Daily Independent*, August 21, 1890, p. 2.

15. Fred Hedde, "The Hall," The Grand Island *Daily Independent*, August 19, 1890, p. 2.

16. Fred Hedde, "The Hall," The Grand Island *Daily Independent*, August 22, 1890, p. 2.

17. Ibid.

18. Ibid.

19. Fred Hedde, "The Hall," The Grand Island *Daily Independent*, August 26, 1890, p. 2.

20. Fred Hedde, "The Growth of Grand Island," The Grand Island *Daily Independent*, August 26, 1890, p. 2.

21. Fred Hedde, "The Sugar Palace," The Grand Island *Daily Independent*, August 28, 1890, p. 3.

22. Ibid.

23. Fred Hedde, "A Big Card," The Grand Island *Daily Independent*, September 2, 1890, p. 3.

24. Fred Hedde, "The Hall," The Grand Island *Daily Independent*, September 10, 1890, p. 2.

25. Fred Hedde, "The Prohibition Debate in the Sugar Palace," The Grand Island *Daily Independent*, September 19, 1890, p. 2.

26. Ibid.

27. Ibid.

28. Fred Hedde, "The Growth of Grand Island," The Grand Island *Daily Independent*, August 26, 1890, p. 2.

29. F.S. Harris, Ph.D., The Sugar-Beet in America (The McMillan Company, New York, 1919) 6-19.

30. Ibid.

31. Ibid.

Sidney Corn Palace at the
Cheyenne County Harvest Festival
(Courtesy of City of Sidney, Nebraska)

Sidney
Corn Palace
1923-1924

For more than a decade after its founding in the 1860s, Sidney, Nebraska, was tagged with nicknames such as "Sinful Sidney" and "Wicked Burgh" by rival towns — most notably Cheyenne, Wyoming.[1] Indians were prevalent in the area, and it was claimed that Sitting Bull learned the English language while in the Sidney vicinity.[2] Run-of-the-mill outlaws took part in numerous gunfights and robberies, although there was no report of wrongdoing by Butch Cassidy while he owned a livery stable there, nor by Jesse James during a brief visit.[3]

Sidney's reputation for lawlessness was somewhat similar to Deadwood's in the 1870s, and the towns also had two early residents in common, Wild Bill Hickok and Calamity Jane, as well as cemeteries named Boot Hill.[4]

Perhaps the most significant Deadwood connection was Sidney's effort to stake its future on the claim that it was on the most direct route to the Black Hills in general and to Deadwood in particular.[5] Getting wagon trains of supplies, settlers and Pony Express riders to travel directly north from Sidney to Deadwood provided the economic stimulus to the older town that gold did to the younger. But what Sidney later had that Deadwood never did was a Corn Palace. The modest structure, built in 1923, was set smack dab in the middle of Central Avenue and Second Street (now Tenth Avenue and Illinois Street), the busiest intersection in town, making the route to Deadwood slightly less direct but certainly more scenic.[6]

In September 1922, the Sidney *Telegraph* editor printed a list of the town's strengths and weaknesses. He claimed that Sidney already had excellent sewer and water systems, schools, churches and businesses, a splendid climate and, of course, the best weekly newspaper in Nebraska, but among the things still needed were a pickle factory, playgrounds, a community center, a way to get rid of criminals and a way to "conserve child morals."[7] Few if any of these ideas came to fruition anytime soon, but by the following year, the community got automobile parking along the sides of the streets instead of down the center,[8] a county fair and the first Corn Palace in western Nebraska.[9]

The parking issue became heated and controversial, but the Corn Palace plan sailed through without any noted opposition whatsoever. The idea for the Corn Palace has been credited to local attorney W.P. Miles, who was quickly appointed to a Corn Palace committee along with three other men. The committee decided to build an octagon-shaped structure 20 feet in diameter around the city's flag pole.[10] Each of the eight sides was constructed off-site and then hauled to the intersection to be fastened together. Initial measurements must have been accurate because the building was put up in one day — September 25, 1923[11] — by contractors Daniels & Erickson and several volunteers.[12]

Ear corn for decorating the palace was easy to find because farmers were harvesting a bumper crop, with some areas yielding 50 to 60 bushels an acre and an average of 25 to 30 bushels across the county.[13] The corn for the palace was cut in half lengthwise and then nailed

Cheyenne County
FALL FESTIVAL
OCTOBER 4-5
SIDNEY,   NEBRASKA
TWO BIG EDUCATIONAL DAYS
filled with knowledge, fun and thrills

WONDERFUL EXHIBITS
of
FRUITS, GRAINS, VEGETABLES
CALVES, SWINE, POULTRY
COOKING, CANNING, SEWING
SCHOOL WORK ETC.

AIRPLANE THRILLS
Sensational exhibition of looping the loop, side banks, tail spins etc. Also the hair-raising, spectacular, dare-devil
PARACHUTE DROP
from a speeding airplane. This big attraction is worth coming miles to see

FREE   FREE
Baseball Game   Band Concert
each afternoon   each evening

Parades - races - sports - dancing - merry-go-round
FOUR BANDS--SOMETHING DOING EVERY MINUTE
Come and enjoy yourself, bring the children with you, have a good time

(Newspapers courtesy of Sidney Public Library)

THE FALL FESTIVAL
WAS HUGE SUCCESS
County's Most Gorgeous Exposition of Progress and Achievement.

to the frame. Various designs adorned the exterior walls as well as the following phrases: "Welcome Hogs, Cows, and Corn;" "Fall Festival, October 4th, 5th;" "Pigs is Pigs;" and "Cheyenne County." In front of the building stood a corn man and a corn pig,[14] both designed by P.J. Ackels, which the newspaper declared a bit freakish.[15]

The Corn Palace couldn't begin to hold the nearly 1,500 exhibits, a number far beyond the expectations of festival officials, so entries were spread among the Tobin Opera House, the Byars building and others. As for the quality of the items, the *Telegraph* declared, "To say these exhibits were beautiful would be meaningless. They simply were as fine as the world ever saw, or could expect to see. To appreciate them one would have to see them, then words to describe their beauty would fail them."[16]

The town itself was declared pretty, and businesses offered prizes for the prettiest unmarried female as well as the prettiest married female in attendance. A week after the Fall Festival concluded, the *Telegraph* reported it was still unable to learn the identity of the prettiest married female, concluding that the results were sidetracked "to keep peace in the family."[17]

Without question, the 1923 Fall Festival was considered a success, with nearly 7,000 visitors (2,000 on Thursday and 5,000 on Friday) enjoying the exhibits, parades, races, bands, baseball games, merry-go-round, Ferris wheel, stunt flying and parachute jumping by Daredevil Jim. Although the Fall Festival was to become a permanent event for Cheyenne County, the Corn Palace itself proved temporary and was dismantled within a month of the festival's closing.[18] A new Corn Palace was constructed for the 1924 festival, and a placard was placed in front that read, "1923 — Cheyenne County produced 4,000,000 bushels of corn. 1924 — Better corn; Better quality; Better price. This corn was gathered from 45 fields of the county."[19] No records have been found indicating the existence of a Corn Palace in Sidney after 1924.

If anyone had asked why he or she should attend a Sidney Fall Festival, the Sidney *Telegraph* had a ready

FALL FESTIVAL NEXT THURSDAY AND FRIDAY WILL BE CHEYNNE COUNTY'S GREATEST OUTDOOR EVENT

Pageant of Progress and Achievement—Educational and Entertaining—Musical Program, Monster School Parade, Baseball Games, Races, Airplane Parachute Jumping, Other Attractions.

(Newspaper courtesy Sidney Public Library)

First western Nebraska Corn Palace
(Courtesy of Sidney Public Library)

answer: "Because it enables you to see at a glance Cheyenne county agricultural and educational progress. Because it is a composite presentation of your county's wealth and resources. Because it reflects the county's actual economic and social conditions. Because you will see the results of Cheyenne county's men and women's best efforts. Because you will find a happy combination of pleasure and profitable education. Because you can see Cheyenne county at a glance."[20]

It's interesting to note that Sidney's first festival was likely held in an effort to "one-up" the nearby town of Dalton, which held a Fall Festival in 1922. Ironically, the Sidney Fall Festival eventually became an Octoberfest while the Dalton Fall Festival continued. But, alas, they never built a Corn Palace.

(Newspaper courtesy of Sidney Public Library)

Footnotes for Sidney Corn Palace, 1923-24

1. Loren Avey, Lynchings, Legends, & Lawlessness (Hughes Design LLC, Sidney, Nebraska, 2006), 184.

2. Ibid, 197.

3. Ibid, 10.

4. Ibid.

5. Ibid, 119.

6. Gary Person, interview by author, Sidney, Nebraska, April 14, 2009.

7. Guy V. Doran, "Sidney Has Much But Needs More," Sidney Telegraph, September 22, 1922, p. 1.

8. Guy V. Doran, "Change Car Parking From Center To Curb," Sidney Telegraph, July 13, 1923, p. 1.

9. Guy V. Doran, "The Fall Festival Was Huge Success," Sidney Telegraph, October 12, 1923, p. 1.

10. Guy V. Doran, "Corn Palace Committee Makes Definite Plans," Sidney Telegraph, September 21, 1923, p. 1.

11. Guy V. Doran, "Fall Festival Next Thursday and Friday Will Be Cheynne (sic) County's Greatest Outdoor Event," Sidney Telegraph, September 28, 1923, p. 1.

12. Guy V. Doran, "Western Nebraska's First Corn Palace," Sidney Telegraph, October 12, 1923, p. 1.

13. Guy V. Doran, "Bumper Corn Crop Now Out Of Danger," Sidney Telegraph, October 12, 1923, p. 8

14. Guy V. Doran, "Western Nebraska's First Corn Palace," Sidney Telegraph, October 12, 1923, p. 1.

15. Guy V. Doran, "Fall Festival Goes Beyond Expectations," Sidney Telegraph, October 5, 1923, p. 1.

16. Ibid.

17. Guy V. Doran, "Fall Festival From The Sidelines," Sidney Telegraph, October 12, 1923, p. 1.

18. Guy V. Doran, "Western Nebraska's First Corn Palace," Sidney Telegraph, October 12, 1923, p. 1.

19. Cheyenne County History Book Committee, History of Cheyenne County, Nebraska (Curtis Media Corporation, Dallas, Texas, 1987), 181.

20. Guy V. Doran, "Fall Festival Next Thursday and Friday Will Be Cheyenne County's Greatest Outdoor Event," Sidney Telegraph, September 28, 1923, p. 1.

1912

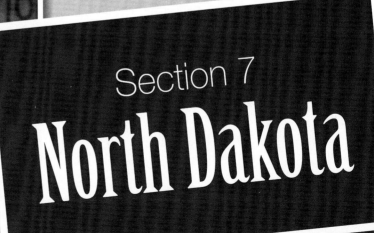

Section 7
North Dakota

Ray Grain Palace
(Courtesy of Doris Langager and the Ray Centennial Committee)

Ray
Grain Palace
1912

Section 7 ❖ North Dakota
CHAPTER 1

Ray, North Dakota, which lies in Williams County near the Montana and Canadian borders, was established on a rail line in 1902. A year later, the town boasted 31 businesses, a sure sign that it was growing along with the state, which had increased in population by 170,000 since statehood in 1889. South Dakota, by comparison, had increased by only 50,000,[1] though perhaps it should be mentioned that North Dakota's population in 1890 was only 190,983, compared to South Dakota's 328,808. By 1910, the two states were nearly tied in population, with North Dakota counting 577,056 citizens, and South Dakota 583,888.[2]

Ray grew along with the rest of the state, and on its 10th anniversary the town's citizens decided it was time to celebrate. Their annual 4th of July celebrations weren't enough for one year, or even one month, so the town organized a Grain Palace Festival for July 26 and 27, 1912. The headlines in the Ray Pioneer touted $500 in prizes and great barbecue, which was assumed to bring in "thousands."[3]

The Commercial Club was in charge of the festivities and promised an event that would be "educational and also one continual round of pleasure for two days and nights."[4] The main feature at the festival was to be a Grain Palace, which would involve the renovation of a large building near the Great Northern depot that was owned by the lumber yard. The exterior would be decorated with grains and grasses, and the interior would add fruits and vegetables to its grain displays. The local paper proudly boasted that its palace would be "a standing advertisement of the great productiveness of the rich soil in this vicinity and [was] destined to be the pride of the community."[5]

For entertainment, on opening day the crowds would get to hear speeches by three candidates for Congress and the following day

---

THE RAY PIONEER

Friday, July 12, 1912

———

**Ray's Grain Palace Festival
July 26 and 27**

———

$500   IN PRIZES $500

———

Great Barbecue Will be Feature

———

Thousands of People to Attend

Our enterprising city will have another celebration. The 4th of July was a success in every way and several thousand people are convinced that the city is a royal entertainer.

(Newspapers courtesy of State Historical Society of North Dakota)

THE RAY PIONEER

Friday, July 26, 1912

———

Great White Way Illuminates City

———

Smallest City in the United States to Have White Way System

———

Entire Northwest is Watching the Progressive Ray

———

Thursday evening July 25 marked an epoch in the history of the most progressive and hustling little city in the entire northwest. The electric currant was switched onto the street lights of the Great White Way lighting system which lines both sides of the main street. The entire street every evening is one dazzling ray of white light making the dark hours of the evening as light as day.

---

more speeches by two candidates for governor. Those attending the State Fair in Fargo the same weekend would have to settle for watching two stunt pilots doing "dips of death and such demonstrations never seen in the northwest before."[6] An American, Jimmy Ward, would be flying his Curtiss biplane named Shooting Star and competing against a French aviator, George Mesach, and his Borel-Mathis monoplane. They were expected to "show how possible it is to drop from the clouds great bombs that would almost annihilate an army."[7] One can only appreciate the significance of this achievement when one is aware that only four years earlier, at a demonstration in which sculptor Gutzon Borglum was an official timekeeper, the Wright Brothers failed to convince the government of the military potential of their airplane.[8]

In preparation for the coming Grain Palace Exposition, the city made a large investment with the Great White Way lighting company and lined both sides of Main Street with dazzling electric lights. There were four lights per block on each side, each mounted on a 12-foot ornamental cast iron post weighing 350 pounds. Each pole had "a cluster of three lights, one large 60-candle power light at the top and two 40-candle power lamps on the sides, thus making 140 candle power light for each post."[9]

When the lights were switched on during the evening of July 25, 1912, the editor of the Ray Pioneer was proud to say "the best lighted little city in the Northwest is today attracting the attention of thousands of people in Minnesota, North Dakota and Montana."[10]

A program was advertised for a two-day event, which was notably different from other expositions of a similar nature. Ray's catered to the area's youth with a juvenile baseball game, footraces for boys, girls and adults — and even a fat man's race, with prizes awarded by the local drug store. Even more unusual, there was a water carnival with a boat race, swimming races for men and boys but not for girls, and a log rolling contest. A high-dive exhibition into Lake McLeod by Professor Haacke was the final event preceding the "Big Dance After Show."[11]

Also helping to attract crowds was the opening of the new Bijou Theater, which was "putting on the best of moving picture films, changing the program on Mondays, Wednesdays and Fridays."[12] The following sentence probably wouldn't mean much to a modern movie audience, but moviegoers were undoubtedly thrilled at that time to learn "the films [were] each about 1,000 feet in length" and four different pictures were shown each evening.[13]

All efforts seemed to pay off as approximately 8,000 excursionists visited Ray during the two-day festival. The editor declared the event "one of the greatest celebrations ever held in the town and … an historical date for the future generations to look back upon with pride."[14] He declared Ray "the most progressive

place of its size in the west," which was partially proven by its hosting the first Grain Palace Festival in the state of North Dakota.[15]

On July, 27, 1913, The Ray *Pioneer* announced that a second Grain Palace Festival would be held on August 7 and 8. Though the first festival was called a wonderful success, it was "but a starter and paved the way for something greater and better."[16] Committees under the sponsorship of the Commercial Club already were putting together programs and prizes. The program, which was announced the following week, was similar to the previous year's, though there appeared to be more local confidence in at least one event, as evidenced by the following statement: "Tug of War — RAY against the world."[17]

One significant boost for the Ray Grain Palace Festivals was the excellent support from the town's businesses. They placed large ads in the paper promoting the festival along with their merchandise and made sure the festival had the largest and boldest type. On July 25, there was an announcement in the paper that a new grain palace was being built and that it was almost finished. It was reported that "the main building [would] be 30x30 which [would give] 900 square feet of floor space. Large towers [would] be built giving the palace a beautiful appearance. The new building [would be] a substantial one and [would] be permanent."[18]

Ray's 1913 Grain Palace Festival promised to be bigger and better than the previous year's, and more interesting as well. Instead of politicians monopolizing the speaker's platform, the list of prominent speakers would include the

(Newspapers courtesy of State Historical Society of North Dakota)

president of Minot Normal, the superintendent of the government experiment station and a special agent of the Better Farming Association. As an added attraction for the young people, the Cash Carnival Company would provide amusements. As one ad stated, "If you stay away you will miss the time of your life."[19]

Other than a hot air balloon being destroyed by fire shortly before ascension, the second annual Festival went off without a hitch. The horse races were fast, the kids' races were good and the jousting tournament entertained hundreds who had never before seen that type of a contest.[20]

The announcement of the third annual Festival in 1914 was accompanied by the news that Ray would be building a new city hall — a 26- by 34-foot building that would house the city commissioners, the fire hall and the city jail. The city obviously was going for economy over comfort and apparently was hoping for few law-breakers. Other news centered on the town's successful baseball team, the annual Alfalfa Picnic that was expected to empty the town of its citizens, the annual Gopher Day in a nearby community and Texas Bill's Wild West Show that was coming soon as a part of the Enormous Yankee Robinson Three Ring Circus.[21]

The Grain Palace was remodeled in the Japanese bungalow style, which promoters hoped would help keep interest strong for the 1914 Exposition.[22] New shingles were put on the roof, and additional shelves and tables were placed inside in order to display more products. Farmers were encouraged to take a couple of days off from fieldwork and enjoy a mini-vacation at the Grain Palace.[23]

Enough farmers did so to enable the third annual Exposition to be as successful as the previous two. Most prominent in the parade were automobiles supplied by three dealerships in Ray, with the Ford and Buick dealers displaying the most advertising.

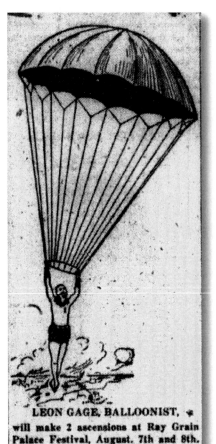

LEON GAGE, BALLOONIST, will make 2 ascensions at Ray Grain Palace Festival, August 7th and 8th.

(Newspaper courtesy of State Historical Society of North Dakota)

July 24, 1914, issue of The Ray *Pioneer*
(Courtesy of State Historical Society of North Dakota)

The Ford was billed as The Universal Car, bought for what it does. A runabout could be purchased for $500 and a touring car selling for $550 — f.o.b. Detroit — was declared "the lightest — the strongest — the most economical car on the market."[24]

Buicks, which came in three sizes and six styles from $950 to $1,985, had been in service for more than nine years and claimed to last more than 100,000 miles. They were advertised as "the car of Power, the car of Strength, the car of Speed, the car of Service."[25] The previous year, a young boy on a bicycle had been struck and killed by a speeding Ford runabout on Williston's Main Street. At 28 miles per hour, the driver was traveling at a speed "so unnatural and reckless" that two policemen prior to the accident had yelled to the driver to cut his speed.[26]

Also in the parade were motorcycles provided by the local Harley Davidson dealership. The 1914 Harley was advertised as having many improvements, including a self-starter, selective two-speed and double-brake control. With the self-starter, which was referred to as a Step-Starter, "if the rider accidentally stalls the motor it [was] no longer necessary to hold up traffic on a crowded street, find a level place in the road, get off in the mud, and set the machine on the stand to start it."[27]

During the 1915 Grain Palace Festival, it was claimed that at least 650 automobiles were parked in town for the event. The cars kept coming and the Festival's popularity continued through 1924. The Grain Palace was torn down in the 1930s and the lumber was used to build grandstands at the baseball park. In 1980, the local Jaycees decided to reinstitute the Grain Palace Festivals of old. Thanks to a donation of $30,000, a new building was constructed that could be used for a Festival each August and for storage during the other months. The plan has worked for more than 25 years.[28]

Ray's annual festivals rank second in longevity only to Mitchell's. During the first 12 years of their existence, the success of Ray's festivals probably could be attributed to strong support from the local newspaper, which gave

The newest Grain Palace
(Courtesy of Ray Centennial Committee)

The building was remodeled in 1914, rather than 1913, as marked.
(Courtesy of Doris Langager and the Ray Centennial Committee)

At least one Ray banker recognized the growing buying power of women.

the festivals first page attention instead of relegating them to page three, as many papers did. Ray's palace was also small enough that it didn't require a great deal of money for upkeep, and the local businesses continued to show their support. Perhaps the remoteness of the town also helped in the sense that there was not a great deal of nearby competition for crowds.

There are two ways of looking at Ray's success: Its population of 600 in 1914 is approximately the same as its population in the 21st century, so the Grain Palace Festivals can't claim to have contributed to the town's growth, but on the other hand, perhaps they were partially responsible for the town's stability. The bottom line is, both the Festival and the town still survive.[29]

Footnotes for the Ray Grain Palace 1912-Present

1. Ray, North Dakota: The First 100 Years, 1902-2002 (Ray, N.D.: Ray Centennial Committee, 2002), 11.
2. U.S. Census Bureau, Resident Population and Apportionment of the U.S. House of Representatives, 2000.
3. Edwin J. Knudson, "Ray's Grain Palace Festival July 26 and 27," The Ray Pioneer, July 12, 1912, p. 1.
4. Ibid.
5. Ibid.
6. Edwin J. Knudson, "Races Between Two Bird Men," The Ray Pioneer, July 12, 1912, p. 3.
7. Ibid.
8. Howard Shaff and Audrey Karl Shaff, Six Wars at a Time (Sioux Falls: The Center for Western Studies, 1985), 88.
9. Edwin J. Knudson, "Great White Way Illuminates City," The Ray Pioneer, July 26, 1912, p. 1.
10. Ibid.
11. Edwin J. Knudson, "Grain Palace Festival Programme," The Ray Pioneer, July 19, 1912, p. 2.
12. Edwin J. Knudson, "Bijou Theater Attracts Crowds," The Ray Pioneer, August 2, 1912, p. 1.
13. Ibid.
14. Edwin J. Knudson, "First Annual Grain Palace Festival Success," The Ray Pioneer, August 2, 1912, p. 1.
15. Ibid.
16. Edwin J. Knudson, "Ray Will Hold Second Annual Grain Palace Festival," The Ray Pioneer, June 27, 1913, p. 1.
17. Edwin J. Knudson, "Program First Day," The Ray Pioneer, July 4, 1913, p. 1.
18. Edwin J. Knudson, "Building Grain Palace," The Ray Pioneer, July 25, 1913, p. 1.
19. Edwin J. Knudson, "Grain Palace Festival Next Week a Record Breaker," The Ray Pioneer, August 1, 1913, p. 1.
20. Edwin J. Knudson, "2nd Annual Grain Palace Festival Was a Great Success," The Ray Pioneer, August 15, 1913, p. 1.
21. Edwin J. Knudson, "Dates Set for Grain Palace Festival," The Ray Pioneer, June 26, 1914, p. 1.
22. Edwin J. Knudson, "Grain Palace Being Remodeled," The Ray Pioneer, July 10, 1914, p. 1.
23. Edwin J. Knudson, "Grain Palace Festival Next Week," The Ray Pioneer, July 24, 1914, p. 1.
24. Edwin J. Knudson, "Ford, The Universal Car," The Ray Pioneer, May 5, 1914, p. 4.
25. Edwin J. Knudson, "150,000 Buicks," The Ray Pioneer, April 20, 1914, p. 10.
26. Williston Herald, "Williston Boy Run Down and Killed by Automobile," The Ray Pioneer, August 29, 1913, p. 1.
27. Edwin J. Knudson, "Harley-Davidson," The Ray Pioneer, April 20, 1914, p. 10.
28. Ray, North Dakota: The First 100 Years, 1902-2002 (Ray, ND: Ray Centennial Committee, 2002), 56-57.
29. Ibid.

Section 8
Wyoming